THE

INVESTMENT TRUSTS HANDBOOK

2020

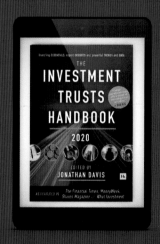

INVESTMENT TRUSTS HANDBOOK

2020

*Investing essentials, expert insights and
powerful trends and data*

EDITED BY

JONATHAN DAVIS

www.ITHB.co.uk

HARRIMAN HOUSE LTD
3 Viceroy Court
Petersfield
Hampshire
GU32 3LJ
GREAT BRITAIN
Tel: +44 (0)1730 233870

Email: enquiries@harriman-house.com
Website: www.harriman-house.com

First published in Great Britain in 2019.
Copyright © Harriman House Ltd.
Original chapter text and photographs remain copyright © of individual authors or firms.

Hardcover ISBN: 978-0-85719-806-8
eBook ISBN: 978-0-85719-807-5

British Library Cataloguing in Publication Data
A CIP catalogue record for this book can be obtained from the British Library.

www.ITHB.co.uk

CONTENTS

INTRODUCTION

T HE 2020 EDITION of our annual publication *The Investment Trusts Handbook* incorporates a range of new features, as well as an expanded reference section and directory. The content falls naturally into three main categories: (1) a series of seven articles reviewing the year that has elapsed since the last edition was published; (2) 15 articles containing professional perspectives on some of the key topics of the moment; and (3) a new, more comprehensive, reference section that includes data, analysis, and an expanded directory of the largest investment companies.

The topical issues covered include: the outlook for investment returns; the collapse of Woodford Investment Management and its fallout; the role of corporate governance in the trust business; the remarkable impact that new technology is having on investment returns; and the way that investment trusts are having to change the way that they market themselves, and communicate with investors in today's digital age. More than 95% of the content in this year's handbook is either new or completely updated. Unless otherwise stated, all the data and graphs included here were accurate as at the start of October 2019.

As I noted last year, investment trusts remain the connoisseur's choice when it comes to investing, but that does not mean that the sector can afford not to move with the times. The need to 'adapt or die' is a theme that runs through this year's edition. I am aware, from reader feedback, that many of you have found the 'How to' articles that we have published in previous editions very helpful in learning more about how investment trusts work, and why and how they can make a material difference to your wealth.

As a result, the publishers and I have decided to make a selection of the best introductory articles from previous editions available, as a free archive on the handbook website (www.ithb.co.uk), for anyone who buys the latest edition. In addition, I hope to produce an expanded version of the section on 'Analysing investment trusts', which featured in the previous two editions as a short standalone guide, that can be downloaded in pdf format. My Editor's Notes will this year also be available to download from the handbook website.

Against a background of endless Brexit negotiations, an evolving US–China trade war, a slowing world economy, and persistently low interest rates, the outlook for investors going into 2020 remains as challenging as ever. Those of us who rely mainly on investment trusts to ensure our financial well-being can take comfort in the knowledge that trusts have navigated many worse things in the century and a half since the first one appeared and, today, still offer a wide variety of flexible and diversified solutions suitable for most needs and risk profiles. To profit from this choice does, however, require a commitment to further your knowledge and experience, something which the handbook is designed to help you achieve.

JONATHAN DAVIS MA, MSC, MCSI is one of the UK's leading stock market authors and commentators. A qualified professional investor and member of the Chartered Institute for Securities and Investment, he is a senior external adviser at Saunderson House and a non-executive director of the JUPITER UK GROWTH TRUST. *His books include* Money Makers, Investing With Anthony Bolton *and* Templeton's Way With Money. *After writing columns for* The Independent *and* Financial Times *for many years, he now writes a private circulation newsletter and is researching two new books. His website is: www.independent-investor.com.*

We strive to explore further.

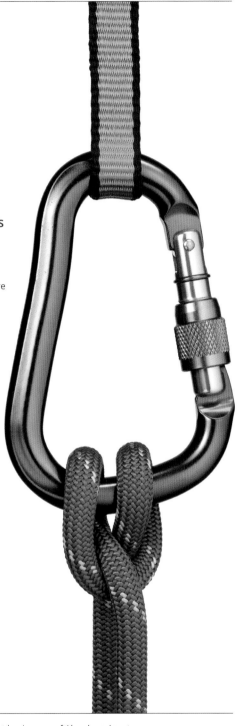

Aberdeen Standard Investment Trusts ISA and Share Plan

We believe there's no substitute for getting to know your investments face-to-face. That's why we make it our goal to visit companies – wherever they are – before we invest in their shares and while we hold them.

With a wide range of investment companies investing around the world – that's an awfully big commitment. But it's just one of the ways we aim to seek out the best investment opportunities on your behalf.

Please remember, the value of shares and the income from them can go down as well as up and you may get back less than the amount invested. No recommendation is made, positive or otherwise, regarding the ISA and Share Plan.

The value of tax benefits depends on individual circumstances and the favourable tax treatment for ISAs may not be maintained. We recommend you seek financial advice prior to making an investment decision.

Request a brochure: **0808 500 4000**
invtrusts.co.uk

Aberdeen**Standard**
Investments

ACKNOWLEDGEMENTS

Compiling *The Investment Trusts Handbook 2020* has once again been an intensive and collective effort. Thanks to all of those who have helped to bring it to fruition, whether as contributors or handmaidens to the production process.

At Harriman House: Stephen Eckett, Myles Hunt, Sally Tickner, Christopher Parker, Tracy Bundey and Tim Clarke.

Contributors (past and present): Robin Angus, John Baron, James Burns, Charles Cade, James Carthew, Geoffrey Challinor, Sandy Cross, Susie Cummings, Richard Curling, Piers Currie, Mark Dampier, Alex Davies, Alex Denny, Clare Dobie, Simon Elliott, George Kershaw, Max King, John Newlands, Ian Sayers, William Sobczak, Peter Spiller, Bruce Stout, Tony Yousefian.

Research: Charles Cade, Ewan Lovett-Turner (Numis), Simon Elliott, Kieran Drake, Emma Bird (Winterfloods), Christopher Brown (J.P.Morgan Cazenove), Alan Brierley (Investec), Annabel Brodie Smith, David Michael (the AIC), Ross Leckie (Artemis), Richard Pavry (Devon Equity Management), William Heathcoat Amory (Kepler Intelligence), Ed Marten (Marten & Co/Quoted Data), David Elliott.

At the publishing partners: Alex Denny, Claire Dwyer (Fidelity), Piers Currie, Louise Bouverat (Aberdeen Standard), Natalie McNab (Jupiter), Vik Heerah, Gary Corcoran, John Regnier-Wilson (Polar Capital).

INVESTMENT TRUST BASICS

For first-time investors in trusts, here is an overview of investment trusts – what they are and how they invest – from editor JONATHAN DAVIS.

What is an investment trust?

INVESTMENT TRUSTS, ALSO known as investment companies, are a type of collective investment fund. All types of fund pool the money of a large number of different investors and delegate the investment of their pooled assets, typically to a professional fund manager. The idea is that this enables shareholders in the trust to spread their risks and benefit from the professional skills and economies of scale available to an investment **management firm.**

Collective funds have been a simple and popular way for individual investors to invest their savings for many years, and investment trusts have shared in that success. Today more than £190 billion of savers' assets are invested in investment trusts. The first investment trust was launched as long ago as 1868, so they have a long history. Sales of open-ended funds (unit trusts, OEICs and UCITs funds) have grown faster, but investment trust performance has generally been superior.

How do investment trusts differ from unit trusts and open-ended funds?

There are several differences. The most important ones are that shares in investment companies are traded on a stock exchange and are overseen by an independent board of directors, like any other listed company. Shareholders have the right to vote at annual general meetings (AGMs) and vote on the re-election of the directors. Trusts can also, unlike most open-ended funds, borrow money in order to enhance returns. Whereas the size of a unit trust rises and falls from day to day, the capital base of an investment trust remains fixed.

What are discounts?

Because shares in investment trusts are traded on a stock exchange, the share price will fluctuate from day to day in response to supply and demand. Sometimes the shares will change hands for less than the net asset value (NAV) of the company. At other times they will change hands for more than the NAV. The difference between the share price and the NAV is calculated as a percentage of the NAV and is called a discount if the share price is below the NAV and a premium if it is above the NAV.

What is gearing?

In investment, gearing refers to the ability of an investor to borrow money in an attempt to enhance the returns that flow from his or her investment decisions. If investments rise more rapidly than the cost of the borrowing, this has the effect of producing higher returns. The reverse is also true. Investment trusts typically borrow around 10–20% of their assets, although this figure varies widely from one trust to another.

What are the main advantages of investing in an investment trust?

Because the capital is largely fixed, the managers of an investment trust can buy and sell the trust's investments when they wish to – instead of having to buy and sell simply because money is flowing in or out of the fund, as unit trust managers are required to do. The ability to gear, or use borrowed money, can also potentially produce better returns. The fact that the board of an investment trust is accountable to the shareholders can also be an advantage.

Another advantage is that investment companies can invest in a much wider range of investments than other types of fund. In fact, they can invest in almost anything. Although many of the largest trusts invest in listed stocks and bonds, more specialist sectors, such as renewable energy projects, debt securities, aircraft leasing and infrastructure projects such as schools, have also become much more popular in recent years. Investment trusts offer fund investors a broader choice, in other words.

And what are the disadvantages?

The two main disadvantages are share price volatility and potential loss of liquidity. Because investment trusts can trade at a discount to the value of their assets, an investor who sells at the wrong moment may not receive the full asset value for his shares at that point. The day-to-day value of the investment can also fluctuate more than an equivalent open-ended fund. In the case of more

Cut through
with conviction

FIDELITY INVESTMENT TRUSTS

Truly global and award-winning, the range is supported by expert portfolio managers, regional research teams and on-the-ground professionals with local connections.

With 372 investment professionals across the globe, we believe this gives us stronger insights across the markets in which we invest. This is key in helping each trust identify local trends and invest with the conviction needed to generate long-term outperformance.

Fidelity's range of investment trusts:

- Fidelity Asian Values PLC
- Fidelity China Special Situations PLC
- Fidelity European Values PLC
- Fidelity Japan Trust PLC
- Fidelity Special Values PLC

Past performance is not a reliable indicator of future returns. The value of investments can go down as well as up and you may not get back the amount you invested. Overseas investments are subject to currency fluctuations. The shares in the investment trusts are listed on the London Stock Exchange and their price is affected by supply and demand.

The investment trusts can gain additional exposure to the market, known as gearing, potentially increasing volatility. Some of the trusts invest more heavily than others in smaller companies, which can carry a higher risk because their share prices may be more volatile than those of larger companies.

To find out more, go to fidelity.co.uk/its or speak to your adviser.

specialist trusts, it may not always be possible to buy or sell shares in a trust at a good price because of a lack of liquidity in the market. Investors need to make sure they understand these features before investing.

How many trusts are there?

According to the industry trade body, the Association of Investment Companies, there are currently around 400 investment trusts with more than £190bn in assets (as at the end of September 2019). They are split between a number of different sectors. The largest trust has approximately £7bn in assets.

How are they regulated?

All investment companies are regulated by the Financial Conduct Authority. So too are the managers the board appoints to manage the trust's investments. Investment trusts are also subject to the Listing Rules of the stock exchange on which they are listed. The board of directors is accountable to shareholders and regulators for the performance of the trust and the appointment of the manager.

How do I invest in an investment trust?

There are a number of different ways. You can buy them directly through a stockbroker, or via an online platform. Some larger investment trusts also have monthly savings schemes where you can transfer a fixed sum every month to the company, which then invests it into its shares on your behalf. If you have a financial adviser, or a portfolio manager, they can arrange the investment for you.

What do investment trusts cost?

As with any share, investors in investment trusts will need to pay brokerage commission when buying or selling shares in an investment trust, and also stamp duty on purchases. The managers appointed by the trust's directors to make its investments charge an annual management fee which is paid automatically, together with dealing and administration costs, out of the trust's assets. These management fees typically range from as little as 0.3% to 2.0% or more of the trust's assets.

What are tax wrappers?

Tax wrappers are schemes which allow individual investors, if they comply with the rules set by the government, to avoid tax on part or all of their investments. The two most important tax wrappers are the Individual Savings Account (or ISA) and the Self-Invested Personal Pension (SIPP). The majority of investment trusts can be held in an ISA or SIPP. There are annual limits on the amounts that can be invested each year (currently £20,000 for an ISA). Venture capital trusts (VCTs) are a specialist type of investment trust which also have a number of tax advantages, reflecting their higher risk.

Where can I find more information?

The best place to start is with the website of the Association of Investment Companies (AIC), which has a lot of basic information, as well as performance and other data. The *Money Makers* website has detailed tables summarising the main features of the most important trusts. Most online broker platforms, such as Hargreaves Lansdown, Fidelity Funds Network and The Share Centre provide factsheets, performance data, charts and other information. Many trusts now have their own websites too.

Independent research sites, such as FE Trustnet, Interactive Investor, Citywire, DigitalLook, Morningstar and periodicals such as the *Financial Times*, *MoneyWeek*, *Money Observer* and *Investors Chronicle* also regularly provide updates and recommendations on investment trusts. Citywire has a dedicated online investment trust newsletter. *Investment Trusts* is an independent subscription-only newsletter.

Lastly, head to www.ithb.co.uk for our official handbook website – where a wealth of valuable content and data can be accessed.

KEY TERMS EXPLAINED

Investment trusts (aka investment companies) pool the money of individual and professional investors and invest it for them in order to generate capital gains, or dividend income, or both. These are the most important factors that determine how good an investment they are:

SHARE PRICE
The price (typically in pence) you will be asked to pay to buy or sell shares in any investment company. You want it to go up, not down.

SPREAD
The difference between the price per share you will need to pay if you want to buy and that you will be offered if you wish to sell – can be anything from 0% (good) to 5% (bad).

MARKET CAPITALISATION

The aggregate current value of all the shares a trust has issued – in essence, therefore, what the market in its wisdom thinks the investment company is worth today.[*]

NET ASSET VALUE (NAV)

The value of the company's investments less running costs at the most recent valuation point – typically (and ideally) that will be yesterday's quoted market price, but for some types of investment trust it might be one or more months ago.

NET ASSET VALUE PER SHARE

This is calculated, not surprisingly, by dividing the NAV (see above) by the number of shares in issue. You can compare it directly with the share price to find the discount.

DISCOUNT/PREMIUM

When the share price is below the investment company's net asset value per share it is said to be trading 'at a discount'; if it trades above the NAV per share, then the trust is selling 'at a premium'.

DIVIDEND YIELD

How much a trust pays out as income each year to its shareholders, expressed as a percentage of its share price.

THE FUND MANAGER

The person (or team) responsible for choosing and managing the investment trust's capital. Will typically be professionally qualified and highly paid. How much value he or she really adds is hotly debated.

THE BOARD

Investment companies are listed companies, so they must comply with stock exchange rules and appoint a board of independent directors who are legally responsible for overseeing the company and protecting the interests of its shareholders, which ultimately means replacing the manager or closing down the trust if results are no good.

GEARING

A fancy word for borrowing money in order to try and boost the performance of a company's shares – a case of more risk for potentially more reward.

---

[*] The market is not always wise and would be a duller and less interesting place if it were.

ACTIVE

High Conviction Fund Management since 1985

At Jupiter, we encourage our fund managers to follow their convictions and actively look for new investment opportunities.

For over thirty years, this culture of freethinking and individuality has allowed us to search for the best investments, as we look to grow our clients' money. We believe it's this confidence to be truly active, that sets us apart.

As with all investing, your capital is at risk.

Discover the Jupiter difference. Visit **jupiteram.com** or search **JUPITER ASSET MANAGEMENT**.

VISIT **JUPITERAM.COM**

JUPITER
Asset Management

FEES AND CHARGES

What it costs to own shares in an investment trust – a figure that (confusingly) can be calculated in several different ways. More important than it sounds on first hearing.

SECTORS

Investment trusts come in many shapes and sizes, so for convenience are categorised into one of a number of different sectors, based on the kind of things that they invest in.

PERFORMANCE

A popular and over-used term which tells you how much money an investment trust has made for its shareholders over any given period of time – by definition, a backward-looking measurement.

TOTAL RETURN

A way of combining the income a trust pays with the capital gains it also generates (you hope) over time, so as to allow fair comparisons with other trusts and funds.

RISK AND RETURN

Riskier investments tend to produce higher returns over time, typically at the cost of doing less well when market conditions are unfavourable and better when they are more helpful. Risk comes in many (dis)guises, however – some more visible than others.

IS THERE ANY DIFFERENCE BETWEEN AN INVESTMENT COMPANY AND INVESTMENT TRUST?

Basically no. Strictly speaking, investment trusts are investment companies but not all investment companies are investment trusts. Feel free to use either term interchangeably, without fear of embarrassment.

CLOSED-END FUNDS

Investment trusts are an example of what is called a 'closed-end fund', meaning that its capital base is intended to be fixed and permanent (unlike unit trusts and OEICs, which take in and return money to investors on a daily basis and are therefore called open-ended). The distinction is no longer quite as important as it was, as it has become somewhat easier for investment companies to raise new money through share issues.

USEFUL SOURCES OF INFORMATION

Industry information

The Association of Investment Companies | www.theaic.co.uk

Data, news and research

The Investment Trusts Handbook official website | www.ithb.co.uk

Morningstar | www.morningstar.co.uk

FE Trustnet | www.trustnet.co.uk

Citywire | www.citywire.co.uk

DigitalLook | www.digitallook.com

Platforms

Interactive Investor | www.iii.co.uk

Hargreaves Lansdown | www.hl.co.uk

The Share Centre | www.share.com

Fidelity International | www.fidelity.co.uk

Alliance Trust Savings | www.alliancetrustsavings.co.uk

Research

Edison | www.edisoninvestmentresearch.com

QuotedData | www.quoteddata.com

Trust Intelligence (Kepler Partners) | www.trustintelligence.co.uk

Specialist publications

Investment Trust Newsletter (McHattie Group) | www.tipsheets.co.uk

Investment Trust Insider (Citywire) | www.citywire.co.uk

Money Observer (regular supplements) | www.moneyobserver.com

Publications that regularly feature investment trusts

Financial Times | www.ft.com

Investors Chronicle | www.investorschronicle.co.uk

MoneyWeek | www.moneyweek.com

Polar Capital Technology Trust plc

Digital Disruption:
Transforming the world bit by bit

Twenty years after the dawn of the commercial internet, nearly every sector is now being challenged, improved or replaced by disruptive technology. The Polar Capital Technology Trust – managed by a team of dedicated technology specialists – has a proven track record with the ability to spot developing technology trends early on and to invest in those companies best placed to exploit them.

Find out more about how the
Polar Capital Technology Trust
is helping to transform the world bit by bit.

London Stock Exchange Ticker: PCT

Visit **polarcapitaltechnologytrust.co.uk**
Available to purchase through all major platform providers, stockbrokers and/or your financial adviser.

YEAR IN
REVIEW

MONTH BY MONTH IN 2019

W<small>E SUMMARISE HERE</small> some of the main events of the year to date in the investment trust world.

JANUARY 2019

Corporate activity

BIOPHARMA CREDIT announced that it had received a payment of $370 million after a loan was repaid early. The fund now has cash equivalent to 55% of net assets. GREENCOAT UK WIND is looking to invest £452m in two Scottish wind farms and will look to raise up to £131m to help fund the deal. PRIMARY HEALTH PROPERTIES and MEDICX FUND revealed an all-share merger, while Andrew Rose will retire as the manager of SCHRODER JAPAN GROWTH at the end of June, to be succeeded by Masaki Taketsume.

Sector outperformed in January

The UK market bounced back in January, erasing the losses seen in December and providing the best start to a year since 2013. Investment trusts outperformed for the third time in the last six months, with the FTSE Equity Investment Instruments Index up 4.6% in January compared with a rise of 4.2% for the FTSE All-Share Index.

Recent issuance

January was a reasonably quiet month for issuance, with just £350m raised across the sector. This compares with £213m for the previous month and £267m for the equivalent month in 2018. The difficult fundraising conditions last month were highlighted by the postponement of the launch of THE GLOBAL SUSTAINABILITY TRUST. BLACKSTONE/GSO LOAN FINANCING issued 134m C shares relating to a partial rollover from CARADOR INCOME, while placings included AXIOM EUROPEAN FINANCIAL DEBT* (£6m) and M&G CREDIT INCOME* (£25m).

[19]

Another £242m was raised through smaller, secondary issuance in January including: SCOTTISH MORTGAGE (£56m), SMITHSON IT (£53m), CITY OF LONDON (£22m), FINSBURY GROWTH & INCOME* (£21m), CAPITAL GEARING (£12m), BB HEALTHCARE (£9m), PERSONAL ASSETS (£9m), FIDELITY SPECIAL VALUES (£8m), and WORLDWIDE HEALTHCARE* (£8m).

FEBRUARY 2019

Corporate activity

In recent developments, Jeroen Huysinga, who has been involved in the management of JPMORGAN GLOBAL GROWTH & INCOME* since 2008, will retire later this year. Raj Tanna and Helge Skibeli will join Tim Woodhouse as the fund's joint portfolio managers with effect from 14 March. WOODFORD PATIENT CAPITAL* announced the issuance of 75m new shares to Woodford Equity Income Fund in exchange for a portfolio of five unquoted companies. The open-ended fund now owns 9% of the investment trust's share capital.

Sector underperformed in February

The UK market enjoyed another positive month in February, with the FTSE All-Share Index up 2.3%. Investment trusts underperformed the UK market for the fourth time in the last six months, with the FTSE All-Share Equity Investment Instruments Index up 1.9% in February. However, so far this year the sector is just ahead of the FTSE All-Share Index, with the sector up 6.7% to the end of February compared with 6.6% for the index.

Recent issuance

February saw a pick-up in issuance activity, with £614m raised across the sector, compared with £350m in January. So far, in 2019, £964m has been raised across the investment trust sector, a 28% increase on the £755m raised in the first two months of 2018. The largest fund-raising came from TRITAX BIG BOX, which raised £250m through issuing shares at a 15% discount to NAV, in order to fund a strategic acquisition. TRITAX BIG BOX now has a market cap of £2.4 billion. February also saw GREENCOAT UK WIND raise £131m in order to pay down its credit facility. A number of funds continue to regularly issue shares at a premium to NAV, and we estimate that £164m was raised through smaller, secondary issuance in February, compared with £242m in January. This included: SMITHSON IT (£27m), FINSBURY GROWTH & INCOME* (£25m), SCOTTISH

MORTGAGE (£24m), CAPITAL GEARING (£11m), WORLDWIDE HEALTHCARE* (£10m), PERSONAL ASSETS (£9m), and CITY OF LONDON (£6m).

MARCH 2019

Corporate activity

In recent developments, the Board of JPMORGAN AMERICAN* proposed a change of investment approach for its large cap portfolio that combines the best ideas from both JPM's growth and value investment teams into a high-conviction portfolio. If shareholder approval is forthcoming Jonathan Simon and Tim Parton would replace Garrett Fish as the fund's lead manager. SYNCONA announced that it would look to reduce its investment in third-party managed funds and increase its weighting to cash. The WELLCOME TRUST reduced its stake in the fund from 37% to 28% last month, following an institutional placing.

Sector underperformed in March

The UK market continued to rise in March, with the FTSE All-Share Index up 2.7%, while investment trusts underperformed for the third time in the last four months. The FTSE Equity Investment Instruments Index was up 1.5% in March. Unsurprisingly, so far this year the sector is behind the FTSE All-Share Index, with the sector up 8.3% in the first quarter of the year compared with a 9.4% rise for the index.

Recent issuance

March was a good month for issuance, with £1,228m raised across the sector compared with £614m in February. So far, in 2019, £2,191m has been raised across the investment trust sector, a 52% increase on the £1,444m raised in the first three months of 2018. The first IPO of the year, with the launch of THE SCHIEHALLION FUND* by Baillie Gifford, raised $477m from the firm's existing institutional clients. The largest placing in March was for THE RENEWABLES INFRASTRUCTURE GROUP (£302m), while GREENCOAT RENEWABLES raised €148m. Property remains in favour, with WAREHOUSE REIT and SUPERMARKET INCOME REIT raising £76m and £45m respectively.

Other issues in March included: TUFTON OCEANIC ASSETS ($50m), TWENTYFOUR INCOME (£23m), and RM SECURED DIRECT LENDING (£14m), while WOODFORD PATIENT CAPITAL* issued 81m shares at NAV to LF Woodford Equity Income Fund, in exchange for cash of £6m and a portfolio of unquoted assets valued at £73m.

APRIL 2019

Corporate activity

The board of AEW UK LONG LEASE REIT announced that it was reviewing options for the fund's future after a major tenant went into administration. The Social Housing Regulator published a report outlining its concerns over providers who lease their property portfolio. Both CIVITAS SOCIAL HOUSING and TRIPLE POINT SOCIAL HOUSING are exposed to providers that were judged as 'non-compliant'. Lord Rothschild announced that he would stand down as Chairman of RIT CAPITAL PARTNERS in September.

Sector outperformed in April

The UK market rose for a fourth consecutive month in April, with the FTSE All-Share Index up 2.7%. Investment trusts outperformed the UK market for the first time in the last three months, with the FTSE Equity Investment Instruments Index up 3.5%. However, so far this year the sector is behind the FTSE All-Share Index, with a rise of 12.1% in the first four months of the year compared with 12.3% for the index.

Recent issuance

April was a quieter month for issuance, with £735m raised across the sector compared with £1,229m in March. So far, in 2019, £2,952m has been raised across the investment trust sector, a 43% increase on the £2,064m raised in the first four months of 2018. The month saw the second IPO of the year with the launch of the US SOLAR FUND, which raised $200m. April also saw a number of recently launched funds return to the market to raise additional capital. This included HIPGNOSIS SONGS (£142m), MERIAN CHRYSALIS (£100m), and SDCL ENERGY EFFICIENCY INCOME (£72m), while SUPERMARKET INCOME REIT issued shares worth £11m as part of the acquisition of a supermarket in Nottingham. Another £258m was raised through regular issuance in April, including: SCOTTISH MORTGAGE (£56m), SMITHSON IT (£53m), FINSBURY GROWTH & INCOME* (£24m), CITY OF LONDON (£15m), TWENTYFOUR INCOME (£13m), BB HEALTHCARE TRUST (£10m), and EDINBURGH WORLDWIDE (£8m).

MAY 2019

Corporate activity

The board of THE EUROPEAN INVESTMENT TRUST announced that it was reviewing the fund's management arrangements following a period of disappointing returns. Michael O'Brien and Sandip Patodia were promoted to portfolio manager and assistant portfolio manager, respectively, of FUNDSMITH EMERGING EQUITIES, with Terry Smith providing support in his role as CIO of Fundsmith. The management team of JOHN LAING ENVIRONMENTAL ASSETS GROUP* is to move to Foresight. The board of MARTIN CURRIE ASIA UNCONSTRAINED proposed that shareholders be offered either cash or a rollover into an equivalent open-ended fund, due to structural challenges preventing buying interest in the investment trust.

Sector outperformed in May

The UK market saw its first monthly decline of the year in May, with the FTSE All-Share Index down 3.0%. However, investment trusts outperformed the UK market for the second time in the last three months, with the FTSE Equity Investment Instruments Index down 2.6% in May. As a result, so far this year the sector is slightly ahead of the FTSE All-Share Index, with a rise of 9.2% in the first five months of the year compared with 9.0% for the index.

Recent issuance

May was a strong month for issuance, with £1,121m raised across the sector compared with £735m in April. So far, in 2019, £4,072m has been raised across the investment trust sector, a 50% increase on the £2,718m raised in the first five months of 2018. Two IPOs were seen: RIVERSTONE CREDIT OPPORTUNITIES INCOME, which raised $100m, and AQUILA EUROPEAN RENEWABLES INCOME FUND, which raised €154m. The largest fundraising in May was in the Environmental Infrastructure sector, with GREENCOAT UK WIND raising £375m, while GRESHAM HOUSE ENERGY STORAGE FUND raised £50m. Demand for specialist property funds remains strong with fundraising from TRITAX EUROBOX (€135m), IMPACT HEALTHCARE REIT* (£100m), and GCP STUDENT LIVING (£5m). In the Property Debt sector, REAL ESTATE CREDIT INVESTMENTS raised £78m, and STARWOOD EUROPEAN REAL ESTATE FINANCE raised £40m. Other issues included: TWENTYFOUR INCOME FUND (£80m), CVC CREDIT PARTNERS EUROPEAN OPPORTUNITIES* (£24m), and AVI JAPAN OPPORTUNITIES (£13m).

JUNE 2019

Corporate activity

In recent developments, Jupiter Fund Management announced that Alexander Darwall was planning to launch an investment management business, Devon Equity Management. The board of JUPITER EUROPEAN OPPORTUNITIES is investigating the possibility of appointing Devon to advise on its investment portfolio. Also last month, SYNCONA published its annual results and announced that it had sold its holding in Blue Earth. We estimate that cash/liquidity now represents around two-thirds of net assets.

Sector underperformed in June

The UK market enjoyed a positive month in June, with the FTSE All-Share Index up 3.7%. However, investment trusts underperformed the UK market for the third time in the last six months, with the FTSE Equity Investment Instruments Index up 3.3% in June. So far, this year, the sector is slightly behind the FTSE All-Share Index, with a rise of 12.8% in the first six months of the year compared with 13.0% for the index.

Recent issuance

June was another good month for issuance, with £967m raised across the sector, although it was down 14% from May when £1,121m was raised. So far, in 2019, £5,039m has been raised across the sector, a 70% increase on the £2,968m raised in the first six months of 2018. The largest fundraising in June was for SEQUOIA ECONOMIC INFRASTRUCTURE INCOME (£216m), while the Infrastructure sector also saw BBGI raise £75m. AQUILA EUROPEAN RENEWABLES INCOME FUND started trading after raising €154m through its IPO.

Other fundraising last month included: LXI REIT (£200m), HGCAPITAL TRUST (£64m), GCP ASSET BACKED INCOME (£63m), AUGMENTUM FINTECH (£29m), CVC CREDIT PARTNERS EUROPEAN OPPORTUNITIES* (£24m), BB HEALTHCARE (£17m), and PICTON PROPERTY INCOME (£7m).

JULY 2019

Corporate activity

ATLANTIS JAPAN GROWTH announced a series of measures ahead of its continuation vote that included the adoption of an enhanced dividend, and the removal of its periodic redemption mechanism. PERSHING SQUARE HOLDINGS faced criticism from two shareholders following the issue of debt worth $400m. The Board of WOODFORD PATIENT CAPITAL* announced that, as well as closely monitoring the situation at Woodford Investment Management, it had held preliminary discussions with other management groups. In early July, Neil Woodford sold 1.75m shares in the fund, representing 60% of his personal holding.

Sector outperformed in July

The UK market enjoyed another positive month in July, with the FTSE All-Share Index up 2.0%. Investment trusts outperformed the UK market for the third time in the last four months, with the FTSE Equity Investment Instruments Index up 2.7% in July. So far, this year, the sector is slightly ahead of the FTSE All-Share Index, with a rise of 15.8% in the first seven months of the year compared with 15.2% for the index.

Recent issuance

July was the quietest month of the year so far for issuance, with £312m raised, down 68% from June, when £967m was raised. So far, in 2019, £5,351m has been raised across the sector, a 36% increase on the £3,923m raised in the first seven months of 2018. The largest fundraising was for REGIONAL REIT, which raised £63m through a placing at an 8% discount to its year-end NAV, while ABERDEEN STANDARD EUROPEAN LOGISTICS INCOME raised £46m (€52m) through issuance at an 8% premium. In the Infrastructure sector, GORE STREET ENERGY STORAGE and GRESHAM HOUSE ENERGY STORAGE raised £31m and £15m respectively, while other fundraising in July came from AUGMENTUM FINTECH, which raised £29m. Another £162m was raised through regular issuance, including: SMITHSON IT (£31m), CAPITAL GEARING (£22m), and PERSONAL ASSETS (£21m), while SCOTTISH MORTGAGE did not issue any new shares in a month for the first time since March 2018.

AUGUST 2019

FTSE UK Index changes

The results of the latest quarterly FTSE UK Index Review were announced on 4 September, with the changes taking effect after the close of business on Friday 20 September. There will be two investment companies involved in the changes to the FTSE 250, with WOODFORD PATIENT CAPITAL* to be relegated, while FORESIGHT SOLAR FUND will be promoted from the FTSE Small Cap. In addition,

MERIAN CHRYSALIS and SDCL ENERGY EFFICIENCY INCOME will be promoted to the FTSE All-Share and FTSE Small Cap indices, while RDL REALISATION will be relegated.

Sector outperformed in August

The UK market fell in August, with the FTSE All-Share Index down 3.6%. Investment trusts outperformed the UK market for the fourth time in the last five months, with the FTSE Equity Investment Instruments Index down 2.6% in August. So far, this year, the sector is ahead of the FTSE All-Share Index, with a rise of 12.8% in the first eight months of the year compared with 11.1% for the index.

Recent issuance

August was the quietest month of the year so far for issuance, with just £182m raised, down 41% from July, when £312m was raised. So far, in 2019, £5,533m has been raised across the sector, a 36% increase on the £4,067m raised in the first eight months of 2018. The largest fundraising seen last month was for HIPGNOSIS SONGS, which raised £51m through a placing at a small premium to its share price, while GORE STREET ENERGY STORAGE raised £6m to invest in energy storage projects in Northern Ireland and the Republic of Ireland.

A further £125m was raised through smaller, secondary issuance in August including: PERSONAL ASSETS (£26m), CAPITAL GEARING (£23m), BB HEALTHCARE (£10m), SMITHSON IT (£9m), FINSBURY GROWTH & INCOME* (£7m), CITY OF LONDON IT (£6m), BAILLIE GIFFORD SHIN NIPPON (£6m), and ALLIANZ TECHNOLOGY TRUST*(£6m).

SEPTEMBER 2019

Corporate activity

In recent developments, GABELLI VALUE PLUS+ announced that Investec Wealth & Investment, one of its largest shareholders, was looking to requisition a general meeting in order to propose a continuation vote. The board of JUPITER EUROPEAN OPPORTUNITIES announced the imminent appointment of Devon Equity Management, Alexander Darwall's new investment management company, as manager. WOODFORD PATIENT CAPITAL* announced a series of write downs, while its board continues to evaluate its portfolio management arrangements.

Sector underperformed in September

The UK market rose in September, with the FTSE All-Share Index up 3.0%. Investment trusts underperformed the UK market for only the second time in the last six months, with the FTSE Equity Investment Instruments Index up just 0.7%. So far, this year, the sector is behind the FTSE All-Share Index, with a rise of 13.6% in the first nine months of the year compared with 14.4% for the index.

Recent issuance

September was a decent month for issuance, with £723m raised across the sector. This was up 297% from August, when £182m was raised, and up 142% on the same month last year. So far, in 2019, £6,256m has been raised across the investment trust sector, a 43% increase on the £4,366m raised in the first nine months of 2018. September saw the sixth IPO of the year with the launch of JPMORGAN GLOBAL CORE REAL ASSETS, which raised £149m. The largest fundraising was for MERIAN CHRYSALIS (£175m), while specialist property funds also remain in demand, with fundraisings for SUPERMARKET INCOME REIT (£100m) and TARGET HEALTHCARE REIT (£80m). Other recent fundraisings have included TUFTON OCEANIC ASSETS ($31m) and REAL ESTATE CREDIT INVESTMENTS (£17m). Another £147m was raised through smaller, secondary issuance in September including: FINSBURY GROWTH & INCOME* (£25m), CAPITAL GEARING (£22m), SMITHSON IT (£19m), PERSONAL ASSETS (£12m), IMPAX ENVIRONMENTAL MARKETS (£10m), SCHRODER ORIENTAL INCOME (£10m), and BB HEALTHCARE (£9m).

These month-by-month summaries are extracted from the excellent monthly investment trust reports prepared by the Winterflood Investment Trusts research team and are reproduced here with their permission.

---

*   Denotes a corporate broking client of Winterflood Securities.

FIRST QUARTER 2019

Figure 1: Best performing funds in price terms in Q1 *

	(%)
Leaf Clean Energy	62.2
Pershing Square Holdings	30.7
3i	27.3
Allianz Technology Trust	25.4
JPMorgan Chinese	25.0
Fidelity China Special	24.6
Edinburgh Worldwide	23.4
Schroder UK Mid Cap	22.8
Lindsell Train	21.9
Premier Global Infrastructure	21.8

Source: Morningstar, * excluding funds with market cap. below £15m

Figure 2: Best performing funds in NAV terms in Q1 *

	(%)
Pershing Square Holdings	33.8
Allianz Technology Trust	31.3
JPMorgan Chinese	26.7
Premier Global Infrastructure	21.1
Fidelity China Special	21.0
Smithson Investment Trust	20.7
BB Healthcare	18.9
Independent Investment Trust	18.1
Edinburgh Worldwide	17.9
Manchester & London	17.3

Source: Morningstar, * excluding funds with market cap. below £15m

Figure 3: Worst performing funds in price terms in Q1*

	(%)
Doric Nimrod Air One	(17.3)
RDL Realisation	(15.6)
Doric Nimrod Air Three	(15.3)
Adamas Finance Asia	(15.2)
Marble Point Loan Financing	(13.6)
Better Capital PCC 2012	(13.2)
Riverstone Energy	(12.7)
Doric Nimrod Air Two	(12.4)
Amedeo Air Four Plus	(11.6)
Ground Rents Income Fund Plc	(10.6)

Source: Morningstar, * excluding funds with market cap. below £15m

Figure 4: Worst performing funds in NAV terms in Q1 *

	(%)
Ashmore Global Opportunity USD	(9.0)
Miton UK Microcap	(6.6)
3i	(6.4)
Alpha Real Trust	(6.2)
Marwyn Value Investors	(6.2)
Reconstruction Capital II	(5.1)
Downing Strategic Micro-Cap Inv. Trust	(4.4)
Sanditon Investment Trust	(4.3)
Green REIT	(4.1)
Blackstone/GSO Loan Financing	(3.8)

Source: Morningstar, * excluding funds with market cap. below £15m

Figure 5: Money entering the sector in Q1 2019

	£m
The Schiehallion Fund	$477.3
Tritax Big Box	334.2
Smithson Investment Trust	97.7
Scottish Mortgage	88.8
Finsbury Growth & Income	76.9
Tufton Oceanic Assets	67.5
BlackRock Frontiers	47.0
Supermarket Income REIT	45.4
City of London	41.4
Capital Gearing	33.3

Source: Morningstar, * approximate value of additional capital at 30/03/2019

Figure 6: Money leaving the sector in Q1 2019

	£m
Edinburgh Dragon	(215.4)
Carador Income Fund USD	(85.0)
NB Global Floating Rate Income GBP	(72.4)
Templeton Emerging Markets	(22.7)
JPEL Private Equity	(15.7)
Third Point Offshore USD	(13.5)
Alcentra Eur Floating Rate Inc	(11.4)
Biotech Growth	(10.3)
Witan	(9.4)
Funding Circle SME Income Fund	(9.3)

Source: Morningstar, * approximate value of shares bought back at 30/03/2019

SECOND QUARTER 2019

Figure 1: Best performing funds in price terms in Q2 *

	(%)
Leaf Clean Energy	350.0
Green REIT	25.9
JPMorgan Russian Securities	25.2
Lindsell Train	24.6
Kubera Cross-Border	22.9
BH Macro USD	21.0
Montanaro European Smaller	20.5
Gresham House Strategic	20.1
EPE Special Opportunities	19.6
Jupiter European Opportunities	19.4

Source: Morningstar, * excluding funds with market cap. below £15m

Figure 2: Best performing funds in NAV terms in Q2*

	(%)
EPE Special Opportunities	32.6
Baring Emerging Europe	18.4
JPMorgan Russian	17.6
Lindsell Train	16.5
Baker Steel Resources	15.4
JPMorgan Brazil	14.0
Aberdeen New Thai	13.6
Marwyn Value Investors	12.9
Jupiter European Opportunities	12.9
BlackRock Greater Europe	11.7

Source: Morningstar, * excluding funds with market cap. below £15m

Figure 3: Worst performing funds in price terms in Q2*	(%)
CATCo Reinsurance Opportunities	(38.6)
Woodford Patient Capital	(29.3)
Phoenix Spree Deutschland	(22.9)
Triple Point Social Housing REIT	(17.4)
Ceiba Investments	(14.6)
Syncona	(13.4)
Civitas Social Housing	(10.9)
Drum Income Plus REIT	(10.7)
Aberforth Split Level Income	(9.4)
AEW UK Long Lease REIT	(9.1)

Source: Morningstar, * excluding funds with market cap. below £15m

Figure 4: Worst performing funds in NAV terms in Q2 *	(%)
CATCo Reinsurance Opportunities	(15.7)
Woodford Patient Capital	(14.7)
India Capital Growth	(7.3)
Aurora	(5.3)
Fidelity China Special	(5.0)
Aberforth Split Level Income	(3.5)
Independent	(2.5)
Temple Bar	(2.4)
Edinburgh Investment	(2.3)
Perpetual Income & Growth	(2.1)

Source: Morningstar, * excluding funds with market cap. below £15m

Figure 5: Money entering the sector in Q2 2019	£m
Greencoat UK Wind	398.0
Renewables Infrastructure	341.4
Globalworth Real Estate	304.2
Sequoia Economic Infrastructure	227.4
Aquila European Renewables Income**	€154.3
US Solar Fund**	153.0
Hipgnosis Songs	145.7
Smithson Investment Trust	144.9
Tritax EuroBox	117.5
Merian Chrysalis	111.8

Source: Morningstar, * approximate value of additional capital at 28/06/2019. ** proceeds raised from the initial public offering

Figure 6: Money leaving the sector in Q2 2019	£m
Carador Income Fund USD	(66.8)
NB Global Floating Rate Income GBP	(61.4)
Biotech Growth	(28.8)
Third Point Offshore USD	(22.7)
Alliance Trust	(20.0)
Templeton Emerging Markets	(18.7)
VPC Specialty Lending Investments	(17.7)
NB Distressed Debt	(13.9)
Witan	(13.3)
NB Global Floating Rate Income USD	(13.1)

Source: Morningstar, * approximate value of shares bought back at 28/06/2019

THIRD QUARTER 2019

Figure 1: Best performing funds in price terms over Q3 *	(%)
CATCo Reinsurance Opportunities	54.9
UIL	31.2
Golden Prospect Precious Metal	22.7
Triple Point Social Housing REIT	15.2
Third Point Offshore USD	14.5
Secure Income REIT	14.1
Pershing Square	13.7
VPC Specialty Lending	12.9
Livermore Investments	12.6
Ecofin Global Utilities & Infrastructure	12.2

Source: Morningstar, * excluding funds with market cap. below £15m

Figure 2: Best performing funds in NAV terms over Q3*	(%)
RDL Realisation	19.1
Golden Prospect Precious Metal	17.2
VietNam Holding	11.7
Fidelity Japan	11.3
Ecofin Global Utilities & Infrastructure	11.2
Menhaden	10.8
Doric Nimrod Air Three	10.4
Pershing Square	10.0
Doric Nimrod Air One	9.1
Doric Nimrod Air Two	8.6

Source: Morningstar, * excluding funds with market cap. below £15m

Figure 3: Worst performing funds in price terms over Q3*	(%)
Riverstone Energy	(31.1)
Adamas Finance Asia	(25.0)
Lindsell Train	(23.5)
Woodford Patient Capital	(19.8)
Hadrian's Wall Secured	(15.1)
Reconstruction Capital II	(14.1)
Mobius	(13.9)
EPE Special Opportunities Macau	(12.2)
Property Opportunities	(10.6)
Better Capital PCC 2012	(10.5)

Source: Morningstar, * excluding funds with market cap. below £15m

Figure 4: Worst performing funds in NAV terms over Q3 *	(%)
Marwyn Value	(11.7)
Biotech Growth	(11.4)
Woodford Patient Capital	(9.8)
Carador Income USD	(7.9)
BlackRock Latin American	(7.6)
BB Healthcare	(7.4)
Miton UK Microcap	(7.1)
Blue Planet	(7.0)
Downing Strategic Micro-Cap	(6.9)
BlackRock World Mining	(6.8)

Source: Morningstar, * excluding funds with market cap. below £15m

Figure 5: Money entering the sector over Q3 2019	£m	Figure 6: Money leaving the sector over Q3 2019	£m
Merian Chrysalis	175	NB Global Floating Rate Income GBP	(60.4)
JPMorgan Global Core Real Assets	148.9	Edinburgh	(58.2)
Sequoia Economic Infrastructure Target	138.8	Pershing Square	(56.8)
Healthcare REIT	80	Third Point Offshore USD	(51.4)
Capital Gearing	68.9	Leaf Clean Energy	(50.7)
Personal Assets	65.4	Perpetual Income & Growth	(37.8)
Regional REIT	60.4	Templeton Emerging Markets	(27.5)
Smithson	59.5	Witan	(24.8)
Hipgnosis Songs	52.1	Alpha Real	(23.2)
Finsbury Growth & Income	45.2	TwentyFour Income	(19.9)

Source: Morningstar, * approximate value of additional capital at 28/06/2019, **
proceeds raised from the initial public offering

Source: Morningstar, * approximate value of shares bought back at 28/06/2019

These charts are drawn from the invaluable monthly and quarterly roundups of investment trust news produced by the research firm QuotedData. In addition to these regular charts, the roundups also provide news and commentary on recent trends in the investment trust sector and are free for private investors who sign up at www.quoteddata.com.

SIGNIFICANT DEVELOPMENTS IN 2019

Investment trusts

Discounts widened a little, but remain narrower than ten-year average. Capital raised up 20% on 2018 at £6.6bn, led by private equity and infrastructure. Capital returned to shareholders of £2.1bn, well down on 2018. WOODFORD PATIENT CAPITAL switched mandate to Schroders after former manager Woodford Investment Management closed down.

Economy and markets

The Federal Reserve reversed course on interest rates. Bonds had big inflows and gold rallied in the face of global economic slowdown. Equity markets recovered well after sharp declines in Q4 2018. US/China trade war rumbled on. Brexit did not happen (but edged nearer?).

DON'T WORRY, BE HAPPY

Investment trust expert MAX KING *reviews the performance of equity investment trusts in 2019.*

A MID ALL THE political and economic turmoil, the dark forebodings for the future, and continuing investor scepticism, it's been easy to forget that this has been a good year for equity markets. The negative returns of last year, 9.4% in dollars and 3.8% in sterling on the MSCI All Countries World index, have, as of 8 October, been fully recovered with a dollar return, including income, of 13.5%, and a sterling one of 18.3%. Admittedly, the fall in sterling has enhanced returns for UK investors, but some of that is due to general dollar strength, with the Dollar Index (DXY) rising a little over 3%.

For many UK investors, however, it has been a frustrating year. While the US market has regularly been hitting new peaks, passing the 3,000 mark on the S&P 500 index in the summer, the All-Share index languishes 10% below the peak reached in May 2018. The US market continues to power ahead, returning over 20% in the year to date, compared with 5.3% for the UK, 14% for the rest of Europe, 14.3% for Japan, and 9.7% for emerging markets. The UK's underperformance is commonly ascribed to the Brexit effect, but this is far from the whole explanation. The UK economy has performed better than expected, overseas earnings account for about 70% of the total, and the rating of the UK market has not been falling relative to the World index.

The persistence of US outperformance is shown by the fact that while the US market is up 335% since the start of the current bull market ten years ago, the World ex-US is up just 104% in dollars, and 115% in local currency. The US market now accounts for 56% of the MSCI All Countries Index, while the UK is under 5% – a sobering thought for investors anchored to high UK exposure, forlornly hoping that the tide will turn in their favour. In the past, it has been possible to escape the curse of the UK's mega caps by investing in mid and smaller companies, but this year, as last year, they have underperformed both in the UK and internationally.

US outperformance in 2019 has not been driven by earnings growth but by a market re-rating. Analysts expect earnings to advance just 2% this year, after 24% in 2018, much of that the result of Trump's tax cuts. The rise in the S&P index means that the forward multiple of US earnings has risen from 14.3 in December to 17.1 at the end of September. Analysts are expecting a rebound in US earnings growth to 10.1% in 2020, but that is probably discounted in recent market levels. For the S&P index to move much above 3,000 in the next year, without a subsequent setback, will be a challenge.

The driving force behind the strength of the US market is the continuing outperformance of growth stocks over value. As the fact sheet of any technology or health care fund will show, the US dominates the world in these sectors, and its global market share rises inexorably. This dominance extends to other sectors in which technology plays a key part, such as retailing (e.g. Amazon), media (e.g. Netflix), and cars (e.g. Tesla). Innovation has turned around the historic US dependence on energy imports, and its financial sector goes from strength to strength. Surely, desperate value investors argue, this can't go on? Isn't the sort of reversal seen in 2000–2003 overdue?

There was some evidence in September for at least a respite for value investing but, as Nick Schmitz of Verdad Capital notes, "portfolios of the cheapest stocks have underperformed growth portfolios by 152% in the last 12 years, which was only exceeded briefly at the peak of the dotcom bubble. What's more, the same portfolio has underperformed growth in nine of the last 12 calendar years, which has never happened historically. Growth stocks are now more expensive than value stocks (based on market-to-book-value spreads) by margins not exceeded since the peak of the dotcom bubble and the Great Depression."

Schmitz, however, is in no hurry to join the crowd of Eeyores predicting another dotcom crash. The valuation of value stocks has remained stable at 1.1x book, and around 7x cash flow, while growth has been re-rated from 2.5x book to 4x, and from 11x cash flow to 18x. This suggests that the valuation of growth stocks is stretched, but the re-rating can be explained by the fall in the yield on government bonds, which increases the valuation of distant cash flows. If bond yields rise, growth stocks will probably lag, but the violent switch-back which followed the bursting of the dotcom bubble looks unlikely. With technology now far more embedded in the global economy than then, and the path of its progress much clearer, it is not obvious that the information technology sector is expensive on a 15% premium to the S&P's forward multiple of 17. Consumer staples trade at a similar premium, and healthcare at a 15% discount.

Ed Yardeni describes the long bull market since 2009 as interrupted regularly by 'panic attacks' relating to geopolitics, the economic outlook, or other imagined threats. He has counted 64 of these panic attacks, followed by 64 relief rallies. Throughout the bull market, investors have been nervous, cautious, and defensive. For contrarians, this is very positive as bear markets are usually preceded by investor euphoria, with sky-high valuations, money pouring into the market, and a flood of new issues. There is little sign of this in the US, where 'unicorn' private companies with a valuation above $1 billion have struggled to make the transition to the public market. The share prices of Uber, Lyft, and Peloton have fallen by an average of 28% since flotation, while the much-hyped $47bn flotation of office space rental company WeWork has been postponed indefinitely. Pinterest and Zoom have done well, so it's not all gloom for the investment bankers, but the real test will come with the proposed flotation of Airbnb next year.

Nowhere, surely, have investors been more gloomy than in the UK. Monthly outflows from equity funds, according to the Investment Association, have averaged over £500 million and exceeded £1,500m in August. Outflows have been strongest in the UK and Europe, but positive in the North America and Global sectors. These outflows are balanced, to some extent, by the growing popularity of passive ETFs, but there is no doubting investors' aversion to equities. At first sight, issuance by investment companies contradicts this, with £6.6bn raised in the first nine months of 2019, a 20% increase on 2018, while the capital returned of £2.5bn was down nearly 50%. Only £1.6bn of the issuance, however, has been from equity funds, with the rest from the alternatives sector – generally, funds that are expected to have a high yield, low volatility, and low correlation to equity markets. This area now accounts for 48% of the £180bn investment company universe and is mostly comprised of bond proxies – an alternative to government or investment grade bonds at a time when real yields, and often absolute yields, around the world are negative.

Within that total, there have been only five new issues raising money, the lowest number for 20 years. Only one of those, Baillie Gifford's £360m SCHIEHALLION TRUST, investing in private equity, can be regarded as an equities trust, though private equity is classified as being alternative. That leaves £1.6bn of secondary issuance, of which over £1bn was accounted for by six trusts raising over £100m each: SMITHSON (over £300m), FINSBURY GROWTH & INCOME (nearly £200m), CAPITAL GEARING, SCOTTISH MORTGAGE, PERSONAL ASSETS, and BB HEALTHCARE.

With SCOTTISH MORTGAGE now trading at a discount to net asset value, owing to increased scepticism about its high-growth strategy, its issuance has stopped.

Two thirds of the capital returned has been from equities trusts. Notable have been £220m from EDINBURGH DRAGON's 30% tender, £150m from the wind-up of MARTIN CURRIE ASIA UNCONSTRAINED, and £110m from LAZARD WORLD TRUST FUND. Over £100m has been returned by the two Invesco trusts, EDINBURGH INVESTMENT and PERPETUAL INCOME & GROWTH, both formerly managed by Neil Woodford's team. When he left, the managers had an opportunity to break away from the Woodford style, but failed to do so, and subsequent performance has been poor.

Investors will remember 2019 not for the solid gains enjoyed, nor the commendable outperformance generated by many managers in the investment trust sector, but by the Woodford disaster. PATIENT CAPITAL shares have now lost two thirds of their value in five years, and 45% in the year to date. Though their shares trade at an apparent discount of more than 40% to net asset value, there can be little confidence in those asset values. Investors in Woodford's open-ended funds, meanwhile, are locked into a sinking ship. How so many intelligent investors, respected advisors, and experienced commentators, came to be sucked into what was always a deeply-flawed proposition will probably remain an utter mystery.

A less-comprehensible casualty of 2019 has been RIVERSTONE ENERGY, down 24% in net asset value and 45% in share price. Riverstone invests in private equity energy in North America, and should have been a beneficiary of the growth of fracking, and a benign oil price – which rallied from $50 a barrel to $75 in the Spring, but then retreated to $60. Unfortunately, though, and as shown by the share prices of the energy majors, investors just aren't interested in fossil fuel companies.

Given the unexpected, but long overdue, rally in the gold price, it is not surprising that the list of winners in the year to date has been headed by the tiny GOLDEN PROSPECT, up 54% in net asset value and 76% in share price terms. JPMorgan's emerging markets team is on a roll; not only does the core JPMorgan EMERGING MARKETS TRUST continue to perform well ahead of its somewhat disappointing benchmark, but its Russian and Chinese trusts also did well, gaining around 35% in net asset value terms. Russia may be hated by the political and media establishment, but investors who took a different view have been rewarded, as confirmed by the 24% gain for BARING EMERGING MARKETS, while JPMorgan's performance in China has been far ahead of Fidelity's.

Contrarians who stuck with technology against the prevailing consensus, in late 2018, that the sector was overvalued have been rewarded with 27% gains for both Polar Capital and Allianz's trusts. BAILLIE GIFFORD JAPAN, FIDELITY JAPANESE VALUES, and ATLANTIS JAPAN, have also recovered strongly from the sell-off in growth stocks, returning 27%. Copious share issuance hasn't stopped FINSBURY GROWTH & INCOME returning 25%, and IMPAX ENVIRONMENTAL, also up 25%, shows that concern for sustainability is no barrier to good performance.

Blockbuster new issues are rarely a good augury, so when Fundsmith raised £820m for SMITHSON, a trust investing globally in mid and smaller companies, in October 2018, investors could be excused for being sceptical and cautious. But Smithson's 29% return this year, despite a substantial secondary issue in the Spring, shows that rules are made to be sometimes broken. Finally, 25% plus return from global trusts MID WYND, SECURITIES TRUST OF SCOTLAND, and MARTIN CURRIE GLOBAL, show that trusts don't have to be specialists to be great performers.

Public opinion, however, focuses on the Woodford disaster. UK investors are not just reluctant to invest in equities, but disinvesting at a time when valuations are, at worst, up with events (US growth stocks) and, at best, significantly undervalued (Japan and UK smaller companies). There are risks aplenty – an economic downturn, Brexit, inflated bond valuations, trade disruption, authoritarian governments – but no worse than we have seen and overcome in the past. The outlook continues to be for long-term gains interrupted by regular panic attacks.

MAX KING *was an investment manager and strategist at Finsbury Asset Management, J O Hambro and Investec Asset Management. He is now an independent writer, with a regular column in* MoneyWeek, *and an adviser with a special interest in investment companies. He is a non-executive director of two trusts.*

NOT ALL PLAIN SAILING

MAX KING *continues his review of the year by looking at the alternative assets sector.*

FIFTEEN YEARS AGO, the 'alternatives' category was a moderate part of the investment trust sector, comprising a modest number of listed private equity funds, an ailing group of listed hedge fund vehicles, and a few extras. Despite the continuing shrinkage of the hedge funds, alternatives now account for 48% of the £180 billion investment company universe, covering infrastructure, property, renewable energy, bonds, debt, and specialist finance funds.

Though the pace of new issuance slowed in 2019, secondary issuance by already-listed funds accelerated. The focus continues to be on funds offering a high yield, low volatility, and low correlation to equity markets, but the launch of SCHIEHALLION (£360 million) and the £275m raised by MERIAN CHRYSALIS shows that there is also an appetite for relatively high-risk private equity funds without a yield.

From where did this market spring, and from where is the demand for stock coming? The answer lies in the breakdown of, or loss of confidence in, the balanced fund model of investment. Many investors have always been happy to sacrifice some of the long-term return from equity investing for lower volatility, recognising that volatility scared clients out of long-term investment decisions, usually at precisely the wrong time. Historically, they achieved this trade-off through diversification into cash and bonds, an approach pioneered by American economist Harry Markowitz, in 1952, in a doctoral thesis. He advocated a 60/40 equity/bond portfolio, a mix that has been shown to both improve performance, and reduce volatility, over long periods of time.

In recent years, though, it became apparent that bonds could no longer be relied upon for diversification. The inverse correlation of bond and equity performance would not necessarily continue – they had been positively correlated in the past. Bond yields have fallen to such an extent that, according to Deutsche Bank, 43% of global investment-grade bonds outside the US trade at negative yields. Yields are still positive in the UK and US but, with inflation of 2%, real yields are negative. Diversifying a portfolio with bonds that are guaranteed to lose money in real terms, if held to redemption, and which may not even dampen equity volatility, is hardly in the investor's interest.

But what if other asset classes can be brought into the equation? Asset classes which offer a better yield than government or corporate bonds, whose performance is not correlated with equities, which have lower returns but also lower risk than equities, but are readily tradable? Hence the hunt for alternatives – funds with listed securities that act as bond proxies (but with a better yield), reduce portfolio risk, and smooth returns. Moreover, diversification within alternatives means that every sub-category doesn't need to have all the same characteristics, such as a decent yield. For example, a portfolio might include listed private equity even though it is relatively risky and often low-yielding.

The typical model portfolio of a wealth manager will still include an allocation to bonds, and some cash, alongside equities, but also a growing allocation to these alternatives, with the proportions determined by the compliance department's assessment of the client's risk appetite, and the manager's view of prospective returns. Some of the wealth managers were slow to catch on and are now trying to catch up, hence the continuing demand for new issuance. According to the Association of Investment Companies (AIC) and Numis Securities, the alternatives sector now comprises 31 Real Estate Investment Trusts (REITs – focused on income rather than property development or trading) which account for £25bn of the assets of the alternatives sector, 20 private equity funds (£22bn), 18 infrastructure including renewables funds (£16bn), 38 debt and leasing companies (£13bn), and 8 hedge funds (£7bn). Of the latter, PERSHING SQUARE, accounting for most of the assets, is arguably now a pure equity fund, while there are also a few sector specialists with around £3bn of assets in total.

The number of funds continues to grow, although new issuance in 2019 has been light; just five funds raising £880m in total, with one or two more likely in the fourth quarter. Of this total, SCHIEHALLION, Baillie Gifford's new private equity fund, raised £361m. Secondary issuance has been much more prolific with over £4bn raised, including £1bn in renewable energy, £1.5bn in REITs, £760m in debt funds, and £275m for the MERIAN CHRYSALIS private equity fund. INTERNATIONAL PUBLIC PARTNERSHIP (INPP), the infrastructure fund, raised £116m on 1 October, and a further £66om of secondary issuance – including £300m for HIPGNOSIS SONGS and £230m for 3I INFRASTRUCTURE – was then underway.

All of this issuance was at a premium to net asset value to finance expansion, from which it is clear that many managers are not finding it difficult to find investment opportunities, or investors to back them. The flow of funds, however, has not all been one way. NB GLOBAL FLOATING RATE INCOME FUND bought back £213m of shares; though the shares yield 5%, they trade at a 5% discount to net asset value, and 10% below their issue price seven years ago. The CARADOR INCOME FUND returned £110m to investors, and HIGHBRIDGE MULTI STRATEGY FUND £180m.

Not all strongly-performing funds have rushed to raise more money; 3i, the £11.3bn giant of the private equity sector, returned 54% in the first nine months of the year but sees no need for extra capital. In the same sector, HGT and Harbourvest both returned over 30%; the former raised a modest £64m, but the latter still trades on a 15% discount to net asset value. Fund-raising by the non-renewables infrastructure sector stalled after share prices were hit by political concerns last year. It has since recovered strongly and INPP and 3I INFRASTRUCTURE have recently announced share issues for acquisitions. ECOFIN GLOBAL UTILITIES & INFRASTRUCTURE, which invests only in listed shares, has returned 31% in share price, and 27% in net asset value terms, but still trades on a 7% discount.

Performance has not all been one way. As always, some funds have gone off the rails, and initial optimism about some sub-sectors has turned to scepticism and disillusion. Disaster of the year has again been CATCO, the retrocessional insurance fund. It raised over $500m from investors in a late-2016 C share issue, to take advantage of better pricing following the natural disasters which had hit its core fund. More disasters followed, and the cost of earlier disasters kept escalating. The fund is now committed to returning to investors what little money it has left.

The five aircraft leasing companies, not included in the AIC numbers, have all dropped sharply, partly due to the phasing out of the Airbus A380, to which they are heavily committed, partly due to a perception of default risk on Norwegian Air Shuttle, a key customer. Their business models are heavily dependent on obtaining new leases on aircraft when the initial ones expire, and investors clearly have doubts that they will be able to do that.

The social housing funds, launched with the laudable aim of providing affordable housing for rent, have seen their shares drop to significant discounts, especially CIVITAS, because of regulatory concerns. The core problem is that the finance they provide to housing associations is relatively expensive; better-managed and organised housing associations can finance their expansion more cheaply elsewhere.

The worst performer in net asset value terms was ASHMORE GLOBAL OPPORTUNITIES, which lost 38% and is now finally close to the end of a protracted wind-up initiated six years ago. It is now tiny but its experience carries two important lessons. One is that hanging on to a lame duck on a large discount rarely pays off (it was launched in late 2007, and was in trouble within a year) and the second is that waiting for a wind-up is usually worse than biting the bullet and selling today. At least by selling you have a chance to recoup and redeploy some of your investment. The opportunity cost of waiting for the wind-up is often very high.

The list of poor or disappointing performers among alternatives is growing, and this highlights a key problem in much of the sector. The return they offer investors, given their generally higher management costs, requires either a demanding return on capital, or for that return to be enhanced by the copious use of debt. This means that the funds are often much riskier than investors realise. AEW UK LONG LEASE REIT, for example, seemed solid as a rock until one of its major tenants went bust. The shares now trade 29% below the issue price. Most of the casualties have been in the bonds, debt, and asset finance category, notably in the small sub-group of peer-to-peer lending. In the latter case, investors failed at launch to ask a simple question: if the portfolio has a junk bond-scale yield, can it really be low risk?

In addition, there is always the potential for regulatory change, politicians changing the rules, and management mistakes. Most of the funds require hands-on management. It is more than just sitting back and collecting the cash. This means operational risk, whether in student accommodation, private equity (note the disappointment of BETTER CAPITAL 2009, and the disaster of its 2012 fund), or the management of royalty streams. There will be more accidents, because investors are still rushing to invest in vehicles with unproven or changing business models. HIPGNOSIS SONGS, for example is currently seeking to double in size, but it has yet to demonstrate that its purchases have been shrewd. Renewable energy funds are prolifically issuing new shares, but the subsidies which anchored the original thesis have now gone for new projects. Land may retain its value, but buildings on them can become obsolete, so may need to be depreciated.

Investors in alternative assets need to tread carefully. Established funds whose management has a strong record of adding value will continue to do well, but most investors would be well advised to be more sceptical about share issuance, and to look at business models with a forensic eye, rather than relying solely on the headline yield. This could be a good time to look through your portfolios with a view to a bit of a clear-out.

MAX KING *was an investment manager and strategist at Finsbury Asset Management, J O Hambro and Investec Asset Management. He is now an independent writer, with a regular column in* MoneyWeek, *and an adviser with a special interest in investment companies. He is a non-executive director of two trusts.*

CAN THE VCT MARKET'S RESILIENCE CONTINUE?

VCT specialist and founder of Wealth Club ALEX DAVIES *explains how the market for VCTs has changed, but continues to set new records.*

WHEN YOU LOOK at the events of the past year, you might wonder what future generations will make of it. Will it go down in the annals of history as the UK's annus horribilis? The year 2018 was certainly tough for the UK investment industry, which saw net fund sales plummet by £41.3 billion (85%) compared to 2017. UK equities were among the top losers, with investors selling out in every single month of the year. The Investment Association, which tracks and produces the figures, attributes this to a "perfect storm of uncertainty".*

Venture capital trusts (VCTs), however, have bucked this trend. Last tax year, a record £731 million was invested in VCTs, the highest amount at the current rate of tax relief, and the second highest amount ever. The largest VCT raised £227.7m, another record. This year, we might well see the first £1bn VCT.

HITTING NEW RECORDS

Why are VCTs bucking the trend and hitting new records? The chief reason is that VCTs are one of the last decent, and relatively simple, tax-efficient investment options left for wealthier investors. Tax pressure in Britain is at a 49-year high. Higher earners have been hit the hardest; they have been at the receiving end of a two-pronged tax attack. Their tax burden has increased and, at the same time, many of the traditional avenues to invest in a tax-efficient way have been blocked.

The draconian restrictions on pensions, and the government's crackdown on buy-to-let, are examples. Only ten years ago, for instance, investors could contribute up to £235,000 to their pension. Importantly, those contributing the

---

* www.professionaladviser.com/professional-adviser/news/3070704/net-fund-sales-plummet-more-than-gbp40bn-in-2018

full amount were able to claim nearly £100,000 in income tax relief. Ten years on, it's a completely different story. Some higher-earning investors are restricted to annual pension contributions of as little as £10,000, and the maximum tax relief they can receive is £4,500.

It is hardly surprising investors have started to look at alternatives. VCTs are a natural next port of call for many. Like pensions, they offer valuable income tax relief but, unlike pensions, there are no complex and punitive contribution rules. Unlike ISAs, where there is an annual limit on contributions of £20,000, you can contribute significant amounts.

VCTs offer:

1. Up to 30% income tax relief when you invest.
2. The potential for regular dividends, which are tax free. So, if a VCT pays a dividend of 5%, this is what you actually get in your hand. By way of comparison, to get the same income from a unit trust, an additional-rate taxpayer would have to receive a gross dividend of more than 8%.
3. Simplicity: you don't need to declare VCTs – or any dividends you receive – on your tax return.
4. A generous allowance of £200,000 a year for everyone. That's it – no tapering, no additional rules.

Tax relief is not the only way investors can benefit, however. In the last tax year alone, VCTs have cumulatively paid £294m in dividends. Over the last ten years, the top 20 VCTs have all at least doubled investors' money on a net asset value total return basis. That's before including tax relief. When you do, the returns are considerably higher.

In addition, returns tend to be largely uncorrelated to the performance of other assets and the stock market, which can be an attractive feature, particularly since there is currently no indication that the 'perfect storm of uncertainty' could resolve itself any time soon.

CAN THE GOOD RUN CONTINUE?

As with any investment, only time will tell if the good run of VCTs can continue. That said, looking at how VCTs work, and where they invest, might support some cautious optimism. Like investment trusts, VCTs are companies listed on the stock market. Each trust typically has a fund manager or investment adviser who chooses where to invest. They are closed funds, but they open every so often to raise new money, which they deploy by investing in new companies, or by providing follow-on investment to existing portfolio companies.

When you invest, you acquire shares in the trust, not in each of its investee companies. This is important, because it means that, if you invest today, you get exposure to the whole portfolio – typically 30–70 investments – irrespective of when they were originally made.

So what kind of investments could you expect? Today, most VCTs fall into one of three categories: generalist, AIM, and specialist. Generalist funds invest predominantly in unquoted businesses across several sectors; AIM VCTs, as the name suggests, invest in companies listed on the Alternative Investment Market; and specialist funds focus on a particular sector, e.g. healthcare.

Established VCT managers will see from a few hundred to a few thousand opportunities each year. Out of these, they will handpick their portfolio companies (usually 15–20 new investments each year), depending on their investment strategy, mandate, and style. All investments must, however, meet the prevailing qualifying rules set by HM Revenue & Customs, which have changed – and become more restrictive – over time.

For instance, management buy-outs, renewable energy projects, and asset-backed businesses, which were for years a staple of many VCTs' portfolios, are no longer allowed. They can still be part of the portfolio – and continue to support dividend payments – but cannot receive any further investment. Since 2015, all new investments must be made into young, fast-growing companies.

No two VCTs are the same, and each will have its own distinctive portfolio. That said, there are some recurring themes. For instance, were you to invest in some of the longest-established VCTs, such as NORTHERN and BRITISH SMALLER COMPANIES VCTs, you would get exposure to a diverse portfolio made up of large and mature companies (mostly management buy-outs), as well as recently added earlier-stage companies.

The same is true of other popular VCTs, such as MAVEN and MOBEUS. These VCTs have a long track record of paying generous tax-free dividends. The old-style companies in the portfolio could continue to support this, while earlier-stage companies have a chance – and time – to grow.

At the other end of the spectrum, there are VCTs, like OCTOPUS TITAN and the two PROVEN VCTs, which have always exclusively invested in fast-growing, early-stage companies. Over the years, both OCTOPUS TITAN and the PROVEN VCTs have paid investors regular dividends, with occasional years of bumper dividends, typically the result of a particularly profitable exit from a portfolio company. As these portfolios currently include a large number of companies at various stages of maturity, there could be further exits on the horizon.

To complete the picture, there's a raft of newer VCT offerings. As can be expected, they have smaller portfolios of relatively new, early-stage investments. The most established amongst them is PEMBROKE VCT, which launched in 2013, and has now been paying dividends since 2016. Some of its earlier investments should now be approaching the stage where they might come to fruition, although there are no guarantees.

What about AIM VCTs?

AIM VCTs are slightly different. They, too, invest in young, potentially fast-growing companies, but they must be listed on AIM (either new listings or new share issues). If they do well, so will the VCT and its investors. However, AIM companies tend to be subject to greater fluctuations in value compared to unquoted ones. The leaders in this field include Hargreave Hale, Unicorn and Octopus. They've all historically paid regular dividends, but recent performance has, to some extent, been affected by the vagaries of the AIM market.

CAN VCTS REALLY BACK TOMORROW'S WINNERS?

Statistically, only a small minority of acorns turn into mighty oaks. Risk capital is called risk capital for a reason. The performance track record within the VCT industry reflects this. Some companies fail, others languish, a good number achieve profitable exits, but only very few turn into headline-grabbing stars.

Zoopla is probably the best-known example. OCTOPUS TITAN VCT invested in this company right at the start. However, it wasn't such a leap in the dark as it might seem. Zoopla's founder Alex Chesterman had previously co-founded the company that eventually became LoveFilm. The investment team behind OCTOPUS TITAN invested early on, and reaped the rewards when LoveFilm was sold to Amazon for close to £200m.

When Alex Chesterman went on to set up Zoopla, Octopus backed him again. It turned out to be an even bigger success. Five years on from Octopus's investment, Zoopla Group floated on the London Stock Exchange with a value of £919m, and later became the first VCT-backed £1bn company.

More recently, Watchfinder, the leading retailer of pre-owned premium watches, was sold to Richemont, the Swiss luxury goods holding company, which owns brands such as Cartier, Montblanc, Vacheron Constantin, and Van Cleef & Arpels. Watchfinder first received investment from Beringea, manager of the PROVEN VCTs, in 2014, and subsequently grew rapidly. Turnover trebled between 2015 and 2018. The trade sale to Richemont was completed in July 2018. The size of the deal was undisclosed, but the VCT achieved its exit at 8.7x the value of its investment.

WHICH VCT TO CHOOSE?

Few investors, if any, would invest all their money in just one unit trust, or a single share – no matter how good they believed it was. The same logic should apply to VCTs. Indeed, although each VCT offers, in itself, some diversification – because its portfolio typically includes 30–70 companies – most people invest in a number of VCTs, which naturally increases diversification.

For instance, if you were to invest in OCTOPUS TITAN VCT, as well as the NORTHERN VCT or MOBEUS VCT, you would get exposure to significantly different portfolios, all run by very experienced managers. If you wanted to diversify further, you could consider something like PEMBROKE VCT and, if you can withstand the volatility, an AIM VCT such as Hargreave Hale or Octopus. All the VCTs mentioned are open (or due to open) for subscription in the 2019/20 tax year. The minimum investment depends on the VCT, starting from as little as £3,000.

WHO INVESTS IN VCTS?

The average age of our clients who invested in VCTs last year was 59. The youngest was 21, the eldest 100. Males accounted for 84%, females only 16%. They invested £34,948, on average, typically spread across a number of VCTs. The average amount invested in each VCT was £12,390. We don't record occupation, but those investors we speak to are, mostly, professionals such as doctors, lawyers, higher earners in the City, business owners, but also head teachers, and civil servants. What do they all have in common? Nearly all are affected by the pension restrictions in some way.

For someone who doesn't have sufficient assets or earnings, and doesn't clearly understand the risks, VCTs are unlikely to be a suitable investment. Young, small companies are more likely to fail than older, larger ones. If something goes badly wrong for a small company, it is much harder for it to recover than it is for a large and well-established company. They are also a lot more illiquid, as are the VCTs themselves. Diversification can help mitigate some of these risks. In addition, you have a 30% cushion in the form of tax relief, should things go wrong.

However, if you have sufficient assets elsewhere, have already used your pension and ISA allowances, and have a certain level of financial sophistication, VCTs may well be a worthwhile option to consider. As a rule of thumb, VCTs should be no more than 10–15% of your total portfolio.

ONE FINAL THOUGHT

It is not just investors who can benefit from VCTs. The UK economy benefits, too, which is the reason why the government offers such generous tax relief to incentivise investment. The £731m that was raised last year will be put to good use. It will provide much needed funding to young, small, and ambitious companies. The latest figures show small, high-growth businesses create an average of just over 3,030 new jobs a week – around 20% of all jobs created. They are also estimated to have contributed around 22% to the UK's economic growth.[*] These companies are the future. So, by investing in VCTs, you are making an investment in the country's future (and earning tax-free dividends, and valuable tax relief, in the process).

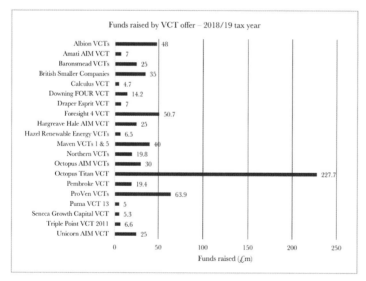

Source: Wealth Club. Chart shows funds raised before dividend reinvestment

ALEX DAVIES is the founder and CEO of Wealth Club, the largest investment platform for tax-efficient investments, which specialises in analysing and marketing tax-efficient investments, including VCTs and Enterprise Investment Scheme investments.

* Octopusgroup.com/wp-content/uploads/Octopus-High-Growth-Small-Business-Report-2018-1.pdf

TRUSTS AND THE WOODFORD SAGA

Trust analyst and commentator JAMES CARTHEW *argues that investment trusts have the edge when it comes to making investments in illiquid assets.*

ANAGERS OF OPEN-ENDED funds, such as unit trusts, OEICS and UCITS funds, always have to worry about being able to hand cash back to investors on demand. By contrast, the money in an investment company is there for the long term and, consequently, they make ideal vehicles for accessing illiquid investments, defined as those that are hard to turn into cash at short notice.

Illiquid assets include property, infrastructure, renewable energy, some debt securities, and private equity (investments in companies that aren't traded on a stock exchange). There are vastly more unquoted companies than quoted ones. Among the ranks of unquoted companies are some of the most innovative young companies poised to become the big quoted companies of the future; well-established, cash-generative companies with strong market positions; and companies that are trading well, but where the owners are thinking of retirement, or the founding family is looking for an exit.

All these types of company may feature as investments in private equity funds. Private equity, then, is a catch-all term for a wide range of different investment strategies.

- Venture capital backs early-stage businesses, providing them with the money to do things like get a product in the shops, put the finishing touches to their software, or kit out a factory.

- Growth capital supplies the money to help proven businesses expand, maybe by opening new branches, or making acquisitions.

- Buyout funds put up the money to help a management team either buy the company that they work for (a management buyout, or MBO), or take control of another company (a management buy in, or MBI). The deal may be funded by debt, making it a 'leveraged' buyout.

- Special situations, or distressed funds, invest in companies that are struggling for one reason or another, and try to turn the business around.

A debate has been raging for some time about whether open-ended funds should be allowed to hold any illiquid assets. The argument got going when many open-ended property funds were forced to prevent investors from withdrawing their money in 2016. This seemed only to compound investors' fears and make the problem worse. We, and many others, called for all open-ended property funds to be converted into real estate investment trusts (REITs), to avoid lock ups of this kind occurring in future. That call fell on deaf ears, however.

The problem reared its head again in the spring of 2019. After a long period of poor performance, investors in the LF Woodford Equity Income Fund (WEIF) had been deserting it in droves. Despite having built an impressive reputation over a 25-year career at Invesco Perpetual, before setting up his own firm, Neil Woodford had, for reasons that many of us found hard to fathom, sprinkled his equity income fund with a wide selection of unquoted investments which did not provide any income.

WEIF is a UCITS fund and the rules that govern this kind of fund are explicit in saying that they can hold no more than 10% of their assets in unquoted securities (technically defined as those that cannot be dealt in on an eligible market). As WEIF shrank, it sailed through this limit. Woodford attempted to get around the problem by listing some of his unquoted companies on Guernsey's International Stock Exchange. The trouble was that there was no meaningful trading in these companies; in effect they were no more liquid than before.

Everything came to a head when Kent County Council's pension scheme asked to cash in a £260 million stake in WEIF. Trading in WEIF's units was suspended and, given that most investors will now want an exit, the fund is being closed and its portfolio liquidated.

WEIF had a sister fund, though, WOODFORD PATIENT CAPITAL (WPCT). WPCT is an investment trust, one of the largest ever launched. It has a chance of surviving the collapse of WEIF, although it will have a different manager as Woodford Investment Management is shutting up shop. WPCT's closed-end nature means that it can choose to take a longer-term view and look through

"IF YOU WANT EXPOSURE TO ILLIQUID ASSETS, IT MAKES SENSE TO DO IT THROUGH AN INVESTMENT COMPANY. IF MARKETS ARE PANICKY, YOU WILL BE ABLE TO SELL IF YOU ABSOLUTELY HAVE TO, BUT YOU CAN ALSO TAKE A LONG-TERM VIEW" this painful period. Unlike the open-ended Woodford fund, it is not at risk of becoming a forced seller of the investments it owns, a crucial distinction.

WEIF and WPCT are both in the riskier venture/growth capital end of the private equity market. A successful investment here can make a multiple of your original investment. The hit rate for these two funds has not been great so far, however, and a number of high-profile investments have been written down in value. This is the problem with venture capital; it is quite easy to lose all or most of your investment. In my career, I have seen a few venture funds launched with great fanfare only to disappear in ignominy.

One of the positive aspects of the Woodford funds was that they were providing capital to early-stage UK companies, which have struggled to find funding in the past. Remember all those headlines about the brain drain from the UK to the US? WPCT was supposed to help stem this. By contrast, in the US, money for start-ups seems to flow like water. Vast companies have been created, sometimes without a clear path to profitability. Some of these have now listed their shares, while others say they intend to stay private for the foreseeable future.

This contrast is evident in HERALD INVESTMENT TRUST's portfolio. This trust focuses on quoted small and medium-sized technology and media companies. Over more than 25 years, it has made investors almost 16 times their money. In the UK, many technology companies come cap in hand to the stock market to fund their growth. Herald is often the cornerstone investor in these companies' initial public offerings (IPOs) and fundraisings. It reaps the rewards if they succeed. In the US, IPOs provide a way for venture capital investors to cash in after the early gains have been made. Herald's manager Katie Potts often finds that these companies are too expensive.

I should make the point that the liquidity problems can apply to some small quoted stocks as well, where there are only a few buyers and sellers, and the spread between buying and selling prices can be quite wide. That is why it makes sense for Herald to be structured as an investment trust. Notwithstanding this, it maintains a diversified portfolio because, in the technology sector, as in the specialist biotech sector, the dividing line between success and failure can be quite narrow, and there is a higher degree of stock-specific risk.

The end of 2018 saw the launch of a new trust, MERIAN CHRYSALIS (MERI), which is aiming to provide growth capital to a relatively small number of companies whose likely next move would be to IPO. Using the Herald analogy above, MERI hopes that its investments will allow companies to follow more of the US path to an IPO than the UK one. It holds eight companies, accounting for about half the portfolio, and expects to end up with a maximum of 15 investments. Investors seem to love the idea; the fund has grown from £100m at launch to around £400m in less than a year.

Some caution is merited here, however. In the US, the recent IPOs of Uber, Lyft, and Peloton, are trading well below their IPO price; others, including WeWork and Endeavour, have pulled their IPOs. It could be that we are about to enter a period when IPOs are difficult to achieve. That doesn't mean that MERI won't be able to cash in any of its investments. Many more companies are acquired by other private equity firms, or by competing companies, than advance to an IPO.

MERI wasn't the only new fund in this area to launch in the past year. We also saw Baillie Gifford list the SCHIEHALLION FUND. This was a pre-existing fund of unlisted investments, but it took the opportunity to raise more money in its IPO, and now has assets of about $500m. It had eight investments at the end of July 2019, and some of these I'd pigeonhole more towards the venture end of growth capital. These only represented 17% of the fund, though. It intends to build a more diverse portfolio slowly. Again, for now, investors seem to love it, and it is trading at a significant premium to asset value.

The vast bulk of listed private equity funds are focused on buyouts. Some, such as HG CAPITAL, make investments directly. Others, such as STANDARD LIFE PRIVATE EQUITY (SLPE) and HARBOURVEST, are funds of funds. These invest in limited partnership vehicles which, in turn, make direct private equity investments. Although SLPE does also make some direct co-investments, buying into an unquoted stock alongside a limited partnership fund that is managed by someone they know and trust.

There is a misconception, in some quarters, that buyout investors just shove as much debt into a target company's balance sheet as they can, asset strip it by selling off the profitable stuff, fire a lot of staff, and walk away if the indebted company runs into trouble, having already booked substantial profits.

The buyout funds would refute that strongly. They have a wide universe of companies to choose from, so they can be picky. They look for companies that generate attractive cash returns on invested capital and can sustain them. They put great effort into getting to know a potential investment before they commit. Academic research has shown that, when private equity companies buy quoted companies, they do shed staff but, for the vast majority of transactions, where private equity is buying unquoted companies, the size of the workforce increases.

SLPE's managers, for example, make a point of working with managers that they know are going to roll up their sleeves and work with the companies they invest in, to achieve operational improvements. Rather than targeting struggling businesses (they leave those to the distressed funds), the buyout funds look for growing companies that they can nurture and support over the long-term. Sometimes, that means making difficult decisions; often it means making investments that pay off in the long rather than the short-term, something that would be penalised in the quoted company market.

As an aside, I think it is important to consider the long-term damage that quoted market investors can inflict on companies. Average holding periods can be measured in seconds, despite share registers being dominated by passive index-tracking funds. Small disappointments are punished with savage share price declines. CEOs, whose bonuses are often linked to share prices, focus on what they can do to push the share price higher rather than what is good for the long-term health of the business.

This is one reason, perhaps, why over the long term, the buyout funds tend to outperform funds which invest solely in quoted equities. Over the short term, the story can be different. If you look at share price and discount graphs for the listed private equity funds, you can see that they suffered in the financial crisis of 2008–2009. This is illustrative of one problem that affected some funds at the time and, conversely, one of their great strengths.

Source: Morningstar, Marten & Co. Figures for Apax Global Alpha, BMO Private Equity, Dunedin Enterprise, Electra, Harbourvest, HG Capital, ICG Enterprise, JPEL, LMS Capital, NB Private Equity, Oakley, Pantheon, Princess and Standard Life Private Equity.

The problem was that many private equity managers had made legally-binding commitments to invest in limited partnership vehicles, in anticipation that cash would flow back from existing investments (as underlying companies were sold or recapitalised). The financial crisis made freeing up cash from this source much harder. A few found they were overcommitted; they couldn't borrow the money they needed to meet their obligations, and so they were penalised heavily when they had to break their contracts. This destroyed some value permanently. However, it did not affect all funds, and I'd like to think that the managers have learned their lesson.

The strength was that, in the general panic, the listed private equity funds could bide their time. Those that had free cash could take advantage of the situation and pick up investments cheaply from desperate sellers. Investors in these funds could cash in their investment at any time, provided that they were prepared to accept they would get a discounted price. Had these been open-ended funds, trading would have been suspended while the managers were forced to dump investments at knock-down prices. That strength was evident, too, in 2016 when real estate investment trusts (REITs) were able to pick up some bargains at the expense of the open-ended vehicles.

As we approach the latest period of slower economic growth, private equity funds are actually quite cash rich. They have raised substantial amounts of fresh capital over the past few years and stand ready to commit this when they judge that valuations look attractive.

Source: Preqin

There are some clear messages here. If you want exposure to illiquid assets, it makes sense to do it through an investment company. If markets are panicky, you will be able to sell if you absolutely have to, but you can also take a long-term view and benefit if your manager is able to take advantage of the situation. Providing venture capital is a great thing for an economy, but it is at the riskier end of the investing spectrum. Growth capital can work but you may need to be patient; and private equity funds aren't the bad guys. If anything they are better for companies than quoted equity investors.

JAMES CARTHEW is a director at Marten & Co, which provides research and corporate advice for the investment trust sector and manages the QuotedData website (www.quoteddata.com).

THE SUMMER PORTFOLIO

Investment trust expert JOHN BARON *provides an example of a real portfolio – one of nine such portfolios run in real time by John's company on the website www.johnbaronportfolios.co.uk.*

INVESTMENT PRINCIPLES AND stratagems are best illustrated when put into action. This article hopes to provide an insight as to some of the factors we consider when managing a 'real' investment trust portfolio. Our website's Summer portfolio has been in existence since January 2009, since when other portfolios have been gradually introduced. But before highlighting its composition and strategy, it is important to understand the portfolio's position in relation to the wider investment journey of which it is part.

CONTEXT

The Summer portfolio is one of nine real (i.e. they exist in fact) trust portfolios managed in real time on the website www.johnbaronportfolios.co.uk, courtesy of same-day details of trades, new portfolio weightings, yields, and explanations shortly afterwards. Other website services include investment commentaries, company news, monthly performance updates, and responses to members' questions. Members are informed by email whenever the website is updated.

The portfolios achieve a range of strategies and income levels, with yields of up to 5.5% at the time of writing. Five portfolios reflect an investment journey – LISA, Spring, Summer, Autumn, and Winter. The LISA portfolio helps smaller portfolios capitalise on the Government's recently introduced Lifetime ISA (LISA) proposals and, therefore, now represents the start of the journey. As such, its objective is to deliver strong capital growth via an equity-focused portfolio.

Over time, the five portfolios increasingly diversify away from equities, to help protect past gains, and to generate a higher income. In doing so, they increase exposure to other asset classes which are less correlated to equities, including bonds, infrastructure, renewable energy, commercial property, and cash. The website's open Diversification page provides an overview as to the pace and extent to which exposure to these other asset classes builds over time. Winter finishes with a yield of 5.2%.

The four remaining portfolios pursue distinct objectives:

- The Thematic portfolio focuses on undervalued themes and special situations.

- The Dividend portfolio seeks a high and rising income, and yields 5.5%.

- The Overseas portfolio contains modest UK exposure.

- The Green portfolio focuses on environmental protection and climate change.

Statistic summary (to 4 October 2019)

The website table below is updated on the day of a portfolio change, and at the end of each month – all figures being in percentages, except for the number of holdings.

	LISA	SPRING	SUMMER	AUTUMN	WINTER	THEMATIC	DIVIDEND	OVERSEAS	GREEN
Holdings	8	16	23	22	17	14	18	21	10
Equities	85–95	75–85	65–75	45–55	15–25	90–100	45–55	90–100	0
Other	5–15	15–25	25–35	45–55	75–85	0–10	45–55	0–10	100
Yield	1.4	2.3	3.2	4.4	5.2	1.2	5.5	2.8	3.2

Performance

While never complacent, the portfolios have performed well relative to their respective benchmarks – the website's open Performance page has more details. Portfolio performance is compared to benchmarks, since inception, in percentages rounded to one decimal place, and tables are updated to the end of each month. All performance figures are calculated on a total return basis, and portfolio figures include all costs. One table shows cumulative performance since portfolio inception.

Cumulative performance (to 30 September 2019)

	LISA	SPRING	SUMMER	AUTUMN	WINTER	THEMATIC	DIVIDEND	OVERSEAS	GREEN
Portfolio	87.0	89.6	289.7	222.8	49.6	83.7	40.2	6.5	7.2
Benchmark	37.3	39.7	172.4	133.5	N/A	39.7	N/A	N/A	N/A
Relative	49.7	49.9	117.3	89.3	N/A	44.0	N/A	N/A	N/A

The start dates for the various portfolios are as follows: Summer and Autumn – 1 January 2009; Spring, Winter, and Thematic – 1 January 2014; LISA and Dividend – 1 April 2016; Overseas – 1 January 2018; Green portfolio – 1 April 2019.

The benchmark for the LISA, Spring, and Thematic portfolios is the FTSE All-share. The benchmark for the Summer and Autumn portfolios is the MSCI WMA Growth and Income – the asset allocation weightings of the indices can be found at www.pimfa.co.uk.

No benchmark is used to monitor the performance of the Winter, Dividend, Overseas, and Green portfolios as their focus on higher-yielding investments, and extent of diversification, is difficult to meaningfully monitor by way of benchmark.

A further table on the website's Performance page shows calendar year performance for each portfolio since inception – including 2019 year-to-date. The website's other open pages – Rationale, Diversification, FAQs, and Investment policy – help to explain the rhythm of the website in more detail, whilst the Subscription page allows visitors to register for a trial period.

BREAKDOWN

Below is a breakdown of the Summer portfolio at time of writing. All holdings and weightings are rounded to the nearest ½%, and are updated on the day a portfolio change is made (as detailed on the website's Dealing page which details trades to the nearest 0.1%), and at the end of each month. The relevant stock market Ticker code is also given next to each holding. The portfolio's yield is 3.2% at the time of writing – income growth being achieved over time.

As at 30 September 2019

BONDS	
CQS New City High Yield (NCYF)	7.0%
Henderson Diversified Income (HDIV)	3.5%

UK SHARES	
Finsbury Growth & Income Trust (FGT)	6.0%
BlackRock Throgmorton Trust (THRG)	5.0%
Henderson Smaller Companies (HSL)	5.0%
Schroder UK Mid Cap Fund (SCP)	4.0%

UK SHARES	
The Mercantile Trust (MRC)	4.0%
Montanaro UK Smaller Cos (MTU)	3.5%
Standard Life UK Smaller Cos (SLS)	3.0%
Oryx International Growth Fund (OIG)	3.0%

INTERNATIONAL SHARES	
North American Income Trust (NAIT)	6.0%
Edinburgh Worldwide (EWI)	5.0%
JPMorgan Japan Smaller Cos (JPS)	5.0%
Henderson Far East Income (HFEL)	4.0%
Templeton Emerging Markets (TEM)	3.0%

THEMES	
Herald (HRI)	5.5%
HICL Infrastructure Company (HICL)	4.0%
Allianz Technology Trust (ATT)	4.0%
Bluefield Solar Income Fund (BSIF)	3.5%
Standard Life Private Equity Tst (SLPE)	3.0%
International Biotechnology Trust (IBT)	2.5%

COMMERCIAL PROPERTY	
Standard Life Property Income (SLI)	5.0%
TR Property (TRY)	3.0%

CASH	
	2.5%

TOTAL	
	100%

EQUITIES

As seen from the portfolio breakdown, the portfolio is predominantly invested in equities. This reflects its position in the investment journey. Having progressed through the early stages of that journey, courtesy of the equity-dominated LISA and Spring portfolios, which contain a small but growing number of holdings, this portfolio has a higher number of holdings to help further reduce individual company risk, whilst also allowing an increase in the level of diversification.

Going global

The discipline of diversification does not just relate to different asset classes – the principle should also apply when deciding equity exposure, whether by geography, company size, or sector allocation. A recent paper entitled 'Geographic diversification can be a lifesaver, yet most portfolios are highly geographically concentrated' by Karen Karniol-Tambour, Pat Margolis, and Melissa Saphier, leaves one in no doubt of the conclusion. As noted:

> "There have been many times when investors concentrated in one country saw their wealth wiped out by geopolitical upheavals, debt crises, monetary reforms, or the bursting of bubbles, while markets in other countries remained resilient."

There are certain circumstances when overseas exposure is perhaps not suitable, particularly during the final stages of an investment journey, when diversification to protect past gains is at its zenith. Usually the portfolio's equity exposure is minimal, and what there is tends to be focused on the country of domicile given currency fluctuations are, indeed, an unnecessary risk at this late stage. The Winter portfolio has very little overseas exposure. However, for most equity portfolios, the principle espoused above is sound.

The US market has been one of the best performing in the current decade, but was one of the worst in the previous. And the need for overseas diversification is likely to become more pronounced. Increasing globalisation in the post-war period has led to a higher correlation between markets. Although globalisation has rarely progressed in a straight line, the recent prospect of trade wars and protectionism, and with it greater divergence in performance, suggests diversification overseas will become a more important consideration for investors.

As the paper also highlights, the ability of China to stimulate its economy in a downturn raises the likelihood of an increasingly multi-polar and less-correlated world. Yet, despite its share of global assets being nearly 10%, and global output

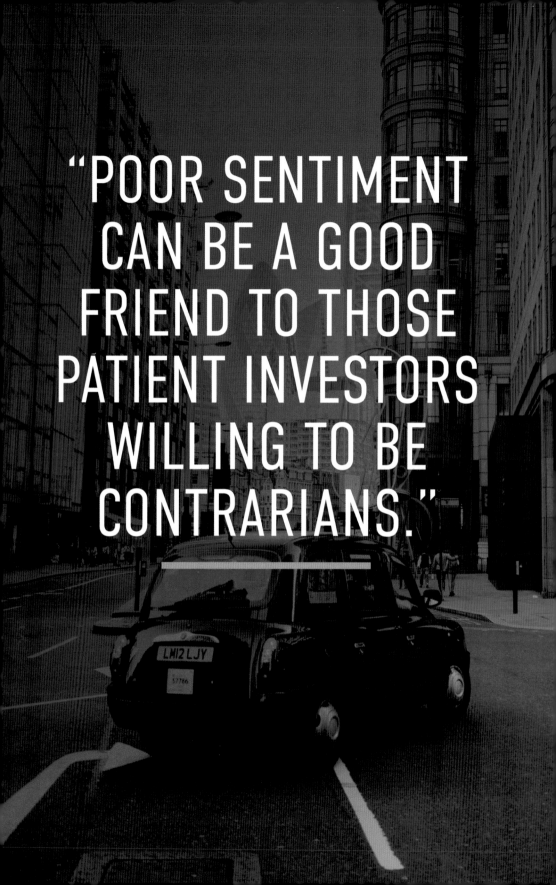

being nearly 25%, its weighting in most portfolios is around 2.5%. This is despite the fact that the market is accessible to investors. Even if a discount is applied given its political disadvantages, this figure still remains too small, and mirrors an underweight exposure to emerging markets generally.

The Summer portfolio embodies this thinking by having a decent exposure to overseas markets, both by way of its international exposure, and exposure to certain themes which, by their nature, involve overseas companies. Japan, the Far East, and emerging markets, in general, tend to be favoured over the US and Europe because of valuations relative to prospects, although appearances can be deceiving at first sight.

The portfolio's direct exposure to the US via NORTH AMERICAN INCOME TRUST (NAIT) is not only complemented by EDINBURGH WORLDWIDE (EWI), which devotes over half its portfolio to the US, but also by some of its thematic holdings including ALLIANZ TECHNOLOGY TRUST (ATT) and INTERNATIONAL BIOTECHNOLOGY TRUST (IBT). Likewise, exposure to Europe might appear non-existent until one considers both STANDARD LIFE PRIVATE EQUITY (SLPE) and TR PROPERTY (TRY).

The Japanese market looks particularly attractive. The equity market's rating looks good value relative to others on a range of metrics. In addition, the Government is encouraging companies to be more shareholder-friendly, and domestic institutions to reverse their traditional underweighting of domestic equities. Improving fundamentals, cautious sentiment, and attractive market valuations, usually furnish healthy returns for the patient investor.

The UK market

Despite the many attractions of certain overseas markets, we also believe that the UK market represents good value and have positioned portfolios accordingly. Brexit has cast a long shadow. International comparisons suggest valuations are at the bottom end of a range of metrics – and not having been this cheap for a number of decades. And yet, in stark contrast, the economy is doing well.

This contrast is partly because of misguided concerns about the economic consequences of voting to leave in 2016, and now undue concern about the effects of a no deal/WTO exit. This ignores the simple fact that investment is largely governed by comparative advantage. The competitiveness of our corporation tax rates, the flexibility of our labour markets, our financial expertise, our skilled workforce, our record on innovation, and top universities are, in aggregate, more important in deciding investment and job creation than WTO terms.

If evidence were needed, the reality is that, since 2016, the performance of the UK economy has been good in the full knowledge that 'no deal is better than a bad deal'. Record low unemployment, record high manufacturing output, and record investment are just some of the important milestones reached. And the economy continues to do well relative to others – the unemployment rate being nearly half that of the EU average. Meanwhile, key European economies teeter on the brink of recession at the time of writing.

So why is this important to understand? The misguided narrative has influenced the market's valuation. Only by analysing the reality, or otherwise, can an investor assess whether, and if so the extent to which, sentiment and fundamentals have parted company. For poor sentiment can be a good friend to those patient investors willing to be contrarians.

Smaller companies

However, though the UK market may look attractive, it sadly has too few pioneering giants – a theme I have highlighted in recent commentaries. With this in mind, within the portfolio's equity exposure, it continues with the LISA and Spring portfolios' focus on smaller companies – particularly at home, but also abroad. The sector's long-term record is impressive. Indeed, it is generally accepted that a small-cap focus is one of the more reliable investment strategies in generating higher returns than the wider market over time.

Smaller companies should continue to do well given the present environment of low interest rates and moderate inflation, an economy that continues to defy the sceptics, the sector's attractive rating relative to earnings outlook, and favourable long-term trends including the advance of technology – which is disproportionately helping many of these companies to compete on a more equal footing with their larger peers. The future is indeed small.

The portfolio's UK exposure is particularly focused on smaller companies courtesy of holdings such as BLACKROCK THROGMORTON TRUST (THRG), HENDERSON SMALLER COMPANIES (HSL), SCHRODER UK MID CAP (SCP), and THE MERCANTILE TRUST (MRC). The portfolios have benefitted from some of these discounts having narrowed somewhat in recent years, but we remain of the view that the UK Smaller Companies sector is one of the most attractively-rated both at a portfolio and trust level relative to prospects.

The portfolio's focus on smaller companies is not confined to these shores. EDINBURGH WORLDWIDE (EWI) has a global growth smaller company remit which is producing handsome returns. JPMORGAN JAPAN SMALLER COMPANIES (JPS) is a further example. Various studies have shown a disproportionate number of extraordinary companies tend to be smaller in size wherever they are located – and have produced returns accordingly.

However, it is also important to remember the importance of maintaining an element of portfolio balance relative to objectives. Whilst positive about the outlook for smaller companies, the Summer portfolio also maintains some exposure to larger companies, especially those with a good track record of dividend growth – again, both at home and abroad. FINSBURY GROWTH & INCOME TRUST (FGT) and HENDERSON FAR EAST INCOME (HFEL) are examples.

This balance between large and smaller companies naturally changes as the investment journey progresses. Those trusts focusing on larger companies assume greater importance over time in part because they tend to exhibit less volatility in extreme market conditions, and because they remain prevalent in producing income.

Thematic investments

The website's portfolios have always benefitted from exposure to individual themes – the Summer portfolio is a particular example. Thematic investing is gaining popularity, generally with wealth managers and private banks, as it offers a number of advantages. Portfolio returns by region or geography tend to be driven by the relationship between macroeconomic performance and market valuations. Such factors are less influential in deciding the returns from thematic investing, and so offer an element of diversification.

Thematic investing also allows investors to embrace a broader perspective, given the investment opportunities available across global equity markets. Although globalisation has not, and will not, be linear in its progress, and key challenges remain, it is offering profitable opportunities that transcend portfolio allocations based purely on region or geography. At a time technology and trade are bringing the world together, a bigger picture view is required.

And portfolio managers are recognising the potential. At a BlackRock presentation on thematic investing in February 2019, Alistair Bishop (the managing director) highlighted a number of global trends that are encouraging structural shifts in many sectors and industries, which in turn are influencing the progress of corporate earnings. As he put it:

> "These forces, which we call megatrends, are giving rise to a new set of powerful investment themes – the advent of disruptive technologies, radical shifts in consumer choices, greater regulatory intervention, and new opportunities for growth.

"By analysing companies across regions and sectors, thematic investing can identify stocks that are favourably positioned to the most rewarding themes, and build portfolios that offer pure exposure to them."

BlackRock are presently focusing on five megatrends – rapid urbanisation, climate change and resource scarcity, demographics and social change, the changing economic power of the emerging markets, and disruptive technologies. The company believes the most powerful investment themes tend to be the result of a confluence of at least two of these megatrends.

Our website portfolios have long benefitted from thematic investing, including that of technology. The Summer portfolio presently holds HERALD (HRI) and ALLIANZ TECHNOLOGY TRUST (ATT) by way of examples. This is a golden age of innovation. The very nature of the latest technology revolution – the internet and, with it, the digital transformation and extensive adoption of more technology-enhanced business models – is ensuring the sector will continue to benefit from its own multi-year cycle, which is still in its early stages.

But the effects will be felt well beyond the sector. Many companies and sectors across the economy are embracing the latest technology solutions to enhance efficiency, improve productivity, and increase revenues. This digital transformation will not only continue to be supportive of technology growth, in itself, but will also help to create new products and markets across swathes of the economy.

The portfolio also pursues the theme of biotechnology, both by way of INTERNATIONAL BIOTECHNOLOGY TRUST (IBT) and, more indirectly, EDINBURGH WORLDWIDE (EWI). The DNA discoveries of Watson and Crick in 1953, the sequencing of the human genome, and the falling cost yet increased power of computer technology, has transformed the potential and efficacy of the biotech companies. Visits to the Francis Crick Institute will confirm an investor's faith in the potential of science.

Indeed, an emphasis on innovation, and the reinvestment of cash flow into R&D, has created a virtuous circle. Little wonder the large pharmaceutical companies have been circling. And because the sector keeps delivering strong earnings growth, at the time of writing, it is still attractively-rated relative to the S&P 500, despite growing at a faster pace. Once again, patient investors will be rewarded.

And long-term horizons will be required. As Professor Bessembinder confirmed, when examining the handful of extraordinary companies which have accounted for the majority of stock market returns over time, it is the long-term compounding effect of share prices which matters. Investors will need to be aware of the life cycle of themes. Alistair Bishop at BlackRock has put it well:

"Themes have longevity because the key megatrends that underpin them tend to persist for a long time. However, across this extended time-span, themes evolve and change shape. Themes overcome hurdles and gain momentum. Themes can be accelerated by innovation, but constrained by consumer inertia. Themes can be reinforced by corporate investments, but hindered by regulatory uncertainty. Thematic investing is non-linear."

OTHER ASSET CLASSES

As the portfolio represents the mid-point in the five-portfolio, risk-adjusted investment journey, the move away from equities towards other less-correlated asset classes continues to gain momentum, in order to assist with diversification and so protect past gains – a process which is continued in a meaningful way by the Autumn and Winter portfolios. The breakdown given earlier in the article suggests the extent of exposure to these other assets accounts for nearly 30% of the portfolio's value.

Increasing exposure to such assets also acknowledges that, whilst one of the key investment principles pursued by the nine portfolios is to remain invested, a modicum of cash and exposure to less-correlated assets better enables volatility to become a friend to those with a long-term strategy – particularly growth investors. They can provide a resource when taking advantage of weaker equity prices.

The website's portfolios recognise Warren Buffett's suggestion that wide diversification is only used when investors are in the dark. The Summer portfolio embraces bonds, infrastructure, renewable energy, commercial property, and a modest level of cash, as a means of achieving this objective. In combination, and whilst accepting few investments will totally escape a major market setback, such investments should help to cushion the blow.

Meanwhile, such investments can also help portfolios achieve higher income levels, which is an objective of the website's five portfolios as the investment journey progresses. This is usually desirable to those approaching their financial goals. But it also acknowledges that the majority of total returns over time originate from re-invested dividends. It is no coincidence that the Summer portfolio offers a yield in excess of that achieved by its benchmark, as do most of the website's other portfolios.

Furthermore, such investments can help portfolios keep up with inflation when generating required income levels. There is presently some concern that economies globally may be seeing the early stages of an inflationary pick-up. History suggests this alone should not cause equities too much trouble. However, the market is also aware that too much inflation, or a sudden pick-up (notwithstanding an inverted yield-curve), could provide a headwind for equities.

The portfolio therefore contains exposure to asset classes where underlying prices have a near-defined correlation with inflation – such as infrastructure (HICL INFRASTRUCTURE COMPANY – HICL) and renewable energy (BLUEFIELD SOLAR INCOME FUND – BSIF). It also contains exposure to commercial property (STANDARD LIFE PROPERTY INCOME – SLI, and TR PROPERTY – TRY) where the correlation is less-defined but inflation nevertheless has usually provided a tailwind.

The Summer portfolio also achieves its income objective, in part, by holding companies which produce a specified income level dependent on the NAV or share price at a particular point, by drawing on capital to supplement, as necessary, the income produced by the underlying investments. An increasing number of trusts are adopting this approach which we support provided companies do not overpromise.

Examples include MONTANARO UK SMALLER COMPANIES (MTU), JPMORGAN JAPAN SMALLER COMPANIES (JPS) and INTERNATIONAL BIOTECHNOLOGY TRUST (IBT) – all of which pay a dividend equivalent to 4% of NAV. Such an approach will result in volatility as to dividends paid but will help the portfolio achieve its income objective. Meanwhile, STANDARD LIFE PRIVATE EQUITY (SLPE) is using its capital to pay a handsome dividend which promises to increase in real terms.

AN HOLISTIC APPROACH

The portfolio embraces a number of theme and sector preferences, but is very cognisant of the need to pursue an over-arching strategy which reflects its position in the wider investment journey. This involves a long-term focus when assessing sentiment and fundamentals, which then better allows volatility to be seen for what it should be – an opportunity.

However, it is worth repeating that enthusiasm for any particular investment theme or stratagem should always be tempered with the need to maintain portfolio balance. No matter how compelling the investment case, an overly aggressive tilt towards a particular holding, or theme, not only raises the portfolio's risk profile, but can unduly affect long-term performance should it go wrong. Resisting temptation is just as important as backing conviction – within balance.

It should also be remembered that the portfolio's preferences, and indeed changes, should not be seen in isolation. An holistic view is taken of each of the nine portfolios. Changes need to be judged as part of the whole, rather than simply a list of individual trades, as their management reflects a range of investment factors and metrics – some in competition, and some not.

As with the other eight real portfolios, the Summer portfolio also balances a range of financial metrics between holdings when deciding on the final combination. Probably the most talked about is the level of discount (or premium) between NAV and price. This can allow investors to take advantage of changes in the level, which are often influenced by swings in sentiment towards a trust and/or its underlying portfolio, and by the extent of debt which can contribute to volatility.

However, while discount levels can be important, particularly when considering an entry point, a range of other factors and metrics are also considered – the importance of which can sometimes be overlooked by investors when deciding on a portfolio's construction. These include:

- The reputation of the manager AND investment house.

- The underlying strategy.

- The outlook for the sector, region, or theme.

- The valuation of the trust relative to its peer group AND the underlying portfolio relative to its universe.

- The level of management and any performance fees.

- The effect on the NAV of the level, cost, and duration, of any debt.

- The extent of dividend cover and revenue reserves (particularly if investing for income).

- The capital structure of the company.

- The nature and effectiveness of any discount-control mechanism.

Some are particularly important, such as the outlook for the asset class in question, together with the manager's long-term record, underlying strategy, and due diligence processes. Meanwhile, the level of NAVs can be materially affected by the extent and cost of debt – something which is not always picked up by discount calculations.

The valuation of the underlying portfolio relative to its universe is a further key determinant which is also often underestimated – again, the attractions of a seemingly-wide discount can be somewhat negated if the portfolio is expensive, without good reason. There is usually no substitute for thorough research.

Some of these factors are best explored through conversations with the trusts' managers themselves. When it comes to the website's portfolios, we rarely make an initial investment without first speaking to the manager – whether they be located in Tokyo, California, or elsewhere. Once a holding is introduced, we then endeavour to maintain contact by way of update – especially when the trust is not well known or covered by analysts.

GOLDEN RULE?

Although cognisant of the various factors at work, perhaps our overriding consideration when managing portfolios is recognition of the benefit gained from investing in good companies over the long term. Changes regarding most of the factors mentioned above can, to varying degrees, influence swings in sentiment and, thereby, the discount and prices. Capitalising on such swings can be profitable in the short term.

However, it should always be remembered that such an approach is usually best employed when initiating a long-term holding. Choosing and sticking with a quality trust which has a good track record often results in better long-term performance than constantly dealing in an attempt to capture short-term price movements. All nine portfolios have benefitted from this approach in the past – and we hope to continue to do so.

JOHN BARON *is one of the UK's leading experts on investment trusts, a regular columnist and speaker at investment seminars, and author of* The Financial Times Guide to Investment Trusts *(a further edition is due shortly). He is a director of Equi Ltd which owns the website www.johnbaronportfolios.co.uk.*

The website reports on the progress of nine real investment trust portfolios, including same-day details of trades, new portfolio weightings and yields. The portfolios pursue a range of strategies, and income objectives, and enjoy an enviable track record relative to their benchmarks.

John has used investment trusts in a private and professional capacity for over 35 years. After university and the Army, he ran a broad range of investment portfolios as a director of both Henderson Private Clients and then Rothschild Asset Management. Since leaving the City, he has also helped charities monitor their fund managers.

TALES OF THE UNEXPECTED

Investors do not always concern themselves solely with heavyweight matters in economic and corporate life, as the entertaining weekly bulletins from ARTEMIS FUND MANAGEMENT *make clear. Here is a selection of the editor's favourite 2019 tailpieces, the short news stories appended to the firm's free weekly email* The Hunters' Tails.

A GAP IN A GARDEN...

"THE BEAUTIFUL SHINJUKU Gyoen National Garden in Tokyo is just a short walk from Shinjuku station," a spokesman for Japan's Ministry of the Environment has said. "We charge visitors an entry fee of ¥200 (£1.50) to help pay for its upkeep, but auditors found a substantial shortfall in revenue of ¥25 million (£180,000) over the past two years. So we began an internal investigation.

"The problem has turned out not to be fraud, but timidity. Because he only speaks Japanese, the 70-year-old ticket-seller was afraid of foreigners, and was letting them in without paying. He even persuaded a colleague in data-processing to hide the discrepancy between actual and recorded revenue, which is why it took so long to uncover. What's especially strange is that although he wasn't collecting any money, he was still issuing tickets, because visitors have to scan the QR code on their tickets to get into the gardens. The ticket-seller has now resigned, and we regard the matter as closed."

SERVILE SLIPPERS...

"THESE SELF-PARKING SLIPPERS are the latest thing in hands-free hospitality," Nick Maxfield of the Nissan Motor Company has told reporters outside a traditional *ryokan* (guesthouse) in Hakone, near Mount Fuji. "Each slipper is equipped with two tiny wheels, a motor, and hi-tech sensors to drive itself across the wooden lobby floor. In traditional inns, like this, the slippers can park themselves at the entrance at the push of a button, ready for guests to use upon their arrival.

"And it's not only the slippers that can propel themselves across the tatami-matted floors of the *ryokan*. The guest rooms also feature floor cushions and *chabudai* (low tables) that can wheel themselves into place. This is a simplified offshoot of the ProPilot Park technology that we are developing for self-driving cars, which we expect to be on city streets around the world by 2020. These self-parking slippers are intended to raise awareness of automated driving technologies, and of their potential non-driving applications."

FEW(ER) FLIGHTS OF FANCY...

EVERY WEEKEND FROM April to September, thousands of British pigeons travel in convoys of customised 'loft-lorries' to 'liberation sites' in France, the Netherlands, Belgium, and Germany. The EU has now warned that it would impose strict checks on birds crossing the Channel. So, the British pigeon-racing season is the latest matter at risk from a no-deal Brexit. "There are a lot of worried people in terms of the impact of no deal. We are getting closer and closer to the racing season. It may be that the season has to be delayed," said Ian Evans, the CEO of the Royal Pigeon Racing Association.

A no-deal could even jeopardise British participation in the Barcelona International Pigeon Race, which is reserved for long-distance birds and seen as the Grand National for pigeons. "There will have to be checks. Physical checks based on risks. There is no special treatment of pigeons," a senior EU official has said in Brussels.

A FLATTER BEAUTIFUL GAME...

"FLAT EARTH FC is the first professional football club whose followers are united by an idea," the club's president, Javi Poves, has said in Madrid's suburb of Móstoles, "and that is the most important thing. Other teams will always belong to a city or a nation, but our re-named club will be the club of anyone in the world who feels the flat earth cause as his own, wherever he lives. We are created to unite the voices of millions of flat earth movement followers who also love football, and who are looking for answers."

Formerly known as Móstoles Balompié, Flat Earth FC will play in the Tercera División of the Spanish football league. "Our mission is to create a community around the team," Javi continued, "a community that is transversal in the world. Creating a terrapiattista team will ensure that we are constantly on the media's lips, and we will bring a new model of relocation to football. Football is the most popular sport, and has the most impact worldwide, so creating a club dedicated to the flat earth movement is the best way to have a continuous presence in the media. Subscriptions for next season are already available on the internet – as are our new jerseys."

AN UNALLIED ARK...

"PEOPLE MAY THINK it is funny that the owners of a life-size replica of Noah's Ark are suing over flood damage," Melany Ethridge of the Creationist theme park, Ark Encounter, has said in Williamstown, Kentucky. "But this lawsuit is no laughing matter. Shortly after we unveiled our 510-foot-long replica of Noah's Ark in 2016, heavy rains caused a landslide and massive damage to our park, but the insurance carriers have refused to cover almost $1 million in damages. Consequently, we are suing Allied World Insurance Co. Holdings, and are asking for a trial."

Ethridge explained that "Our ark was built to the dimensions in the Bible, and is the largest timber-frame structure in the world. It celebrates the Genesis flood narrative through which God spares Noah, his family, and two of each of the world's animals from a world-engulfing flood. Tickets to the ark and the adjacent Creation Museum cost $75, so we lost a huge amount of revenue when our access road collapsed. You've got to be able to get to the boat to be on the boat. Our lawsuit speaks for itself, and we don't have anything to add at this time, other than to say that we are highly confident of a fair resolution to the matter."

THE USE OF A NAME...

A BOY IN INDONESIA'S West Java province has been named Google by his parents, in the hope that he too will become "useful". His father, Andi Cahya Saputra, says he thought about giving their son a name inspired by technology when his wife was seven months pregnant. He was considering Windows, iPhone, Microsoft, and iOS among others – as well as the more traditional Albar Dirgantara Putra. He admitted it took a while for relatives, including the boy's mother Ella, to accept the name.

Andi said he told his father that the name Google has an important meaning because he hopes his son can "help lots of people" and "be a useful person" for others. He says he refused to give Google a surname because it would dilute "the essence" of his name. It has grown on Ella, who says she hopes her son will become "a leader of many people".

LAZARENE LOVE...

"THE FESTIVAL OF Near Death Experiences is an annual event," an unnamed local has said in the Galician town of Las Nieves, "celebrating people who have narrowly escaped death during the previous 12 months. Each year, thousands gather here to give thanks to the town's saint, Saint Martha, whose brother Lazarus was raised from the dead by Jesus.

"During the fiesta, those who have escaped death climb into open caskets, which are carried through the streets by families and friends. They dress as though attending a real funeral, but there's nothing morbid about the experience, it's a celebration of life. People without families carry their own coffin through the streets, while other families carry empty coffins as a mark of respect."

Seventy-year-old restaurant owner Modesto Gomez, who has attended the festival since childhood, declared: "This is a cult of life. It's a celebration, although it's mentally and physically tiring to lie for hours in a moving coffin." Sixty-nine-year-old Maria Rodriguez, who had just been carried through the streets by pallbearers, added: "I did it to thank the saint for saving my dog from cancer. It's spontaneous, it comes from the heart and soul when you love someone."

BUGS IN BUSINESS...

ON THE OUTSKIRTS of Jinan, capital of China's eastern Shandong province, a billion cockroaches are being fed with 50 tonnes of food waste a day. It goes to a plant run by Shandong Qiaobin Agricultural Technology Co., where it is fed through pipes to cockroaches in their cells. Shandong Qiaobin plans to set up three more such plants this year, aiming to process a third of the food waste produced by Jinan, home to about seven million people. "Cockroaches are a bio-technological pathway for the converting and processing of kitchen waste," said Liu Yusheng, president of the Shandong Insect Industry Association.

In Sichuan, a company called Gooddoctor is rearing six billion cockroaches. "The essence of cockroach is good for curing oral and peptic ulcers, skin wounds, and even stomach cancer," said Wen Jianguo, manager of Gooddoctor's facility. Researchers are also looking into using cockroach extract in beauty masks, diet pills, and even treatments for hair loss. Asked about the chance of the cockroaches escaping, Wen said that would be worthy of a disaster movie – but that he has taken precautions. "We have a moat filled with water and fish," he said. "If the cockroaches escape, they will fall into the moat and the fish will eat them all."

LOST SOLES...

FOR THE 15TH time since 2007, an unidentified and unattached human foot has washed ashore in British Colombia. Poseidon's latest contribution to the Canadian littoral came wrapped in a grey Nike Free RN shoe with white laces and a white sole. Size: nine and a half. Sock colour: blue. Thus far, DNA tests have been unable to tie the foot to a missing person, so the British Columbia Coroners Service has asked for the public's help in identifying its former owner.

Local authorities seem phlegmatic about their ongoing finds. "We don't see any indication that there is any suspicion of foul play... Sometimes they are natural deaths, or suicides, or accidental deaths (like a fall)." Readers may wonder why feet, rather than any other body parts, keep appearing in this way. The best guess is that it is because of the way humans decompose in Davy Jones' Locker: should the worst happen, a tightly laced-trainer will protect a foot from marine creatures.

As for why the feet only began appearing in 2007, the answer may lie in the evolution of footwear. Sports shoes increasingly make use of air pockets or foam in their construction, cushioning feet (when attached and on land) while providing a useful buoyancy aid (once severed and at sea). Such is progress.

OEDIPAL AND COMPLEX...

"CHILDREN WEREN'T ASKED if they wanted to be brought into a world full of misery," Raphael Samuel has said in Mumbai. "So why should they have to put up with lifelong suffering? People should understand that they do not owe their parents anything, and that we should be maintained by them for the rest of our lives. They should pay us to live with them. That's why I'm taking my parents to court, to sue them for giving birth to me."

Raphael's mother, Kavita Samuel, commented: "I must admire my son's temerity in wanting to take his parents to court, especially as they are both lawyers. If I had met my son beforehand, I confess that I would not have given birth to him. But if he can offer a rational explanation as to how we could have obtained his consent to be born, then I will accept my fault."

Raphael insisted that his case is not a prank, adding that "the suffering we endure from being born includes facing wars, being stuck in traffic, and having to do things we don't want to. If this case makes even one couple think about whether or not to have children, it will have been a success."

BEINGS BEAT BOTS...

"WE HAD 243 robots when we opened the hotel," Hideo Sawada has said in the Henn-na Hotel in Nagasaki. "But we have had to sack half of them for incompetence. The Japanese-speaking android receptionist was unable to answer basic questions from tourists, the robot luggage carriers could only reach 24 of the 100 rooms, and half of the robot dancers never worked. Worse still, Churl, the AI room assistant, kept waking guests up in the middle of the night by asking them questions whenever they made a sound. So, for now, we've hired human beings to replace all the robots."

Guests at the world's first all-robot hotel had complained frequently about problems with the new technology. Atsushi Nishiguchi said: "When I stayed in the hotel, I found there was no phone, because I was supposed to use Churl. But Churl wouldn't connect me to a human being, so eventually I had to use my mobile to call the front desk." Yoshihisa Ishikawa added: "I was repeatedly woken in the night by Churl saying 'Sorry I didn't catch that, could you repeat your question?' But it was just my snoring triggering the system." A member of staff admitted that "it's easier now that we only have to deal with guests. Before, we spent most of our time trying to sort out problems with the robots."

THE WAYWARD WIENER...

A FAN OF THE Philadelphia Phillies baseball team was rushed to hospital for a brain scan after the team's mascot – a furry, green, flightless bird

– accidentally shot her in the face with a hot dog. During a lull in a contest between the Phillies and the St Louis Cardinals, the Phillie Phanatic – dressed in chef's whites for the occasion – jumped aboard his mobile hot-dog launcher and began firing into the crowd from his giant cannon. At the time, Kathy McVay was sitting in prime seats behind home plate, and so had a good view of the action. The trajectory of the flying frankfurter, however, took her by surprise and struck her on the face "like a ton of bricks."

Ms McVay suffered a haematoma in one eye, and severe facial bruising. The Phanatic – whose distinguishing features the club's website lists as "overweight, clumsy feet, extra-long beak, extra-long tongue, gawking neck" – feels terrible about the incident. And although she has vowed to return to the ballpark, Ms McVay has cautioned fellow Phillie fans "to be aware, because you never know. I understand a baseball, but not a hot dog."

AN ATHEIST'S THEOLOGY...

"I'VE BEEN UPFRONT about my atheism for years," Rev. Gretta Vosper has said outside West Hill United Church in Toronto, "and about my non-belief in God, Jesus, and the Bible. My critics say that my beliefs are fundamentally at odds with those of my church. They say it's appalling that an atheist is allowed to be an ordained minister, to stand in a pulpit and proclaim a lack of belief in a theistic, interventionist, supernatural being called God. But most of my congregation are supportive of my views and, after they took a long, hard look at the cost-benefit of a trial for heresy, the church agreed that there's a place for me in it."

The Right Rev. Richard Bott said: "The United Church of Canada is pleased with the settlement. The dance between our core values of a belief in God, and how they interact with and inform each other, is one that we continue to explore as followers of Jesus and children of God."

ANOTHER RESTLESS REFERENDUM...

VOTERS IN A town in north-west Germany have delivered a resounding message to their local council: keep our streets unnamed. Residents of Hilgermissen were asked to decide whether or not their roads should be given names. History dictates that they are only made up of numbers and the name of an old village, Hilgermissen, which was formed from several small hamlets in the 1970s. The town now has 2,200 people living in it, and 60% of those who voted in the referendum said they wanted the current system to be maintained. The council suggested that giving each street a name would make it easier for the likes of ambulances and couriers, but not enough locals agreed.

Public broadcaster NDR said some residents had noted an "irritable atmosphere" between supporters and opponents of the proposal in the build-up to the referendum, but the result is binding for the next two years. It came after three locals campaigned to hold a public vote in a bid to thwart the council's plan, although it has not stopped some streets being given nicknames by residents. One of those is *Bäckerweg*, or Baker's Way, popular in many German towns and cities.

IN THE BUSINESS OF BELOVED...

"THE FATHER OF the petitioner died in September 2009, and was buried in Drayton Parslow churchyard in April 2010. The existing gravestone was set up in 2014 under the authority of the Archdeacon of Buckingham. The inscription sets out the name and dates of the deceased, and describes him as "Father, Teacher, Linguist." There is an empty line before those words in which the petitioner, Mark Alexander, wishes to insert the single word 'Beloved'.

"The incumbent and one of the churchwardens became parties opponent, and two parishioners submitted letters of objection. In 2010, Mr Alexander (the petitioner) had been convicted of murdering his father, and had been sentenced to imprisonment for life. Following the murder, the petitioner had buried his father under concrete, and had pretended that his father was still alive.

"The Chancellor refused to grant a faculty. He concluded that, given the circumstances, it would be inappropriate to allow the word 'Beloved' to be added to the gravestone, as this would be likely to give offence to the local community. Furthermore, the word would have the effect of re-opening old wounds, and might appear to the public as an expression of the petitioner's continuing denial of the offence for which he has been convicted."

PROFESSIONAL PERSPECTIVES

LOOKING AHEAD TO 2020

SIMON ELLIOTT, *head of research at Winterflood Securities, gives his state of the sector views.*

How do you assess the health of the investment company sector as we head towards 2020?

Simon Elliott: While the investment trust sector remains in decent health, it is fair to say that there are some clouds on the horizon. Discount volatility has increased, and the rate of new launches diminished. There is also increasing scrutiny of unquoted holdings, with concerns over valuations and illiquidity. However, we remain confident about the prospects for the sector. The aggregate level of assets in investment companies continues to rise and exceeded £200 billion this year. Furthermore, there is no sign of the demand for income abating, and it is this that has driven the sector's growth in the last ten years.

What is the biggest threat to the industry at the moment?

SE: Regulation and, in particular, the requirement for greater cost disclosure under Key Information Documents (KIDs) is a significant headwind for the industry at present. This is an issue for intermediaries, and the wealth management community has made it clear that it makes it more difficult for them to embrace investment trusts. At the moment, there is no requirement for the equivalent open-ended funds to make comparable disclosures. We are concerned that the focus on costs overwhelms the assessment of potential returns, resulting in poor investment decisions.

Discounts have come off their all-time lows – which way will they be heading next?

SE: The investment trust industry is always susceptible to changing investor sentiment. Historically, there has been a correlation between discount volatility and market moves, and we would expect discounts to widen in the event of a market sell-off. That said, we believe that the downside discount risk is limited by the sector's lower beta to the market than was the case ten years ago. This reflects the issue and growth of alternative asset classes that should, in theory, perform in a very different way to equity markets. Furthermore, we believe that the higher levels of direct retail ownership should provide more stable shareholder bases over the long term.

Has corporate governance of investment trusts really improved that much? What would you like to see more boards doing?

SE: The standard of corporate governance has improved immeasurably over the last 20 years. This has been driven by more stringent regulation and legislation, but also by the quality of non-executive directors. An independent board of non-executives should be a key selling point of the investment trust structure, and it is notable that the FCA is considering imposing a not dissimilar structure on open-ended funds.

The best boards, in my opinion, are those closest to their shareholder bases, whose interests they should be representing. In order to achieve this, direct interaction with key shareholders is crucial. It does not necessarily have to be in the presence of the incumbent fund manager. We believe this will lead to better-informed decision-making.

Alternative assets have been the big growth sector recently, but do you think the sector is peaking (too much supply, style drift, etc.)?

SE: The investment trust sector has seen a renaissance in the last ten years, with over 100 new investment companies launched, providing exposure to a range of new and existing asset classes. While it is true that the pace of new issues has slowed, it is clear that investors are prepared to provide further capital to funds that are delivering on their investment objectives. So far this year, for example, GREENCOAT UK WIND has raised more than £500 million through two placings, while MERIAN CHRYSALIS has raised more than £200m in two placings, more than trebling the size of the company since its launch in 2018.

What have been the most interesting launches in the past 12 months in your view (excluding your own)?

SE: HIPGNOSIS SONGS FUND was launched in July 2018, with the aim of providing income and capital growth from a catalogue of songs and associated music intellectual property rights. After raising £202m through its IPO, it has raised an additional £193m through two subsequent placings, and is looking to raise up to £300m for a C share [on 17 October Hipgnosis announced that it had raised £231m]. To date, it has successfully deployed its capital and is on track to pay a 5p dividend. The key attraction of this fund is that its performance should be uncorrelated to equity or bond markets.

Last year saw Baillie Gifford launch its first new investment trust in over three decades. BAILLIE GIFFORD US GROWTH initially raised £173m at launch, in March 2018, but has grown to more than £300m as a result of further issuance and strong performance. Helen Xiong and Gary Robinson, the fund's managers, invest in US companies with strong growth prospects, and investment can be also made in unquoted companies. Eleven percent of its portfolio is currently invested in private companies, and this proportion is likely to increase in time.

Why has there been a relative dearth of IPOs this year? How will it go next year?

SE: 2019 has been a far quieter year for new issues. The recent launch of JPMORGAN GLOBAL CORE REAL ASSETS, which raised £149m, was only the sixth of the year. However, fundraising overall remains healthy. We estimate that £5.5bn was raised in the first eight months of the year, which represents a 36% increase on the same stage last year. We believe that this reflects investors' preference for supporting existing investment companies with proven track records of successfully deploying capital and meeting investment targets, rather than taking an additional risk by supporting a new launch.

The IPO market in 2020 will be dependent on two key factors: the quality of the potential launches and market conditions. It is far more difficult to launch new investment companies when markets are unsettled, or there is considerable uncertainty. It is no coincidence that the weakest year in recent times for new issues was 2016, when activity fell dramatically both in the run-up to the EU referendum and its immediate aftermath.

What has been the biggest highlight / disappointment over the last 12 months?

SE: The last 12 months have seen good performances from trusts investing in emerging markets, particularly Eastern Europe and Latin America. This has benefited a number of the funds in the JPMorgan stable, including JPM RUSSIAN SECURITIES and JPM BRAZIL, while JPM EMERGING MARKETS also has had a strong run. In contrast, and perhaps not surprisingly given the backdrop, funds invested in UK micro-caps (companies with a small market capitalisation) have had a tough time. These include RIVER & MERCANTILE UK MICRO CAP, MITON UK MICROCAP and DOWNING STRATEGIC MICRO-CAP. Despite this, we believe that this segment of the UK market is attractive on a long-term view and, in our opinion, offers significant opportunities for active managers.

Are investment trusts still competitive enough against passive and open-ended alternatives?

SE: There is a huge focus on fees across the investment management industry, with pressure being brought to bear by both investors and regulators to reduce fee burdens, as well as provide better disclosure of costs. Historically, investment trust companies have benefited from having lower fees than open-ended funds which, before the Retail Distribution Review came into effect, laboured under the need to pay trail commission. This is no longer the case but, in our opinion, investment trust companies continue to compare well against their open-ended counterparts, not least as a result of the efforts of their independent boards. That said, trusts often provide access to specialist asset classes which, by their nature, are more expensive.

Comparison with passive funds is a bit of a misnomer in our view. Investment trusts are actively managed, while passive funds are not. The former commands greater fees, while the latter provides exposure to beta, or the market return, which is increasingly cheap. It follows that the onus is on investment trusts to demonstrate that being actively-managed should produce long-term benefits to investors in terms of performance.

What has been the impact of the Woodford affair on the investment trust sector?

SE: The gating and subsequent proposed liquidation of Woodford's flagship fund was a result of a liquidity mismatch between its open-ended structure and the illiquid nature of its underlying holdings. The fallout has understandably focused on the appropriateness of the structure of the investment vehicle in investing in illiquid assets. In addition, it has raised wider questions for the investment management industry, particularly the benefits of active management. While a prohibition on investing in illiquid assets within open-ended funds may, in theory, prove advantageous to the investment trust industry, it is not clear whether the regulator is minded to endorse this approach.

Interest rates and bond yields have come down again recently – what has been / will be the impact on valuations and discounts?

SE: The low rate environment of the last 11 years has proved a boon for investment trusts. The greater dividend certainty that the structure provides, and the presence of 'dividend heroes' – trusts that have a record of increasing their dividends over twenty consecutive years or more – remains as relevant as ever. In addition, we suspect that demand will, in general, remain high for funds that generate attractive yields from exposure to esoteric asset classes.

"INVESTMENT TRUST COMPANIES CONTINUE TO COMPARE WELL AGAINST THEIR OPEN-ENDED COUNTERPARTS, NOT LEAST AS A RESULT OF THE EFFORTS OF THEIR INDEPENDENT BOARDS."

Are there fewer or more discount opportunities to exploit than there were? (Give one or two examples.)

SE: There are always pockets of value in the investment trust sector. While 100 or so names are trading on a premium or around NAV, and approximately 110 on discounts narrower than 10%, there are 120 trading on double-digit discounts. Admittedly, some of these are in managed wind-down, or are so small as to be virtually uninvestable. However, there are some interesting value plays, particularly for investors prepared to take a contrarian view. We currently favour listed private equity funds on wide discounts, such as PANTHEON INTERNATIONAL and STANDARD LIFE PRIVATE EQUITY*, both of which have strong long-term performance records. In addition, we believe that there is value in the UK commercial property sector at present, and are recommending BMO COMMERCIAL PROPERTY* in this area.

Are boards doing too much or too little in the way of gearing?

SE: Gearing is one of the advantages that the investment trust structure provides. One could make the argument that it is underused. The average gearing level at present, excluding 3i, is 8%, according to the Association of Investment Companies (AIC). On the other hand, many observers would argue that it is probably the wrong point in the market cycle to be increasing gearing, and there is some evidence that gearing has been reduced in some areas. Many managers talk about looking to take advantage of market weakness by deploying additional gearing. Boards should certainly be supportive in these instances, in our opinion.

Are you worried that trusts are paying too much out as income by drawing from capital?

SE: The payment of income from capital has been a controversial development across the sector in recent years. We believe that paying 'enhanced dividends' is one of the advantages of the investment trust structure and, in a number of instances, it has resulted in discounts narrowing following renewed buying interest. The key is disclosure. As long as shareholders are aware how the income is being generated, we believe that the practice is no different to that pursued, for a number of years, by offshore domiciled investment companies which historically enjoyed greater flexibility in determining their dividend levels. In addition, a number of onshore investment trusts have looked to maximise their yield, in the past, through their charging policy – by allocating costs to capital and income.

How big do you have to be these days to launch an IPO (a) for equity trusts, and (b) alternatives?

SE: The average size of the 17 IPOs seen last year was just over £150m, albeit seven were launched with less than £100m of proceeds. £100m still appears to be the minimum size that most institutional investors deem to be viable, and five of last year's launches were at this size, some requiring additional support to reach critical mass. One of the key considerations many investors make when deciding whether to support a new launch is not just its initial size, but whether it has the potential to grow within a relatively short period of time. Assuming capital is successfully deployed, and initial return targets met, most would look to see a fund ramp up in size within a few years, with the intention being to reach a size of £500m, allowing a lower cost base and greater secondary market liquidity.

Where are the biggest gaps in the investment company universe as far as you are concerned?

SE: Historically the sector has been very underweight US equities, despite the allocations of global trusts and specialist funds in the technology and healthcare sectors. While this may prove frustrating to those investors who prefer investment trusts to other vehicles, the reality is that there is a plethora of open-ended funds that provide exposure to this area, while there are those who are willing to use ETFs/passive funds, particularly since the US market has proven difficult for active managers to consistently outperform.

What would be the biggest change you would like to see to grow the sector in future?

SE: Retail demand has been the key driver of the investment trust sector in recent years. In order to see further growth, it would clearly be helpful for the platforms that provide the conduit for retail investors to provide more information, research and recommendations. A number have already embraced this, and we suspect that others will be minded to follow suit. We would also hope that investment trusts are prepared to provide greater disclosure of their portfolios, i.e. regular full disclosure, in order that diagnostic tools can be applied. These allow fund selectors and investors to make more informed investment decisions, in our opinion.

Which sectors do you think will produce the best returns (risk-adjusted if you wish) over the medium term (say three years)?

SE: I personally favour three sectors at present: UK small cap, private equity, and emerging markets/Asian equities. UK equities, in general, are cheap compared with other developed markets, albeit for understandable reasons, and political risk is heightened, not least given the possibility of a Corbyn-led government. Despite this, I believe that the long-term prospects for UK equities are good and, furthermore, there are some impressive managers in this space. Our favoured picks at present are STANDARD LIFE UK SMALLER COS*, managed by Harry Nimmo, and the MERCANTILE INVESTMENT TRUST*, managed by a team led by Guy Anderson.

Emerging markets/Asia will clearly be impacted by the ongoing trade dispute between the Trump administration and Chinese authorities. However, we believe that the long-term prospects remain strong and valuation levels reasonable. Our favoured funds at present are JPMORGAN ASIAN, SCHRODER ASIAN TOTAL RETURN* and JPMORGAN EMERGING MARKETS INCOME*.

Any advice for DIY investors looking to go into the sector for the first time?

SE: Do your homework! There are lots of good information points available, including the AIC, and media services such as *Citywire*, *Money Observer*, *Investors Chronicle*, *FT Advisor*, and *Investment Week*. In addition, there are some highly-experienced journalists covering the sector and writing in the national press, such as Ian Cowie, Jeff Prestridge and Richard Evans, who are all worth following for their insight and views.

SIMON ELLIOTT *has been Head of Research at Winterflood Investment Trusts, one of the biggest broking firms specialising in investment trusts, since 2008. These were his views on 10 October 2019.*

---

*   *Denotes a corporate broking client of Winterflood Securities.*

THE VIEW FROM
THE CENTRE

IAN SAYERS, *chief executive of the Association of Investment Companies (AIC), explains how he got involved with investment trusts and opens up to us about the biggest issues facing the industry.*

How did you get into the investment trust world? Was it something you thought you'd end up doing?

Ian Sayers: No, not at all. It was entirely fortuitous. I started off at Ernst & Young where I did my training. I was in the banking group there. Back in those days, they didn't have investment management as a separate specialism. One day, when I was very junior, somebody grabbed me and said, "What are you doing this afternoon?" I was the only person in the office and I found myself travelling to a company called 3i, which I was only vaguely familiar with at the time. I said, "What is 3i doing and why am I coming?" They said, "They're converting to an investment trust."

So, literally on the journey that we were making, I got a whistle-stop tour about what investment trusts were. I have to say, I didn't really understand an awful lot of it, but I did work as the junior on the conversion and, 3i being as big as they were, the amount of money at stake was huge. Therefore, you absolutely had to dot the i's and cross the t's on everything that you were doing.

Ernst & Young, like most accountancy firms, later formed an investment management division and I went into that, mostly because it wasn't banking – something I really didn't want to do. That might seem like a lot of foresight, but it wasn't really. Banking is fine, but investment management seemed to have more of a clear social purpose. It's helping people save for their future. So, I moved there.

Then I became a tax adviser at the AIC for a year. I went back to Ernst & Young for a year and then got poached back here, to take a broader remit in regulation. I was a tax man by trade, but I did all of the other technical disciplines. When I was pitching for the role, two or three months before I sat down for my interview, the EU put out a piece of regulation called the Alternative Investment Fund

Managers Directive. I'm probably the only person in the world that has a fondness for that piece of regulation, because it's probably one of the reasons that I got the job. That, in a nutshell, is how I got into all this.

And after that?

IS: Having started off on secondment as the tax adviser to the AIC, I first became the technical director, as they called it, and later deputy and, finally, chief executive. I joined the AIC full time at the very end of 1999, so I am coming up to 20 years all in. One of the things you notice about the industry is once people get involved in it, they tend to stay in it for a long time. Not because we can't go anywhere else, or at least I hope not, but because it's much more interesting and diverse than other types of fund structures, and generally people think it's something worth supporting.

What are the biggest, most interesting changes you have seen in that time?

IS: I think that the biggest change is that, when I started, the industry, with the odd exception, was investing mostly in listed shares and securities. There was a bit of private equity, because there was 3i, but over three-quarters of the assets were invested in equities. A lot of people saw that as a problem because the institutions didn't need equities so much any more, and there was a general view that the industry was going to go into permanent decline.

Now, I don't believe that is true for listed shares and securities. If you look at the performance record, trusts have held up very well indeed. But that was the prevailing view then. Roll forward to today and nearly half the industry's assets are in things that we would class as alternatives. Infrastructure is very big, and so are unlisted forms of debt, property, renewables, and so on. Another huge change is that most of these newcomers – not all of them but most – are income generating. That's been a huge change.

I do a directors' induction course and a lot of the directors who are new to the sector look at me as though I've gone raving mad when I tell them that, when I first joined this sector, the idea of paying dividends was seen as quite quaint. 'Oh, pay a dividend? How lovely.' That kind of thing. Because back then it was all about small-cap, emerging markets, low yield, and so on. Again, come forward and you have the perfect storm of ridiculously low interest rates and George Osborne abolishing the requirement to buy an annuity.

As a result, you've had this massive interest in investment companies, because we have advantages when it comes to paying income, not least the ability to smooth payments from one year to the next by using reserves. Over the last ten years, I would say 95% of the new money raised has, in some way, shape or form, been backed by income. Most of it is from alternatives; not all of it, but a lot.

We've also seen a third of the sector now trading at a premium. You never saw an investment company trade at a premium when I first came into this industry. If you did, it was a talking point and it was literally a tiny blip. Today, a third of investment companies are trading at premiums, which means they can issue shares, so they can also grow. I think that's really the single biggest change that I've seen over the time.

It means you now also have a wider range of asset managers. The list of asset managers we have involved in the sector is much longer than we used to have. That raises its challenges. But from an investment perspective, it's the range of asset classes, and the focus on income, which have been completely different if you are comparing the last ten years to my first ten years.

The sector has got a lot bigger but the ownership of investment trusts has also changed, has it not?

IS: When I joined the AIC, most investment institutions, the pension funds, and insurance companies, were still selling out. The industry was becoming progressively more retail owned. It's surprisingly difficult to get decent figures on that, but the industry was moving to being maybe 60%-owned by retail, and maybe 40% by institutions, depending how you defined the universe (which is also not that easy).

It's not gone completely full circle, but I would say it's definitely shifted a bit back in the other direction now. To the extent that we have good information about alternatives, they have a much higher proportion of institutional shareholders. It's probably about 55% retail, 45% institutional. I think it's a nice balance to have. You want to have investors from the widest range of backgrounds that you can.

The one area where the share of buying hasn't changed a lot is people coming through financial advisers. The abolition of commission on open-ended funds was a big change, and we've got figures that show the amount of money being put into investment trusts by IFAs has gone up five-fold since the Retail Distribution Review (RDR) effectively banned it. But the financial adviser share is still a tiny drop in the ocean. The barriers are still high. You have an industry that was built up on commission for 30 or 40 years. You remove commission, but it doesn't change overnight.

It's an area we're still working on, although it is fair to say that investment trusts are not struggling for demand, as you can see by the fact that the average discount this year came into its all-time lowest for the sector. There's plenty of demand out there, but the challenge of breaking into the IFA market is still with us. An extra billion pounds a year coming in from financial advisers is nice, but in an industry of £200 billion, it's not earth shattering.

We all know wealth managers have become much more important in the mix – what difference does that make?

IS: Yes, they are, and certainly some of the largest wealth managers are now virtually institutions. They're behaving like institutions in the sense that most of them say they'll probably keep a large presence in the investment trust sector, but it will shift more and more to alternatives. The equity bit will become less and less, and the alternative bit will become more and more. That is a change we have to adapt to.

I think the question whether you can get more classic pension fund money back is more open. You may have seen that the Business Bank is looking at ways to try and get defined-contribution pension money into venture capital. There's a possibility that could be a new opportunity for the future, because we're saying if you want to do that, the best way to do it is through a closed-ended fund. You could see more traditional pension companies coming back into the market that way.

But, like everything, the whole industry is a cycle. We love dividends; then we're not interested in dividends. Alternatives, equities, institutional retail – it keeps shifting around and you just have to keep adapting to it. I think where the industry is today is much more balanced than it was. The closed-ended structure is definitely better for certain asset classes, and we're exploiting that much more than we were 20 years ago.

Would you agree that one of the better things to have happened in the last 20 years is what Robin Angus calls 'investment trust freedom day', meaning the ability of trusts to issue and buy back shares?

IS: Yes, he is talking about 6 April 1999 and the day that the government abolished Advanced Corporation Tax (ACT). I should know the date; I'm a tax man – I was there listening to the announcement! If you bought back shares before then, there was a big tax cost, because they used to think that that if a company can buy back shares, it's got to have profits to do it, so it must also have profits it can pay tax on. Hence, the ACT. In fact, being trusts we didn't have any corporation tax to pay, so having to pay ACT was just a straightforward added cost of doing business. It meant that 25% of the dividend was lost in tax. That made it uneconomic. The government then abolished that tax.

There were some other changes we had to make on the legal and regulatory side, but what it meant was that, for the first time, you could actually go into the market and buy shares back to try to control the discount. That wasn't the only advantage. If your share has a pound of assets and you're paying 8op for the shares, that's 2op left over for the rest of the shareholders. So you get a benefit for the remaining shareholders. But the real thing is that the trust is out there buying in the market. An extra buyer means a narrower discount. And it will bring the discount in.

Discount control methods have evolved. I describe them as now being probably in their late teenage years. To begin with, people tried various different things and it didn't always work. Over time, we've learnt more and more about how to do them. What we realise now, particularly with alternatives, is there is no one solution. We had a few property funds who put in some very strict discount controls, for example, but then we had the financial crisis in 2008–2009 and they had to abandon them because, as we're seeing with open-ended property funds, you don't want to end up selling the assets in a really bad market.

So, trusts have to learn how to do it. But I agree with Robin Angus. For a big company with a big, liquid portfolio, and plenty of resources, you can manage the discount pretty tightly. The freedom certainly brings discounts in a lot and, on average, discounts over the last five years have never been lower. With other asset classes – you've got to accept that you can't just sell your infrastructure projects, for example, so you have to live with that. You can't magic away all illiquidity.

The other side of the coin is that it makes it easier for trusts to raise new capital by issuing shares. That is quite a significant change from the past when it was a cumbersome process to issue new shares.

IS: Yes. This year, particularly, IPOs (initial public offerings) have been pretty slow, but new issuance has, nevertheless, been at record levels. To issue more shares as a trust, you've got to get the shares to a premium, and it is possible to do that. Trusts that have been at discounts, and tackled the discount, have been able to attract other investors in. Then they see the shares go to a premium and issue those shares back out to the market. That's been a big change.

I think the quid pro quo is that IPOs are getting harder to do. The wealth managers, in particular, usually don't want to get locked in to a £50 million fund. They want £200m, £300m, and it's that much harder to do. The average size of an IPO has gone up steadily. For the moment, it's been relatively slow. But my guess is that these things will come around again. If pension funds or the banks suddenly decide they want to see a whole load of closed-ended funds investing in venture capital, the market will supply that need.

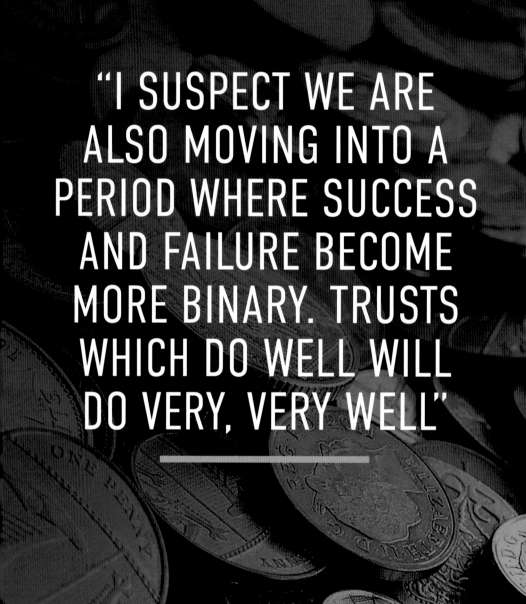

"I SUSPECT WE ARE ALSO MOVING INTO A PERIOD WHERE SUCCESS AND FAILURE BECOME MORE BINARY. TRUSTS WHICH DO WELL WILL DO VERY, VERY WELL"

I suspect we are also moving into a period where success and failure become more binary. Trusts which do well will do very, very well, while the funds that are struggling will probably get taken out a bit quicker. That is not a problem because that's what a market should do. The only thing you have to worry about is whether the really successful ones get too big. That's up to the boards of individual trusts to decide.

Another thing which happened quite early on your watch was the split-capital trust scandal. At the time, people thought it raised a question mark over the future of the whole sector. With the benefit of hindsight, can you more clearly see now why that was able to develop, without either the regulators or the market being able to prevent it happening, and what the consequences have been?

IS: These kinds of issues build over time, and there's possibly a natural tendency to assume that the problem will just go away. Over a hundred split-capital investment companies didn't happen overnight. They started off with a structure that was perfectly reasonable, but then interest rates started to fall (it seems ridiculous in the context of where we are today) but there was pressure to deliver yield. That meant that trusts started to invest in each other, and you ended up with costs on top of costs, gearing on top of gearing, cross investment, and so on.

That position built over time. One of the problems is that you need somebody to look down from above and see it all coming. The regulators were criticised, but back in those days the Financial Services Authority (FSA), as it was, weren't regulating investment companies in the way they are today. Today, they still don't have full control of regulation over investment companies, but they had even less then. They had some control through the listing rules. In a sense, they probably didn't think we were on their watch at all.

It is only when people lose money, and there's a crisis, that it becomes a real issue. I think it wasn't so much a lack of transparency, because trusts published portfolios even then, but it's a question of having to see all the interconnections in a very complex picture. The other thing you learn is that when there are real losses of value in any area of financial services, a good proportion of the time, gearing has something to do with it. I think that one of the consequences of the split-capital saga is that gearing now tends to be quite cautiously used.

You could even argue we're making the reverse mistake now. Even though our members can borrow for 30 years at 2.5%, gearing is still very modest. Now, that may be to do with worries about where we're going, and the Eurozone crisis, and all these kinds of things, but you do wonder if, maybe in 20 years' time, you'll look back and go, "Gosh, we missed a trick there." Because if you can't generate 2.5% off an equity portfolio over 30 years, then why are we here?

What I would say is that the split-capital issue was the low point of my career, because we were having phone calls from people who had been seriously financially disadvantaged. We did run a charity to help people out. But that is not somewhere you really want to be. Quite a number of my team were there at the time, and you don't forget it.

The other lesson I took away is that if something sounds almost too good to be true, and yet those involved still insist that there's an explanation, you will get a healthy dose of scepticism. There were people in the trust business saying that the split-capital issue had been blown out of all proportion and there weren't any problems. A year later, 40 companies had lost all their money. That is not a good way to go.

One of the advantages of the closed-ended structure is that you have flexibility to use financial engineering, but I think there are a lot of grounds for just keeping things simple. People want a fund that performs well. I'm not sure that playing around at the edges on all these kinds of things is necessarily a good idea. In any event, most of that has gone. There are virtually no splits today, at least not of the type that we would have thought of as splits. There's the odd trust using a ZDP (zero-dividend preference share) to gear the portfolio, but they have virtually disappeared, as has most of the financial engineering. I don't think that's a bad thing.

It is said that the quality of corporate governance in investment trusts has gone up. In the old days, boards tended to be made up of people who, even if we don't call them cronies, knew each other well. Boards weren't regarded as being particularly active. What's been the driver behind the change and how far has it gone? How much further does it need to go?

IS: I would say that there is certainly an element of truth in your characterisation of it. I don't think anyone would deny that, but I think it is possibly overstated. There were a lot of good directors around then. I have seen some very good examples of directors doing good things in the splits crisis, and the banking crisis, where they really played a tough role in getting the right result. However, I think you're right to say it was insular as an industry. It was common to meet people with multiple directorships. If you had 50 or 60 people in the industry in a room, that was about the whole industry.

That's changed a lot. For example, I know that we have 1,300 directors in the sector, of which 1,100 have no more than one or two directorships. The vast majority have one directorship. They may have other commitments as well, like charities etc., but that's a big change. The make-up of boards has improved a lot too, although there is still quite a long way to go.

The gender mix is improving. You won't be surprised that 20 years ago, if you went into a room of investment trust directors, you would have barely seen a woman. Today, it's pushing up to around 25%, but there's still further to go. The government wants to get to 33%. The next challenge will be ethnic diversity, which is very low at the moment.

Even if we get to full gender and ethnic diversity, there are other diversities we need to address as well, including social background and skills. There are still boards around with four or five ex-fund managers on the board. Do you really need five? Isn't one or two enough? We're seeing a lot of people being brought in on the marketing and distribution side, which I think is healthy. I'm meeting many more different people from outside the industry. It is fascinating to meet them because they come to our industry without any preconceptions at all. And they just look at you and sometimes they go, "what on earth are you doing that kind of thing for?" I think that's very healthy.

So, overall, it's got a lot better, but it's still got a way to go. I think the process of change has accelerated over the last two or three years, and I think it will continue. I think ethnicity will be a challenge, if only because of the pool you're drawing from. We also have a lag effect because most people who do the non-executive director job tend to be semi-retired. But we mustn't use that as an excuse.

We had a directors' round table recently and, for the first time ever, women outnumbered men. I'm not saying the job is done but you could not have imagined that 20 years ago. We're running some courses now to get more people in from the outside. In the past, trusts rarely used recruitment consultants. It was just a case of "Do you know somebody?" That was perpetuating the problem.

The other difference is that it's very rare now to find someone from a management company on the board of directors.

IS: Yes. I don't have any figures for how that has changed. I wouldn't be surprised if it was over half. Today, I think it's less than 10%. When you do see it, it tends to be just one director. But I certainly remember boards having two or even three people who were connected to the manager. That's virtually disappeared. Of course, some management group directors were also among the most scrupulous and dedicated, but the perception of it being too cosy was unhelpful. If something goes wrong, it doesn't look great. I think the industry realised that it is better to separate it out as far as possible.

Describing investment trusts as the City's best-kept secret, and the low-cost investment option, used to make for a good tagline. But, today, there's a lot more competition from both actively-managed and passive funds. As a result, there's been downward pressure on fees. Do you have a view on whether that's gone too far or hasn't gone far enough?

IS: It has been quite an unnatural evolution in the sense that you needed regulatory intervention in the shape of the RDR to strip out commission payments. But when that happened, it was a slightly double-edged sword. It meant that people were no longer being influenced by commission, which I think has been very positive – although, ironically, probably more positive in the fact that once you abolished commission for financial advisers, you had to do the same for online stockbroking as well. That has been far more beneficial to us because the likes of Hargreaves Lansdown are now some of our biggest shareholders. That's been a really big success, which wasn't what we were aiming for, but it was all part of stripping incentives out of the system.

But the quid pro quo is that you can no longer make the claim that investment trusts are always cheaper than other funds. We've responded by cutting fees, and you see a lot of tapered fees meaning that, as you get bigger, the fees in percentage terms go down. Boards have got to realise that this is a competitive area.

Occasionally, boards go a little bit too far in cutting fees, to the point that management groups say that it's not worth it for them to carry on at that rate. The managers have to allocate their capital where it's most profitable. But I think that's relatively rare. The pressure on fees is going to continue to be downwards, and I think you're going to see active asset management over the next few years becoming cheaper, not necessarily dramatically, but steadily, over time. That's certainly what the regulator wants to see happening.

The key point is that if you're paying an active fee, and you don't beat your benchmark, then you might as well not pay the active fee. Most open-ended funds tend to underperform their benchmark, while investment trusts tend to outperform their benchmark. That's good news for us, but you can see the problem that the Financial Conduct Authority (FCA) has got. You can always say that if you pick the best managers, you will get a good result. But I'm not sure anyone knows of a reliable way to do that. That's where the passive funds come in, although I don't think it hurts our sector as much as some other sectors.

Alternatives are another case, of course, because there are no readily passive alternatives.

IS: Yes, you can't really have a passive alternative asset fund. Alternatives are more expensive as well, although there's a degree to which that's justified, because if you're running equities in a listed structure, and you double the size of the assets, there's no more work to do. But if you double the number of properties you own, you've got double the work to do. So, there's a degree of justification. I think the passive threat is a very serious threat to active open-ended managers, but less so to us because the people who are interested in trusts are more committed to active management. Hopefully we can deliver, because we do tend to outperform. Fingers crossed!

On that subject, what happened to the Cass Business School study which came out last year and got a lot of publicity for claiming to show that investment trusts did, on average, deliver superior performance to open-ended funds? When I contacted one of the authors recently, he said "We've abandoned it because we've got data issues."

IS: We do a lot of, what we call, a sister funds analysis, where you take 30 or 40 open-ended funds and look at how they perform compared to 30 or 40 closed-ended funds doing the same thing. Consistently, it shows us outperforming, but there's no way I'm going to suggest that's an academic exercise. I think the difficulty with the Cass study is that they wanted to break it down sector by sector, and you find that you are comparing 200 open-ended funds to only half a dozen on the closed-ended side. I can see why, academically, it's hard to draw definitive conclusions from that, but we'll keep plugging away.

I've been 20 years in this industry and, even in down markets, I have never seen us not outperforming open-ended funds over the long term – not in the short-term, where you really can suffer, but over the long term. It happens over and over again. That is why you put your money in it, I put my money in it, sensible people put their money in it. Most of the open-ended fund managers still stick their money with us. Everybody in the know sticks their money in closed-ended funds, whilst not necessarily saying that publicly.

So, the popularity is there, but we don't have the mass marketing experience that open-ended funds have always had. It's more difficult for us to break through as mainstream, big, mass market products. An open-ended fund has it much easier to suck in huge sums of money. That's not necessarily a good thing – as we have seen with the Woodford saga – but it is mechanically much easier to do.

How do you assess the fallout from the Woodford debacle on the investment trust sector? Has it been, on balance, net positive or net negative for the sector?

IS: I think it's a bit too early to come down definitively on either side. I think, overall, it will be positive. We have to talk a lot to investors about closed- versus open-ended status, and you watch people's eyes glaze over very quickly. But, this year, that has all changed. To find yourself live on BBC News being asked "Could you explain in 30 seconds, Ian, the difference between an open- and closed-ended fund?" is quite a big challenge. We've had to find a way to do that, and that is important.

What I am worried about, and it's relevant to the Business Bank proposal as well, is if investors confuse the underlying issues. The danger is that retail investors who, let's face it, are generally not that excited or interested about financial services products, get confused and think that it's all about the problem of illiquid assets; that illiquid assets are, therefore, bad and we shouldn't touch them.

Trying to explain to them that this is not the issue with Woodford is difficult. Woodford was running an equity income fund and, while it did have some illiquids in it, they weren't the only reason the fund got into difficulties. I suspect it might have had to shut, even if it had none of those unlisteds. If you say to people, "You can have your money back," and a pension fund says, "We'll have £250m back in one go," I'm not sure how many funds could handle that without experiencing a liquidity problem.

It's not about unlisteds. They're not bad – what is bad is putting them together with daily redemption. We've seen it before with open-ended property funds. They had to shut for six months. Now we've seen Woodford is going to shut for six months. And so, yes, we've been saying that the warning signs have been there for years, but no one's been doing anything about it, other than being quite critical of the regulator.

I think things did change, this year, when Mark Carney intervened and gave his evidence to the Treasury Committee using the infamous "built on a lie" phrase. I think what he's worried about is raising the illiquidity issue to a systemic level. Yes, he is concerned about consumers, but that's not his primary job. His primary job is financial stability. He is worried about seeing a run on funds in the same way as we have had a run on the banks in the past.

Does that mean we are going to see more regulatory change after Woodford?

IS: Something is now going to happen, but I think we've taken an awfully long time to get to where we are. We often talk about the architecture of financial services. We build it up in a certain way, but then if you want to ever change anything, it becomes really complicated. Why on earth are open-ended property funds offering daily redemptions? The reason is that platforms have billed themselves as being able to deal daily. If you offer daily redemption, you're not doing it because that's the right thing to do, for the asset class or the consumer. You're doing it because distribution has gone in a certain direction.

And then take the Hargreaves Lansdown Wealth 50 list. Why does that exclude investment companies? They say that they will have too much money going into too few funds. Well, yes, that's because you promote it that way! It used to be the Wealth 150. Maybe you need to think about a different way, rather than pushing everybody into a smaller and smaller range of funds, and then complaining that they can't give you the liquidity. You created that problem by being huge and very successful and, yes, they are brilliant at what they do, but why then narrow the options? A third of their clients went into Woodford. It was astonishing, extraordinary. Are best buy lists really doing the right thing? I don't know.

These are all questions that the Woodford situation raises. I think it is what I'm most worried about with the Business Bank venture capital proposal. Let's not get into the world of saying – and I've already seen comments online along these lines – "Surely you're not going to put pension investors into venture capital? That's incredibly risky." Actually, I'd say, no, the risk is there, but you're talking about the wrong risk. The risk is you're not going to get the returns that you need for a decent pension income.

Some of these default pension schemes are incredibly cautious. I've seen one that's projecting 4% returns, on average, per annum, compared to an equity fund that might do 7%. Well, put a 3% differential over 40 years into your spreadsheet and see what it means for your retirement income! It's astronomical. But no one talks about that. They just talk about risk. But there are different kinds of risk.

So, I think the debate about where to go next should be positive for our sector, but it's not a slam dunk. The other side will fight back. And they can point to issues for us. You know, we've got discounts, premiums, those kinds of things. I think, overall, it will be a positive thing. I certainly think the days of daily redemption property funds are drawing to a close.

What else is on your agenda at the moment? What's the biggest thing? We haven't talked about Key Information Documents (KIDs), and the wider threat of regulation, for example.

IS: I think the whole closed-ended structure and illiquid assets is probably our biggest issue, at the moment. That's going to take up a lot of time. But, in the background, we still have the key information document issue. That's a really good example of how you shouldn't make regulation. It's not a criticism of the EU; I just think you don't try and create one set of rules that applies to every single product in 27 member states. I don't blame the people who were in Brussels, or wherever they were, not coming up with a great solution. I don't think anyone could've achieved it.

But it has been a frustrating business. The timing wasn't great because, when they first came out, it was after the financial crash. It was ten years ago when they first started looking at this. In the post-crash world, coming from the UK into Brussels, I think there was a, "Why is this lying so-and-so lying to me?" feeling. We said this is not going to work. I've got a letter from ten years ago saying this is not going to work, and these are the reasons why. It was completely ignored and here we are.

So, it would be great to change. I've got a feeling it's not having a massive impact on people. I don't think anyone really looks at these documents, and people are certainly not promoting them. If you look on websites, they're tucked out of the way a bit. The industry has, I think, been quite responsible on that. It's a very odd situation to find yourself in, as a chief executive, complaining about a document that makes our performance look fantastic, and our risks look really low! It's a weird situation to be in, but directors are very concerned about it, so it is still very much on our agenda.

I think the other main issues are related to marketing and distribution. If you look at where the world is going, we have a very loyal base of investors, but all the statistics show they're relatively old. They are hobbyist in nature. They love the industry. They all get converted aged around 45–50. Every statistic shows they get converted at that age, but the question we're wrestling with is, is the next generation going to come on in the same way?

It's not realistic to say we can't bring in younger investors because they don't have any money. If they have any money, they won't go into investment trusts. It's going to go on a deposit for a house. The question is then, when they get to 45–50, will they be converted to investment trusts in the same way? I think we've just got to recognise that the way they're going to get information, and the way they're going to buy products, is going to change.

In fact, it's already changed. With things like the environmental, social, and governance (ESG) issue, the next generation are just going to take that as read. If a product isn't stamped ESG-compliant, they're probably not going to buy it. Talking about green funds sales is a total red herring. They won't believe that they need to buy a green fund, just as they won't go to a green supermarket. They'll expect Tesco to be green and environmentally friendly. And if you don't, they will boycott you. They expect everyone to be doing it. It's not a choice thing. And that's different from my generation. They are going to expect it right across the board.

It is very early days in that debate, and I think fund management hasn't quite worked out what being environmental and sustainable means. Does it mean not buying companies that don't meet certain criteria? Does it mean buying investments that have a positive impact? I'm worried about that because I've heard fund managers say "I'm going to have to sell down these companies [that don't comply]."

I'll give you an example: airlines. Is it more responsible to sell off all your airline stocks, or invest in them, and use your shareholder power to make them behave in a more environmentally-responsible way? Maybe we're all going to give up flying eventually. But, if we're not, maybe it would be worth addressing that issue. You've got to think about that kind of thing. That debate, I think, is still happening.

Ultimately it will come down to the individual shareholders, but I think the fear of some managers is that anything that doesn't meet the criteria will have to be sold. What does that mean for those companies? They get taken private, in which case you've got less influence over what they're going to do. So, we'll have to think about it quite carefully. It is still evolving.

An increasing part of your job, in recent years, has been to deal with the regulator, not just in this country but also in the EU. For the EU, as you say, the whole idea is to standardise everything they can standardise. We don't know what's going to happen with Brexit, but do you think that, after that, there will be any fundamental change in regulation? Or do you think we'll just absorb the EU approach and just rubber stamp it?

IS: I might throw the question back and say, you tell me how we're leaving the European Union and I'll tell you what the answer to that question is! If we leave on a deal, I'm as certain as I can be, the first thing that they'll do is have a two-year standstill to give us time to work out the future relationship with the EU. Nothing will change very quickly.

After that, I think there would be a very interesting debate to be had about what we keep from European regulation and what we don't. That's a sensitive discussion. If you want to have access to the European market you can't strip everything away, because then you'll lose access to their market. It's less of an issue for investment trusts because we have few mainland European investors. To the extent that we access them, we'd probably still be able to do that because the US can access European investors, and as long as the EU treats us the same way, that's fine.

What we've said is that we will end up with a two-tier regulatory system. If you're selling in the domestic market, you should be allowed to diverge from Europe. If you want to sell into the European market, you've got to comply. There are jurisdictions around the world that do that. I don't think the UK would scrap the KID, but it would be able to change it so that it wasn't quite so toxic.

There are quite a lot of other regulations we might want to get rid of, but it's three years away before we start that process. And I was saying that three years ago! So, who knows? But that's what we would do. And that, I think, would work very well for our industry. There's very little demand from mainland Europe because they just don't have closed-ended funds at the moment.

What is the most important thing the AIC does, and how much time do you spend on regulation versus promotion or whatever?

IS: We did a member survey last year. We do one every five years, just to find out that what we're doing is what members want us to do. And you won't be surprised to discover that the top two things that they want from us is lobbying and technical advice. And those go hand-in-hand. If you're trying to change anything, you've got to change it in the law.

That just reflects what the last ten years have been like. There's been an avalanche of regulation. That's the number one thing by far. Beyond that, there are other services that our members probably don't always think of. For example, we produce statistics for the sector that they probably don't even remember, that kind of thing. We have a consumer website. The communication stuff is extremely important.

We're very unusual, for a City trade body, to be actively promoting the product our members offer. It's quite rare. The Association of British Insurers (ABI) doesn't go around touting the value of insurance. They don't need to because their own members already do that. Even the Investment Association (IA) doesn't. It does talk a bit about open-ended funds, but not in that way because, as I said, as an industry, we don't spend that much money on marketing. We have three or four people in our communications team. It's a big part of trying to get the message out.

So, there's that, and then, ultimately, just helping directors do their job as best they can. I think any director who comes onto the board has two things they want to do. They want to make the fund perform well, and they want to make sure they don't trip up on the risk side. We try to help on both, but the risk side – making sure that we understand all of this regulation, what they have to do – is a key part of it.

The directors are there to look after the interests of the shareholders, but most trusts also have to deal with their fund managers and advisers – how do you balance those, sometimes, conflicting interests?

IS: We work with the managers, but we only allow investment companies in as members. We have no associate members. I've always kept that completely clean. If my job is to help a company who's a member, ultimately my job is to help the company to help their shareholders. That drives everything that we do. There are times when we might be on the opposite side of the fund managers on a certain debate. When we did the VAT case, which was one of the big things that I did, that saved us £40m a year, but it cost the managers about £15m because of the way VAT works.

But the board here was very clear. We don't represent the managers. It was the best thing to do, so they took the decision to fight the case. And we won the case, which was a good day. I remember it was a Friday afternoon. I was down the pub. And we got the fax – fax? I think it was a fax. It can't have been that long ago, surely? It must have been. Anyway, we got a letter through, so I had another pint of beer. It was a Friday afternoon. I thought I deserved that one!

Final question: how long are you going to go on doing this job?

IS: I don't want to talk too much about my personal plans, but I will as it's as interesting and challenging today as it was 20 years ago. It's not become stale, because things are changing all the time. There are some people in this world who wouldn't think tackling the Alternative Investment Fund Managers Directive, and reading 27 draft copies of it, is a satisfying thing to do. But, unfortunately, I'm a technical nerd. All it did was preserve the status quo. Some people would think I'm completely mad, but that's my background; that's what I do.

I'm very happy where I am at the moment. I haven't actually added it up, but the top team here must have close on a 100 years' experience at the AIC. No one ever leaves. You wouldn't do that if you didn't enjoy it, and you didn't enjoy the people. There's certainly been times, certainly during the European stuff, where I saw more of Guy Rainbird than I did my wife. You're out in Brussels all the time. You can't do that unless there's a pretty good working relationship. So, I'm here for the time being, but if you asked me, "Would I be here in ten years' time?" I'd say almost certainly not. You don't want to outstay your welcome.

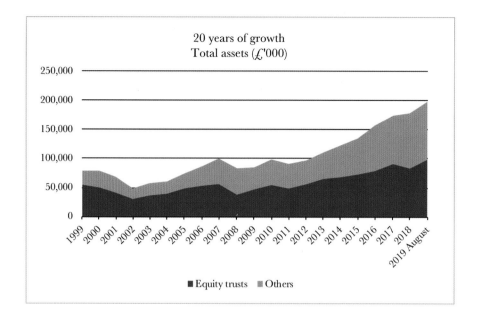

IAN SAYERS *has been working at the Association of Investment Companies since 1999 and its chief executive since 2010.*

COULD IT HAPPEN TO US?

ROBIN ANGUS *itemises the risks that investment trust boards need to monitor on a regular basis and explains how the board of* PERSONAL ASSETS, *where he is an executive director, assesses them.*

INVESTMENT FUNDS HAVE been much in the news recently, and not always for the happiest of reasons. Funds in the Woodford stable have been caught up in a nasty portfolio liquidity crunch and this has had a knock-on effect on the firm's listed investment trust, WOODFORD PATIENT CAPITAL. Elsewhere, LINDSELL TRAIN INVESTMENT TRUST, long prominent in the sector for its stellar price performance, has also run into some unsettling price volatility resulting from questions about the premium to NAV at which its shares sell.

Trusts have also suffered losses from 'torpedo stocks' within their portfolios. The AIM-listed Burford Capital, which specialises in funding lawsuits in exchange for a portion of the proceeds (and in which both Woodford and Invesco's EDINBURGH INVESTMENT TRUST have significant stakes), fell by 65% in a single day after a hedge fund shorted the stock and justified doing so in a damning research note.

Could such misfortunes happen to others? This article offers a mundane but necessary 'risk audit' of problems which can face investment funds in general and investment trusts in particular. My intention is not that of the Fat Boy in *The Pickwick Papers*, "to make your flesh creep", but to stress that a board's awareness of risk needs to be as high as its tolerance of risk is low.

RISKS TO WATCH OUT FOR

Managing a fund is more than just managing a portfolio of investments, and very markedly so in the case of an investment trust, which is not only a fund but also a listed company. Some types of risk are common to all or most funds. Others are very rare, but (if they do occur) can cause major problems – for instance, those in a category not otherwise featured here which we might call **historical risk**.*

The list of risk categories which follows may seem unduly long, but all have at one time or other been raised with me by at least one shareholder or interested investor.

1. PERFORMANCE RISK

The nature of the risk

As Maria von Trapp sings to the children in *The Sound of Music*: "Let's start at the very beginning,/A very good place to start." Every investment fund has performance risk. It is commonly seen as 'risk of underperforming a benchmark', but to us it is 'risk of failure to do what it says on the tin'.

How to guard against it

We have a clearly-stated policy against which every board decision and every action the investment adviser takes is measured. To quote Kipling's *Kim*, it is our "*ne varietur*", our guideline and absolute requirement, which will never change. History unfortunately offers many examples of trusts which have broken faith with their investment policy. Only a few live long enough to regret it.

2. STRUCTURAL RISK

The nature of the risk

Are there aspects of a fund's structure that could hinder performance? Closed-endedness not balanced by a discount and premium control mechanism (DCM) is the most obvious, but others are gearing, a fixed life, or the existence of other classes of capital. WOODFORD EQUITY INCOME'S problem was that under the Open-Ended Investment Companies Regulations 2001 it could invest only 10% of its portfolio in unlisted securities, and for various reasons (e.g. a fall in net assets while the valuation of the unlisteds remained the same) the fund exceeded this limit.

---

* Those with long memories may recall how, in 1996, Fleming American Investment Trust (now JPMORGAN AMERICAN INVESTMENT TRUST) had to pay out several million dollars to the US government to pay for the cleaning up of the site of a creosote factory in Louisiana built in 1882 by one of its predecessor companies, the Alabama, New Orleans, Texas and Pacific Junction Railway.

How to guard against it

Trusts which take on structural risk must live with the consequences. In an ideal world they and their shareholders do so willingly and with their eyes open. PERSONAL ASSETS has the simplest possible structure for an investment trust, consisting only of Ordinary shares. It is not geared, has no fixed life, holds no unlisteds, and operates a discount control policy to ensure that its shares always trade close to NAV.

3. GEARING RISK

The nature of the risk

Gearing is a good servant but a bad master. Maintaining the same amount of gearing with a reducing pool of assets means that the gearing percentage will increase, taking one of the levers of power away from boards and managers. The use of gearing is a two-edged sword.

How to guard against it

At PERSONAL ASSETS we have never borrowed money for investment. We were geared in the 1990s, but our geared exposure to markets came from holding investment trust warrants and the shares of investment management companies. It is possible that at some time in the future we may use short-term borrowings, but it is much more likely that we would use equity index futures.

4. RATING RISK

The nature of the risk

This risk is peculiar to closed-ended funds. PERSONAL ASSETS, while not an open-ended fund in the usual sense, both creates new shares to satisfy demand and buys back shares when demand is exceeded by supply. Over the 15 months to 31 July 2019 we issued 305,354 shares for a consideration of £124 million. Had we not done this, a large premium might have emerged.

Why, then, don't we just 'let the premium rip'? Sometimes, too, people talk as if PERSONAL ASSETS owned an orchard full of low-hanging fruit which the board inexplicably fails to pick. Why should we not at least be a little greedier and go for one or two extra percentage points on the new shares we issue? The reason is that doing either of these superficially attractive things would in fact break faith with our shareholders.

Buyers of new shares are often also existing holders through investment plans. Seeking a bigger increment to net asset value through issuing stock at a higher premium would be merely one hand taking from the other. As regards 'letting rip', for a short-term benefit you would destroy performance in the long term, there being no way to achieve a decent return if you have a double-figure premium that will naturally trend back to zero – that is, net asset value.

How to guard against it

We ensure that our shares always trade at close to NAV through a combination of share buybacks at a small discount and the issue of new or Treasury shares at a small premium when demand exceeds supply. We are, we believe, unique in the trust sector in that this policy is enshrined in our articles of association and could be changed only by a vote by the shareholders themselves in a general meeting. When trusts advertise a DCM but don't do this, it is incumbent on shareholders to make sure they fully understand the scope and limits of the discount policy that has been adopted.

5. REGULATORY RISK

The nature of the risk

AIFMD, FATCA, MiFID II – such strings of initials sound like codes waiting to be cracked at Bletchley Park. Some, like FATCA (the US Foreign Account Tax Compliance Act), were imposed from outside, while others, like AIFMD (Alternative Investment Fund Managers Directive), are imposed by the EU.

How to guard against it

While the Association of Investment Companies (AIC) does sterling work in monitoring and lobbying against the burden of regulation, it is not to be expected that leaving the EU (assuming we actually do so) will be accompanied by a bonfire of regulations. On the contrary, in the wake of the Woodford funds' problems, we would expect regulation to increase. A sizeable slice of every board meeting will therefore still of necessity be taken up with scrutinising these risks and making sure that we are in the clear.

6. SUPERVISORY RISK

The nature of the risk

Is there appropriate oversight of the investment manager or adviser?

How to guard against it

Independent boards are one of the greatest advantages possessed by investment trusts. Their job is not to run the trust on a day-to-day and stock-by-stock basis, but, like the sovereign in Bagehot's definition, they have the right "to be consulted, to encourage and to warn", and they know, too, that there are proper occasions for each of these.

Are independent boards effective? The gentle inquiry, *Are you quite sure that's a good idea?'* from the Queen would be more chilling than any explosion of rage from President Trump. Quite apart from my role at PERSONAL ASSETS, long experience of the sector has taught me that the same is true of advice behind the scenes from a good board.

It is the responsibly of the directors individually and of the board as a whole to make sure that a trust is being run properly. Risk of all kinds has risen higher up the board of PERSONAL ASSETS' agenda in recent years. Twice a year the board considers the comprehensive risk registers we keep, and these are constantly updated as new risks are identified. It is exhausting but essential work.

7. MANAGEMENT RISK

The nature of the risk

Fund management is a people business, and as in all people businesses the people concerned don't always do what you want them to. They lose focus, or retire, or move to other firms, and this can cause problems for the funds they leave behind (or in some cases are still running).

How to guard against it

In 2009 the board of PERSONAL ASSETS drew up our investment advisory agreement to the effect that should the investment adviser undergo a change of control or a change in its corporate structure which might reasonably be expected to be materially prejudicial to our interests, or should Sebastian Lyon cease to be a full-time executive of the investment adviser, PERSONAL ASSETS has the right unilaterally to terminate the agreement.

Since then, ten years of harmonious working together has done much to produce the PERSONAL ASSETS we know today, and Sebastian's personal holding of over 15,000 shares shows the strength of his commitment to the trust. It is well worth reading carefully the agreement that the board of your investment trust has with its adviser or management company.

We also make sure that we stick to our knitting and avoid the example of an investment manager whose trust we once invested in. A value investor, he had after initial success been underperforming for years while growth was king. Over lunch one day he told us that he was still a value investor, but now needed to be a momentum investor at the same time. We never discovered if he could have pulled off this remarkable feat because we sold the shares that afternoon and the trust itself quietly expired a short while thereafter.

8. POLICY CHANGE RISK

The nature of the risk

This is when a trust either puts proposals to shareholders for a change of investment policy or, on attaining a pre-set winding-up date, produces proposals which don't suit all its shareholders. The principle here has to be *caveat re-emptor*. Make sure the new policy still suits your requirements and, if not, 'holler like hell'.

Once upon a time (the early 1980s, to be exact) there was a trust which changed its investment policy from being a global generalist to being an industry specialist. In the short term, however, the change was not a success, because of a sudden unforeseen deterioration in the fundamentals of the chosen industry. At the first AGM after the policy change, a disgruntled shareholder accordingly scrawled on his voting card the NAV at the year end, the (much higher) NAV at the previous year end and the comment: "You must be a shower of bloody idiots."

I also once had a personal holding in a trust nearing its winding-up date. The continuation proposals I had expected didn't materialise and I was faced with either a rollover into a fund I didn't want, or a substantial capital gains tax bill. Only the coincidence of my having capital losses on hand sufficient to offset the gain prevented the wind-up from penalising me financially.

How to guard against it

Τα πάντα ῥεῖ, μηδέποτε κατά τ' αυτό μένειν, as the Greek philosopher Heraclitus reputedly said – '*all is in flux, nothing stays still*'. Investment styles and specialisations come and go, but capital preservation never goes out of fashion. A trust will

"OVER LUNCH HE TOLD US THAT HE WAS STILL A VALUE INVESTOR, BUT NOW NEEDED TO BE A MOMENTUM INVESTOR AT THE SAME TIME. WE NEVER DISCOVERED IF HE COULD HAVE PULLED OFF THIS REMARKABLE FEAT BECAUSE WE SOLD THE SHARES THAT AFTERNOON" usually change its policy in an attempt to improve its rating, but in our case the DCM keeps the share price steady at around net asset value. We therefore have no intention of changing our policy, and since we don't have a fixed life we never need to have a continuation vote. Our investment policy is here to stay.

9. ESG RISK

The nature of the risk

Investors are increasingly conscious of environmental, social and governance (ESG) risk, which has moved from being a minority interest to its current place in the mainstream of investment decision-making. As the importance of ESG factors has increased in the eyes of regulators and consumers, as well as investors, so the potential financial impact of these factors, both positive and negative, has increased.

How to guard against it

It is the board's job to monitor and weigh up both the positive and negative risks. For PERSONAL ASSETS' portfolio, our investment adviser does not exclude companies from its investment universe purely on ESG grounds. Rather, it integrates analysis of environmental, social and governance risks into the research and decision-making process. This entails consideration of both the negative risks and the opportunities for companies that are on the front foot as regards these issues.

Engagement with the management teams and boards of the companies we own continues to be a critical part of the adviser's investment process. The adviser votes all proxies of shares owned and engages with management teams on material issues. It is essential that we keep abreast of how this landscape is evolving and the board will continue to require that the adviser provides updates on how ESG is integrated in response to the changing nature of the risks.

10. REALISATION RISK

The nature of the risk

The Woodford affair has reminded us that this is one of the gravest risks facing investment funds. Is there a danger that the managers will have to disturb investments before they have had the chance to mature, in order to repay departing investors or to meet other demands for cash?

The first forced asset sale on record is in the Bible (Genesis 25:28–34), where Esau, faint from lack of food, found himself having to sell his birthright for a mess of pottage – a famously poor bargain which acts as a warning for all generations to come when assets have to be disturbed prematurely for cash.

It was nearly a quarter of a century ago that I described Thomas Mann's great novel *Buddenbrooks* as an investment classic. It chronicles the rise and fall of a merchant house in the north German city of Lübeck, and how Senator Thomas Buddenbrook, the third of his line, failed disastrously as he tried to live up to the example of his father and grandfather. What I didn't mention then was how the story ends, with the forced sale of the business for well below its true value – a reminder of how serious and sad realisation risk can be.

> *"The liquidation of the business ... took a most deplorable course. ... The pending business was disposed of on hurried and unfavourable terms. One precipitate and disadvantageous sale followed another ... and so the losses piled up. Thomas Buddenbrook had left, on paper, an estate of [650,000] marks. A year after the will was opened it had become ... clear that there was no question of such a sum."*

The last straw was when the family house was sold for a disappointing amount and replaced by a small villa for which Thomas Buddenbrook's executors paid too high a price. (Those who believe house property is a one-way bet, incidentally, should read *Buddenbrooks* and weep.)

How to guard against it

Losses through realisation risk can be severe. Forced sellers rarely prosper. Losses are, however, much less of a danger for PERSONAL ASSETS because our equity portfolio is made up of the bluest of blue chips. While these are not impervious to large swings in value, such as BAT experienced in 2018, if the likes of Microsoft or Unilever were, like Burford Capital, to fall by 65% in a day it would surely be Armageddon and we would have more to worry about than PERSONAL ASSETS' share price.

In his presentation at the annual general meeting, Sebastian Lyon, our investment adviser, tellingly demonstrated how in normal circumstances 95% by value of PERSONAL ASSETS' shareholders' funds could be realised within a single day. Even in abnormal markets PERSONAL ASSETS would be better placed than many trusts in terms of liquidity. For many trusts this is an issue that is rarely discussed, but should be.

What we do nowadays is not much affected by our size. Had we been a specialist fund investing in small companies or unlisteds, the inflows and outflows of money we've experienced over the years would surely have been disastrous. Woodford's traumatic experience this year, being forced to offload a string of unlisted securities into a hostile market, is the most extreme of cautionary tales in this regard.

Today our exposure is almost entirely to large stocks and the average market capitalisation of our equity holdings is £184 billion. Whether we fell to £100m or rose to £10bn we could hold broadly the same portfolio. We are simple, basic and boring, not seekers after undiscovered gems. We look for undervaluation, for good intrinsic value, and for companies which put their shareholders first.

ROBIN ANGUS, *a former stockbroking analyst, has been a director of* **PERSONAL ASSETS TRUST** *since 1984.*

MEASURE FOR MEASURE

Trust analyst WILLIAM SOBCZAK *digs deeper into the issue of what active fund management really means.*

I N RECENT YEARS, active management has been under almost constant attack from the rise of passive funds. Yet threats often give rise to opportunities: we believe that complacency is always the real enemy, and so competition from passive funds can also be seen as a positive development. Active managers have been forced to up their game, and our research shows that the UK closed-ended universe has become significantly more active in response to the challenge of cheap passive products. Here, we discuss this shifting landscape, its implications for investors, and the varying measures for 'activeness' available to investors.

THE ONLY WAY TO GO...

The threat from passive funds has led to active managers becoming more active, and to so-called closet trackers – funds that charge fees for active management but, in practice, hold portfolios very similar to their benchmark – increasingly being pushed out. Academic research has shown that the chance of generating alpha rises with how active a manager is. Cremers and Petajisto's 2009 work verified that the most active stock pickers beat their benchmark, on average, by about 1.26% a year (after fees), while closet indexers essentially matched their benchmark index performance before fees (and underperformed after fees). Cohen, Polk and Silli (2009) examined the performance of stocks that represent the managers' 'best ideas'. They discovered that their best ideas were the ones that consistently delivered the greatest returns.

Yet, because of the way that the investment industry has worked in the past, a highly-concentrated portfolio has not necessarily been optimal for most managers, for a number of (mainly non-investment) reasons, and so the tendency is to introduce stocks into their portfolio about which they have less conviction. For example, large investments in a small number of holdings could, if the picks are bad, put a manager's job security on the line, while a manager has been less likely to be fired for generating returns similar to the benchmark.

Fees are another force driving investors towards passive funds, as active management fees are considerably higher than for passive funds. According to Morningstar, in 2018 an active UK large cap fund would, on average, have an ongoing charge of 0.75%, compared to just 0.12% for a passive proposition. The fee differential has meant that, over the past few years, we have seen demand for passive vehicles dramatically increase.

At the end of 2018 there were 323 exchange traded products (also including exchange traded notes and commodities) listed on the London Stock Exchange, close to double the 177 listed in 2017. According to the Investment Association's April 2019 figures, tracker funds now equate to £200 billion of funds under management, 10% more than just a year before. And in April this year, tracker funds saw £1.81bn of net retail sales, more than ten times the £114 million raised by equity funds.

This pressure has had a positive effect for investors in active funds. Average fees across collective investment funds around the world have seen relentless declines. According to research from Morningstar, the average asset-weighted fee for actively-managed equity funds has fallen by 18% since 2013, compared with a 28% decline in passive funds.

The competitive pressure from passive investments means active managers are having to make greater efforts to justify their existence. The question that arises is: how does one identify those managers that are truly active? In this article we take a look at the different measures for assessing how active a manager is, and their relative advantages, highlighting investment trusts that stand out on each of these measures.

HOW CAN ACTIVE MANAGEMENT BE MEASURED?

Active share is not enough

The most common measure used by investors to gauge how active a manager is, certainly in recent times, is active share. Active share was first developed by Cremers and Petajisto as a tool for representing the extent to which positions in a portfolio differ from the benchmark index's constituents. The measure is expressed as a percentage ranging from 0% to 100%, with a fund which has no holdings in common with its benchmark having an active share of 100%. Their research suggests that funds with an active share rating of 80% or more are best placed to outperform over the long term. For example, Willis Towers Watson assessed 977 global equity funds in 2017. Among these funds, only 256 outperformed their benchmarks over five years. Of those that outperformed, 72% had an active share of more than 80%.

Since the research surrounding active share was published, Baillie Gifford has been a strong proponent of its use. Almost all of its funds and investment trusts report their active share, and EDINBURGH WORLDWIDE INVESTMENT TRUST, managed by Douglas Brodie, boasts an active share score of 99%. Over the past five years, the trust generated 131% total NAV returns against 81.7% from the S&P Global Smaller Companies Index. Even over the tricky past year, the company has generated 7.8% against 6.5% from the index.

Baillie Gifford's other investment trusts boast some of the highest active share ratings across the investment trust universe. MONKS, for example, has a 90% score, SCOTTISH MORTGAGE 94%, and SHIN NIPPON of Japan 93%.

Active share has come under critical scrutiny more recently, particularly if used on its own to measure active management. For example, the measure can be affected by the number of stocks making up a benchmark; the fewer there are, the harder it is to generate a high active share. A single country equity fund would be expected to have a lower active share than a global equity fund, particularly a global small cap fund such as EDINBURGH WORLDWIDE, whose benchmark has no fewer than 8,346 individual stocks.

Another problem is that active share can be gamed. For example, consider an index with a weighting to sector A of 20%, made up of four companies each worth 5% of the index. A manager could put 20% of his or her fund in stock one and thereby add 15% to the active share. If, however, the beta of stock one to the sector is one, then the 20% weighting in the fund will behave very similarly to the 20% weighting in the index. The fund would therefore appear to be highly active, while having less chance of behaving differently from the index than it might first appear. This is an extreme example, but this sort of calculation is the one used to create passive funds without having to buy all the stocks in the index (a process called stratified sampling).

It is, of course, possible that such effects could develop by accident, but managers are also incentivised to exaggerate how active they are in order to attract investors and justify their fees, while at the same time minimising their active risk to avoid losing their jobs. One of the great benefits of the rise of passives is that behaving like the index is unlikely to be enough to keep an active manager's job, so this incentive is diminishing.

In addition to the inherent flaws in the active share calculation, finding the data required for precise measurement is difficult. The most common databases for analysts and investors, Morningstar and FE Analytics, do not offer active share data for investment trusts, and many investment trusts choose not to report it on their factsheets. As such, we think it is important to consider other metrics as well.

ALTERNATIVE METRICS

Tracking error and R2

We think tracking error is an alternative measure that complements active share well. Also known as active risk, tracking error indicates the volatility of the difference in returns between a fund and its benchmark. Typically, the higher the active return (outperformance) in relation to the active risk (tracking error), the better. The advantage is that it is derived from actual returns, so it highlights whether the behaviour of a fund has been unlike the index. The disadvantage is that it is backward-looking, unlike active share which, by examining the current portfolio, is more forward-looking.

HENDERSON OPPORTUNITIES TRUST is a company that stands out for us from our analysis, with a tracking error of 11.3. The trust aims to outperform the FTSE All-Share by investing across the market cap spectrum. The portfolio of circa 90 stocks is dominated by smaller companies, and over 60% is currently invested in AIM. With UK equities being out of favour thanks to Brexit, and small and mid-caps particularly unloved thanks to a perceived domestic bias, the trust is languishing on almost the widest discount (17.2%) in its AIC peer group (Association of Investment Companies).

ABERDEEN STANDARD EQUITY INCOME is another trust highlighted in the list. The trust has long been one of the standout trusts within the AIC UK Equity Income space. Uniquely in that sector, over 60% of the company's portfolio is invested in companies outside the FTSE 100, illustrating the manager's desire to search in areas of the market that other UK equity income managers may be overlooking.

Portfolio concentration

Portfolio concentration is another measure that can give information about how active a manager is. There are two ways that this can be measured: through the number of holdings, and the percentage of total assets which the top holdings account for. In our view, concentration can be seen as a good measure of the confidence a manager has in his or her convictions.

Investment trusts, with their closed-ended structure, are able to allow a manager a huge degree of latitude in running a concentrated portfolio. According to our analysis, within the equity investment trust universe, the average number of holdings has steadily reduced over the past five years, with the average trust now having 75 holdings, compared to 91 in 2013. This represents a decline of almost 20%, which we think is significant. Indeed, this matches anecdotal evidence from manager meetings of an increasing desire from boards for trusts to adopt a more concentrated approach.

Along with the absolute number of holdings, we are seeing a dramatic increase in the percentage of net assets in the top ten holdings. The average trust now has over 40% of their net assets in their top ten holdings, a significant increase from 34% just a year earlier. Recent managers we have met who have told us that they expect to run more concentrated portfolios than they have in the past include JPMORGAN AMERICAN (JAM) and HENDERSON EUROTRUST (HNE).

CONCENTRATION ON THE RISE

However, although we think concentration is an important metric to look at, it has to be considered relative to the concentration of the index. For example, Tencent makes up 14.6% of the MSCI China Index, and Alibaba 13.1%. A fund which had 28% in the two stocks might therefore be highly concentrated but, in this case, this is not telling us much about how active it is. On a similar theme, a trust could have just 30 holdings, but if the index is also relatively concentrated, then the top 20 holdings could be very similarly weighted to the top 30 in the index, and the weights of the remaining 10 companies will be of limited importance to relative returns. A metric such as tracking error would help to uncover this.

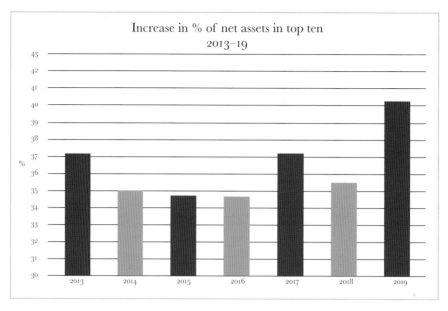

Source: Kepler Partners/Morningstar. All data points are from the first of March of their respective financial year – except 2019 which is from the market close 17 June 2019.

Tactical positioning

In order to understand the active nature of the manager, we can also look at how they shift the portfolio over the medium to short term, what we could call tactical positioning. To assess this, we look at gearing, and the movement between cyclical and defensive companies. In a way, this is the opposite of how we think about some of the managers with the highest active share, such as Nick Train or Terry Smith, who have very long holding periods and low turnovers.

However, it is often the case that trusts which are hit the hardest over short periods are those that are over-geared during a correction, or those that find themselves overexposed to cyclical companies in a recession. You can argue that avoiding such blow-ups is also a valid ingredient in exercising skill as a fund manager.

The past year provides the perfect testing ground for understanding how different managers look to navigate through both corrections and strong rallies. In the second half of 2018, although there was no recession, we saw a very sharp correction across almost every global market, only for markets to rebound strongly in Q1 and Q2 2019. Needless to say, the greater the gearing a trust has, the more risk it has, and the more likely it is to under- or outperform relative to its peers and benchmark. As can be seen below, managers did in fact reduce their gearing over the last half of 2018.

Source: Morningstar

According to Morningstar, the likes of JPMORGAN EUROPEAN SMALLER COMPANIES, HENDERSON EUROTRUST, and SCHRODER ASIA PACIFIC, decreased their gearing by around 5% between June 2018 and December 2018. MITON GLOBAL OPPORTUNITIES reduced gearing by more than 15% over the same period. However, as the graph illustrates, on average, trust fund managers did not have the foresight (or nerves) to re-gear during the rebound. This isn't true of them all though. ABERDEEN SMALLER COMPANIES INCOME, GABELLI VALUE PLUS+, BRUNNER and ABERDEEN FRONTIER MARKETS all increased gearing by more than 5% between December and April 2019.

Below, we show the trusts which have been most active in de-gearing and re-gearing through the second half of last year's market turmoil. While this doesn't show who has been most successful in their tactical positioning (to do that, we need to analyse who de-geared ahead of the market falls rather than after the worst had happened), it does illustrate the managers who take the most active attitude to leverage and market timing.

Largest gearers and de-gearers

LARGEST DE-GEARERS (JUNE–DECEMBER 2018)	GEARING REDUCTION (%)
British and American	- 18.4
Downing Strategic Micro-Cap	-17.8
Africa Opportunity	-16.7
Miton Global Opportunities	-15.6
JPMorgan American	-10.9

LARGEST GEARERS (JANUARY–APRIL 2019)	GEARING INCREASE (%)
Gabelli Value Plus+	+17.5
Temple Bar	+14.0
Aberdeen Smaller Companies	+10.4
Brunner	+8.2
Montanaro European Smaller	+6.5

Source: Morningstar

In terms of movement between cyclical and defensive companies, we see more discrepancies, and this is clearly another area in which we can see how some managers are far more active than others. Across the board, the second half of the year saw the majority of managers move away from cyclical companies, as many believed defensive companies would hold up better through the uncertainty. JPMORGAN CLAVERHOUSE, for example, had the largest shift away from cyclical companies of any investment trust, over the six months to the end of 2018, reducing exposure by 11.3%.

This very much reflects the managers' recognition of uncertainties surrounding global markets, including the US–China trade war, Europe's economic slowdown, and the Brexit negotiations. At the other end of the spectrum, MERCHANTS TRUST increased its cyclical exposure by over 12%. This was largely due to the manager's valuation-led approach to investing, and what is saw as the attractive opportunities in the UK.

These contrasting moves show us one way in which managers can be active and add value, and how differing opinions among managers can drive outperformance relative to peers and, in turn, generate alpha relative to the benchmark. Of course, as with gearing, we have not analysed whether these moves have been, on aggregate, net positive and alpha generating, as our focus is on highlighting the most active managers, not the most successful.

Digging deeper into the numbers

We use tracking error, concentration, gearing, and sector movements to look at how active managers are in the major closed-ended equity sectors: UK All Companies, UK Equity Income, Global, Global Equity Income, Japan, Europe, and North America. We rank the trusts on each metric individually, but also relative to the rest of the sectors. Finally, we discuss which trusts stand out across the different metrics, and establish an overall ranking for each trust which shows how active they are. It is important to emphasise that we are not recommending any specific trusts in this exercise, merely illustrating how trusts differ in their degree of active management. It is for investors to decide how deeply they wish to dig into this kind of analysis.

Tracking error

Also known as active risk, tracking error indicates the volatility of the difference in returns between a fund and its benchmark. The advantage of the measure is that it is derived from actual returns, so it highlights whether the behaviour of a fund has been unlike the index. In order to be considered eligible for the analysis, we used the statistical measure r2 (R squared) to select an appropriate benchmark, first looking for the provider benchmark as held by Morningstar, then substituting or adding to it as appropriate.

The end result ranks 76 trusts across the seven chosen sectors, of which 35 had a tracking error of more than 5% over a five-year period. As can be seen below, the top 15 included a wide spread of strategies and geographies, with INDEPENDENT INVESTMENT TRUST (IIT), taking the top spot with a tracking error of 12.1%. The company is run by long-term manager Max Ward. He follows no formal style or process in his investment approach, believing that this can cause managers to be restrained in their approach. He pays absolutely no attention to an index when building the portfolio, and the end result is a company with an active share of almost 100%.

Alongside IIT, LINDSELL TRAIN (LTI) is another trust that stands out for its high tracking error. We should note that the trust's r2, against the most appropriate benchmark we could find, was below our eligibility limit. This reflects the fact the trust's largest holding is the 46.7% shareholding in its management company Lindsell Train Limited, which is an unlisted company and not, therefore, in any benchmark. While it is difficult to create an appropriate benchmark for this trust, its activeness is not in doubt.*

Another company near the top of the list that might surprise investors is SCOTTISH MORTGAGE (SMT). With close to 90 holdings, a tracking error of 9.5% might seem surprisingly high. However, what differentiates this trust from many of its peers is its high degree of portfolio concentration. Having such a high percentage of its assets in the top ten holdings is, in this case, what produces its active share of 94%.

Trusts with highest tracking error

COMPANY	5-YEAR TRACKING ERROR	RSQUARED
Independent	12.08	74.16
Lindsell Train	10.36	41.04
Aurora	10.30	69.50
JPMorgan Japanese	9.67	68.30
Scottish Mortgage	9.48	76.55
Jupiter UK Growth	8.91	73.77
Aberdeen Standard Equity Inc Trust	8.63	74.28
Canadian General Investments Unit	8.17	85.04
Henderson Opportunities	8.11	85.01
Chelverton UK Dividend Trust	7.96	84.01
Jupiter European Opportunities	7.65	73.25
Aberdeen Japan	7.37	85.45
Baillie Gifford Japan	7.22	85.77
Diverse Income Trust	7.19	78.54
Middlefield Canadian Income	7.12	79.63

Source: Morningstar

Concentration

Portfolio concentration is another measure that can give information about how active a manager is. There are two ways this can be measured: through

---

* [*Editor's comment: It is important not to confuse activeness, in the sense used here, with the amount of portfolio activity, which is exceptionally low in the case of the Lindsell Train investment trust.*]

the number of holdings and the percentage of assets the top holdings make up. As noted earlier, concentration is typically a good measure of the degree of confidence that a manager has in his or her convictions. According to our analysis, 21 trusts have 50 holdings or fewer and, interestingly, the names are similar to those in the tracking error table. There is a significant crossover between our two measures: many of the same names appear in the list of trusts with the fewest holdings, and those with the most concentrated top ten. This is consistent with our finding that there has been a significant decrease in the percentage of net assets in the top ten holdings as closed-ended fund managers respond to the challenge of passive competitors.

Concentration top 15

GROUP/INVESTMENT	% ASSET IN TOP 10 HOLDINGS
Lindsell Train Ord	91.43
Finsbury Growth & Income Ord	82.02
Jupiter European Opportunities Ord	76.47
Aurora Ord	74.62
Value and Income Ord	61.99
Independent Ord	55.29
Temple Bar Ord	50.58
Scottish Mortgage Ord	50.41
Jupiter UK Growth Ord	48.61
Shires Income Ord	47.76
Baillie Gifford US Growth Ord	46.66
Merchants Trust Ord	45.99
Schroder Income Growth Ord	45.30
Edinburgh Investment Ord	43.37
BlackRock Greater Europe	43.18

GROUP/INVESTMENT	# OF HOLDINGS (LONG)
Aurora Ord	13
Lindsell Train Ord	16
Finsbury Growth & Income Ord	25

GROUP/INVESTMENT	# OF HOLDINGS (LONG)
Independent Ord	34
Jupiter European Opportunities Ord	36
European Investment Ord	39
Value and Income Ord	39
Jupiter UK Growth Ord	40
CC Japan Income & Growth Ord	40
EP Global Opportunities Ord	41
Schroder Income Growth	41
BlackRock Greater Europe	42
BlackRock Income and Growth Ord	42
Baillie Gifford UK Growth	43
Middlefield Canadian Income	44

Source: Morningstar

Both of Nick Train's trusts, LINDSELL TRAIN (LTI) and FINSBURY GROWTH AND INCOME (FGT) stand out for having a high allocation to the top ten holdings. Additionally, JUPITER EUROPEAN OPPORTUNITIES (JEO) has a large proportion of its assets in the top 10. Recently, JEO demonstrated the risk of being so concentrated. The trust was hit when Wirecard, its largest holding at 17% of NAV, was caught up in allegations of fraud. The allegations have yet to be proved, and the police investigation in Singapore is ongoing, so the end effect of this situation is unclear, but with such a high percentage of the trust in the stock, any serious fall would be a big blow. However, the manager has expressed his view that the company is being unfairly attacked, and its travails have not stopped JEO from posting good returns this year. Furthermore, the potential in a high conviction approach can be seen in the trust's exceptional long-term performance numbers, with the trust outperforming all AIC Europe peers over three- and five-year periods.

AVI GLOBAL, formerly known as British Empire Securities, is a trust which has seen performance improve following a decision by the manager to invest in a more high conviction manner. The statistics above represent a full look through the portfolio although, if one counts the company's investment in its Japan Special Situations category, which includes 18 different companies with a high degree of overlap to AVI JAPAN TRUST, as one 'position', the portfolio could be considered even more concentrated.

Tactical positioning

Another way of looking at how active a manager is, is to look at their tactical positioning. Some managers move their portfolio quickly in accordance with their market views. When they do this in a direction which is counter to the direction of the market, this amounts to an active approach. To evaluate this, we looked at the changes in gearing and cyclical/defensive positioning over Q4 2018 (the sharp market correction), and Q1 2019, a sharp rally. We looked at the managers who moved against the market, first by looking at how much they changed their gearing and, secondly, by how far they shifted their portfolio into cyclicals when the market was falling, or into defensives as the market was rallying.

We recognise that this is the opposite to how some active managers such as Nick Train or Terry Smith behave. They both have very long holding periods and don't move their positioning on the basis of temporary factors. Nevertheless, this kind of analysis is another aspect of active management worth considering.

Below one can see the top 15 managers who were most active in shifting gearing over the two periods. It is clear that there were smaller movements in Q4 2018, and larger changes in Q1 of 2019, perhaps because Q3 was also a difficult period and so managers had already shifted their positioning somewhat. In fact, in Q4 2018 there was, on average, a movement of just 2.1%, in comparison to changes of 4.1% in Q1 2019.

Changes in gearing

GROUP/INVESTMENT	NET GEARING CHANGE – OCT TO DEC	NET GEARING CHANGE – JAN TO MAR	AVG
Fidelity Special Values	12.75667	21.12185	2.5
Fidelity Japan Trust	5.71099	3.1759	17
Independent	1.99298	7.63109	17
City of London	2.85354	4.38603	17
Baillie Gifford US Growth	3.15677	4.12172	17.5
Merchants Trust	3.92531	3.48853	18
JPMorgan European Growth Pool	2.40996	4.85917	18
Henderson Opportunities	2.78571	4.22873	19.5

GROUP/INVESTMENT	NET GEARING CHANGE – OCT TO DEC	NET GEARING CHANGE – JAN TO MAR	AVG
JPMorgan Mid Cap	2.95421	3.83894	20
Securities Trust of Scotland	2.31641	4.23065	21.5
Schroder Income Growth	1.30813	6.40618	22
Mercantile	1.8	4.25	24
BlackRock Income Growth	1.05	6.7	24
Schroder Japan Growth	3.24	2.35	25
Scottish Investment Trust	1.1	5.03	26

Source: Morningstar

FIDELITY SPECIAL VALUES (FSV) is the only trust that saw double digit movements over both periods. The trust is run by Alex Wright, who aims to identify undervalued companies from across the UK market cap spectrum, and hold onto them until the price properly reflects their value. Alex has employed gearing in a contrarian fashion in recent years, reducing it during the rising market of 2016 and 2017, but increasing it through 2018 as markets have fallen. Somewhat unusually, FSV uses contracts for difference (CFDs) to provide gearing (and to go short). The level of gearing is left to the manager's discretion within an agreed range. INDEPENDENT INVESTMENT TRUST (IIT), CITY OF LONDON (CTY), and BAILLIE GIFFORD US GROWTH (USA), also saw large movements in their gearing levels. When comparing the consumer cyclical movements and the consumer defensive movements, over the two periods, once more the second period saw considerably greater moves. EP GLOBAL OPPORTUNITIES saw the greatest movement in Q4 of 2018 and, in fact, the greatest movements overall. The company has a valuation-led approach, presumably explaining the moves against the grain into cyclicals, and then defensives, during Q4 2018 and Q1 2019 respectively. The trust's investment policy is highly differentiated from its peers, as the board believes its competitors are constrained by having too narrow investment objectives. It is, therefore, unsurprising to see the trust looking highly active in its behaviour.

Over the second period we saw far less marked movements into defensives, during the rally, and only EUROPEAN INVESTMENT TRUST (EUT) moved by over 5%. The company has a highly concentrated portfolio of just 39 companies. The manager, Craig Armour, adopts a long-term approach to investing which is focused on company valuations. During periods of market volatility, he aims to take advantage of any valuation anomalies which emerge.

Tactical positioning

GROUP/INVESTMENT	MOVE TO CONSUMER CYCLICAL FROM OCTOBER–DECEMBER 2018	PERIOD 1 RANKING	MOVE TO CONSUMER DEFENSIVE FROM JANUARY–MARCH 2019	PERIOD 2 RANKING	AVG RANKING
EP Global Opportunities	2.75565	3	4.49465	2	2.5
JPMorgan Mid Cap	0.89991	12	1.74425	5	8.5
Alliance Trust	1.05059	10	0.94599	13	11.5
JPMorgan Claverhouse	1.144	9	0.92096	14	11.5
Dunedin Income Growth	0.65647	17	1.32461	8	12.5
Jupiter UK Growth	0.81074	14	1.19265	12	13
Merchants Trust	0.3196	23	1.52449	7	15
European Investment	0.02801	30	6.2775	1	15.5
JPMorgan Japanese	0.55228	21	1.20065	11	16
Schroder Income Growth	0.0853	26	1.28834	9	17.5
Jupiter European Opportunities	1.6965	6	0.06036	34	20
Fidelity European Values	0.58139	19	0.51084	22	20.5
Troy Income & Growth	0.05904	27	0.72858	17	22
Murray Income Trust	0.26227	25	0.60403	20	22.5
Schroder Japan Growth	0.62949	18	0.27841	29	23.5

Source: Morningstar

The most active trusts...

Before looking at the end result, it is worth reiterating that we recognise that there are two ways of being active. Managers who appear to be very inactive – taking long-term positions relative to the index, and holding them over the long term regardless of temporary conditions – are actually taking active bets against the index by not following it. Examples include the likes of LINDSELL TRAIN, FINSBURY GROWTH AND INCOME, INDEPENDENT, and JUPITER EUROPEAN OPPORTUNITIES, all of which have extremely concentrated portfolios, low turnover ratios, and high tracking errors.

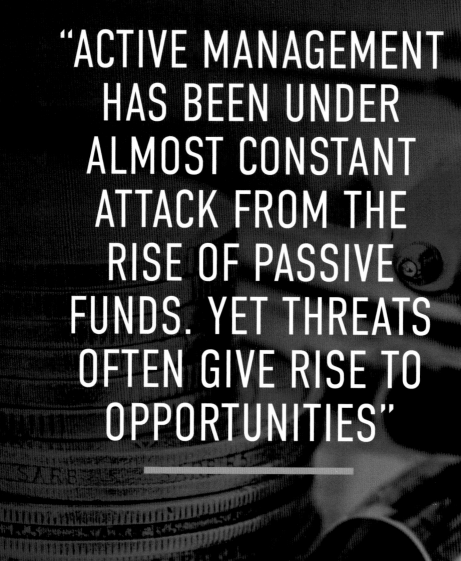

"ACTIVE MANAGEMENT HAS BEEN UNDER ALMOST CONSTANT ATTACK FROM THE RISE OF PASSIVE FUNDS. YET THREATS OFTEN GIVE RISE TO OPPORTUNITIES"

Perhaps more obviously, a manager can be considered active if they move their portfolio around more frequently – as long as they are not just following the market. Examples highlighted above include FIDELITY SPECIAL VALUES, EP GLOBAL OPPORTUNITIES, and JPMORGAN MID CAP, all of which have shifted their portfolios significantly according to the conditions in recent quarters, whether it be through gearing or through cyclical and defensive exposure.

Nevertheless, after collating the data for all of the trusts, across the seven sectors, and the five measures, we can take an average to find which trusts combine all the different elements of active management discussed. Below, we can see the rankings of the top 20 trusts in the different metrics and the final average of their rankings.

| GROUP/INVESTMENT | CONCENTRATION | | TRACKING ERROR | TACTICAL POSITIONING | | FINAL |
	# OF HOLDINGS	TOP 10 AS A % OF NAV		GEARING	SECTOR MOVEMENT	
Jupiter UK Growth	9	9	6	26.5	13	**13**
Independent	4	6	1	17	42	**14**
Jupiter European Opportunities	5	3	10	40	20	**16**
Aurora	1	4	3	47	33	**18**
Lindsell Train	2	1	2	61.5	26	**19**
Merchants Trust	44	12	15	18	15	**21**
Finsbury Growth & Income	3	2	17	58.5	39	**24**
Schroder Income Growth	11	13	56	22	18	**24**
Temple Bar	32	7	31	26.5	24	**24**
European Investment	7	37	24	42	16	**25**
Value And Income	7	5	38	33.5	42	**25**
Shires Income	24	10	28	-	38	**25**
BlackRock Income and Growth	13	16	37	24.5	42	**26**
EP Global Opportunities	11	49	40	36	3	**28**
Troy Income & Growth	15	19	36	50.5	22	**29**
Fidelity European Values	20	20	55	33.5	21	**30**
JPMorgan Mid Cap	45	57	22	20	9	**31**
Edinburgh Investment	34	14	19	55	31	**31**

Source: Morningstar

Some of the most active managers are those investors may have expected, such as INDEPENDENT, JUPITER EUROPEAN OPPORTUNITIES, and the two Lindsell Train trusts. However, there are some trusts that might not immediately spring to mind, underlining how important it is to look at a trust's behaviour across a wide range of measures.

WILLIAM SOBCZAK *has been an investment trust analyst at Kepler Partners since February 2018. Kepler Trust Intelligence offers investors a library of up-to-date investment strategy articles and fund analysis on two separate retail and professional investor sites (accessible via www.trustintelligence.co.uk). This study was completed in H1 2019 and the data mostly refers to performance at the time of first publication.*

ASIA THE PLACE TO BE

BRUCE STOUT, *manager of the* MURRAY INTERNATIONAL *investment trust, says that income-seeking investors should be looking to Asia while the West remains bogged down in debt.*

You are not optimistic about the future for the developed world economies – why is that?

Bruce Stout: The big picture is that the indebted developed world is beginning to get very, very close now to the end of the business cycle, a business cycle that is already the longest in history in the United States, and is predicated on unorthodox monetary policy (printed money, and unsustainable corporate and household debt loads). Arguably, it has delivered pretty poor growth given the amount of stimulus we have had for the best part of 11 years. We are coming to the twilight of that and we have no policy optionality left. We have no fiscal flexibility, no monetary flexibility. I'm talking about the US but it's the same for Europe; it's the same for the UK. What is more, we are approaching the impending downturn with a yield curve that is completely flat and, in many cases, bond yields that are negative.

I think the first thing that has to be said here is that the developed world is actually evolving pretty much in line with what you would expect to happen, when you go down the path of unorthodox monetary policy. What that means is you keep zombie companies alive – there's plenty of evidence of that throughout Europe. Banks can only make money when yields are high, yield curves are steep, and credit spreads are wide – today, you have flat yield curves, very, very low yields, and extremely tight credit spreads. None of the banks can make any money, and I guess what emerges next will be credit quality concerns in the developed world.

There's nothing really changed there, and that's why we have very low exposure to those parts of the world. We have the lowest exposure to Europe for as long as I can remember, we've had the lowest exposure to the UK for as long as I can remember. I'm talking thirty-odd years because that's how long I've been involved with MURRAY INTERNATIONAL. And it's really just getting harder and harder as the headwinds build for corporate profitability to be maintained. And there's nothing the policymakers can do. They have run out of road.

Fortunately there is better news in Asia and emerging markets...

BS: Yes, on the other side of the coin, in the emerging world we look at Asia and many emerging markets today, and we see perfect orthodox policy being followed. We see steep yield curves; inflation rates in countries like India, Indonesia, Brazil, and Mexico well below central bank targets, so there's plenty of scope to cut; we see positive real rates. So, they have all the monetary and fiscal flexibility that they want. They will be able to start to cut rates now that the US has finished raising rates, and may be going lower. That's quite a positive backdrop for Asia and emerging markets.

What is even more compelling, though, is that next year Asia and the emerging world will take over from the developing world as the largest nominal area of economic growth in the world. China will become the largest country, India will move up to number three, and Indonesia will move up to number six. The key here is not the actual size. It's the fact that these economies are being driven now by consumption and investment. In the past they were driven by exports. As they pick up the baton of global consumption from the indebted developed world, it's a very powerful thing for many companies that are exposed to those consumption trends or are interest rate-sensitive beneficiaries.

You could certainly make the argument that it's the worst possible time in history to pick a fight with China. The interesting thing is that Asia becomes the largest economic region in the world in the next few years for the first time in 300 years, as it was up until the 17th century. The British Empire, the German Empire and the Spanish Empire were all founded in the 1600s and took over for 300 years. The natural order is being restored, if you like, because for 2,000 years before the 1700s, the growth of the world was exclusively based in Asia.

To have exposure there, you don't necessarily have to be invested in India and China, but you do have to have companies that are doing business there. You have to look at the potential for interest rate-sensitive businesses, such as banking, for insurance, or indeed pure consumption. We own Auckland Airport in New Zealand and you see a huge amount of Chinese tourism now. Last year, 100 million people left China to go on holiday and they all went back. Thirty years ago, nobody left China.

So these are powerful consumption forces that will drive global growth in the emerging world from now on. Unfortunately, for the developed world, all we can do is contract and watch our standards of living continue to deteriorate.

There are huge unfunded liabilities on the balance sheets of the sovereign states of America, the UK, and Europe. They promised to pay healthcare, education, pensions, and all sorts of things that they can no longer afford. I really don't know how they'll get out of this mess.

You are saying that the emerging world, or Asia anyway, has a comparative advantage in this environment?

BS: Both a comparative and an absolute advantage.

But the emerging world surely can't decouple from what's going to happen in the developed world completely?

BS: Well, interestingly, that is what everybody is likely to say until it happens. If you look at the behaviour of financial markets, they always immediately respond to what happened before. In 2013, when interest rates started to go up in America, and the bond market had its 'taper tantrum', the view was dead simple. Tightening rates in America will quickly destabilise Asia because it happened before. Or tightening rates in America will cause another Tequila crisis in Latin America because that's what happened before.

But there's a lot of water gone under the bridge since these previous tightening cycles, and I think the biggest and most important one is the duration and size of the domestic bond markets in many emerging Asian countries. They all now fund fiscal liabilities in their own currencies with bonds stretching out to 30 or 40 years' maturity. That is related to housing and home ownership, and all the other things that they're beginning to get into. They are in an extremely strong position to manage their growth going forward, at the rate of growth that they want to do. Their dependency on the developed world is reducing all the time. More exports go from Brazil to China than go to the United States now, because these countries are no longer just the commodity producers for the industrial cycle in the West. They are now consuming nations of their own, which is a huge change.

I dare say, in the short term, the markets will make quick and prejudiced decisions as they always do. Where we continue to see the real value is where there is real orthodoxy, because you can actually value companies against their own domestic bond markets. What you can't do in the developed world is look at a company that has no earnings and accurately value it. There have been so many of these so-called unicorns and tech companies, for the last two or three years, that are totally dependent on cheap money to keep going, because there are no profits.

When their revenues slow down, their stock prices go down. That's not the kind of business that we're interested in, anyway, because we're looking for dividends for our shareholders as well. We are coming very close to an inflection point, and I suspect the developed world will become less and less relevant for Asia and emerging markets as we go forward.

In that context how does the trade war fit into your narrative?

BS: The trade war is absolutely bang in line with what normally happens when an economic empire is past its best, and is beginning to lose power and deflate. The first thing that the leaders do is to immediately blame somebody else. In this case, the trade war is predominantly one man's crusade. It's not even the policy of the Republican Party in America. They believe in free trade and globalisation.

It is down to President Trump, who is finding it harder and harder to deliver on his election promises, and now has to find a scapegoat. An easy scapegoat is to blame foreigners. But that's not of any relevance, in reality, because the Germans, for example, are not currency manipulators. They don't sell BMWs because their currency is cheap. They sell BMWs because they're top quality vehicles that people want. And if Americans want to buy BMWs instead of cars from Detroit, then there's not a lot you can do. Trade wars are not going to change that. In the event of protectionism, of course, everybody loses. We will get lower growth and higher inflation.

It is certainly not in the interest of American corporates to close off the consumption markets of Asia at a time when domestic demand in their own country is likely to soften from here. It does seem very, very strange. But it is also what you expect when a country that's been so strong for such a long period of time, sees its powers wane and can't face the prospect of no longer being the big cheese.

Is not Trump's agenda all about the short-term objective of the next presidential election?

BS: It's impossible to know with that particular individual. The truth is that there is only one winner in this and that is the Chinese. They're the only winner because they hold all the trump cards in their hands (excuse the pun). The US, in the person of Trump, is doing this very much from a position of weakness, in order to try to divert attention away from a failing domestic agenda. I have no idea how this is going to resolve because he changes his mind every 24 hours. So, there's no point in even trying to waste your time thinking about it. It could all escalate tomorrow; it could all dissipate tomorrow. You just don't know. For the Chinese, if it ever got to the point where there was no business being done, they will have to adjust the sources of supply. The main imports that China take from the States are food and commodities. That would have to be readjusted over time.

So, as a portfolio manager, this is an external factor that is essentially outside your control?

BS: Absolutely. It's far more important for us what's happened in the rate structure in the world. With the US change in monetary policy, we're now in a position for a lot of Asia to start cutting at some point next year, which should be very positive for interest rate-sensitive stocks, not just for consumer stocks, but all sorts of things; companies wanting access to capital and investment. They've not been able to do that for the last five years, since the US was in tightening mode.

The politics are fractious all over the place in the developed world, and that again is a symptom of excessive debt, of the polarity between those that have and those that haven't, the dwindling few that have and the escalating amount of people who haven't. You see it all over the place. You see it in Europe, you see it in the UK, you see it in America. But, quite frankly, it's been brewing and escalating for the last decade, because they didn't put the right policies in during the financial crisis ten years ago. They kicked the can down the road and this is what's happened. Now they can't kick it any further.

Are you concerned that we are starting to hear ostensibly sensible people starting to advocate yet more extreme monetary stimulus policies?

BS: People are clutching at straws. You've got a convergence between monetary and fiscal policy, in the sense that people essentially want to make them the same thing. The argument, here, is that all the money printed after the financial crisis ended up being non-inflationary. Now, the reason it was non-inflationary is because most of it didn't get into the real economy. A lot of it just went into asset prices, particularly stocks. You also had powerful deflationary forces – high debt loads, which are deflationary, globalisation, which is deflationary, and the most deflationary trend of all, the disruptive technology which is changing all sorts of businesses from retail to services.

It wasn't inflationary. What the exponents of modern monetary theory (MMT) are saying now is let's have more money printing but, this time, rather than letting it go into financial markets, let's put it directly into projects such as infrastructure. That's essentially using monetary means to enact fiscal policy. It is extremely dangerous in as much as it will just be as ineffectual as money printing was the first time around. The biggest danger is that countries with the greatest debt loads could see their currency significantly devalued because, at some point, who's going to want to hold confetti that is printed off the printing presses?

It's difficult to call because printing money and throwing it at heavily-indebted consumers is not going to make much difference; you can take a horse to water, but you can't make it drink. You can cut rates to zero but you can't make people borrow or spend. If the politicians do get hold of the printing presses, and start doing big fiscal expansion projects, there's no longer the same multiplier effect as there was in the past, because they don't suddenly put great squads of people to work. You do it with machines now. The jury is out, therefore, on whether it would have any impact whatsoever.

All the orthodox means have been tried, and when you see so many bond yields around the world negative, and negative out to fifty years in Switzerland, you've got a real issue there. If I'm running insurance money, or a pension fund, and have a liability in ten years, and my Nestlé bond matures today, I've got to go and buy another ten-year Nestlé bond and its yield is minus forty basis points, it is obvious that I'm not going to meet that liability in ten years' time.

There's something severely wrong with the global bond markets when somebody is prepared to buy a bond and pay the issuer for the honour of owning it, whether it be the German government or Nestlé. You don't get any return with a Nestlé bond. You don't even get a Kit Kat! So, I'm extremely sceptical of the sustainability of negative bond yields. At least in the emerging world, they've got orthodox economics, orthodox bond yields, and capital will be allocated efficiently because it's been priced efficiently.

As the manager of a trust with an income mandate, where in this environment are you finding the opportunities to generate that yield?

BS: In Asia, Latin America, and other emerging markets, what we are finding are good quality companies that have got lots of cash, low debt, strong balance sheets, and are throwing off cash, investing, paying dividends and growing dividends – exactly what you want to have as an income fund. And you can diversify globally in a way you couldn't do 20 years ago. Twenty years ago, the UK had a monopoly on yield, there was no yield in Asia, no yield in Japan, no yield in America; it was all being driven by tech. It was very difficult to run a diversified global income fund. You had to have a disproportionate amount of your assets in the UK in order to pick up the yield.

You don't have to do that anymore. We've only got 50 stocks, and we can easily find 50 good businesses around the world that are generating good income. Over the last 15 years, the compound annual growth rate in our dividend has been 8% per annum, but the compound annual growth rate of the revenue per share has been 9.3%. That means we've always been earning that dividend, which is very important to us. Today, you see bond yields all over the world with virtually zero yields. You also see a lot of equities in the developed world today which have big yields but they can't cover the dividends because, when you look at the balance sheet, there's no cash.

In my book, you want to be in things that are transparent, are underleveraged, and that you understand. That, for us, is simplicity. We don't want anything complicated. We don't want anything to do with banks or insurance companies in the developed world, where you can't see into the balance sheet and see what they're owning. Where did all that toxic waste from 2010–11 go, all the debt that came out of Greece, Portugal, Spain and everything? Where is it? It's all stuffed in the European banking system and none of it has been paid down.

So there is a real risk that a credit event will again trigger the next downturn?

BS: There must be credit issues at some point because there has to be. The end of the cycle is always interesting. J.K. Galbraith always used to talk about the "bezzle", remember? (*A bezzle is a financial swindle whose losses only come to light some time after it is perpetrated.*) We don't know what the bezzle is until we see it, but we know there is a bezzle in there again. There always are at the end of the cycle.*

Of course, if things begin to unwind, emerging markets are not going to be immune from this, not by any stretch of the imagination, but you've got to know what you own in this environment. You've got to be very clear why you own it, and whether it has the sustainability to deliver in a tougher environment globally. How will it affect the sale of consumer goods in Indonesia? Probably not a lot. It might affect the valuations on the stocks, but that's a completely different question. It is the underlying business that matters.

What is interesting, today, is that people seem to think that the main drivers of the markets, the Netflixes, Googles and Facebooks of this world, are not cyclical

---

* J.K. Galbraith: "To the economist, embezzlement is the most interesting of crimes. Alone among the various forms of larceny, it has a time parameter. Weeks, months, or years may elapse between the commission of the crime and its discovery. (This is a period, incidentally, when the embezzler has his gain, and the man who has been embezzled, oddly enough, feels no loss.)"

businesses. But throughout my career, advertising has always been cyclical, whether it's done in a newspaper or done on Google. You get a downturn; you will get a downturn in adverts too. In previous downturns or recessions, people cut back on pay TV and other things because they don't have any money. These companies have not been priced with any cyclicality in mind; they are just being priced as pure growth vehicles.

We've not had a recession, or even a significant downturn, for the last 11 years, so they've not been tested. In fact, you could say that is true of the last 20 years, because 2008 wasn't even a real downturn. It was an in-and-out recession and was over if you blinked. It wasn't like 2000, 2001, 2002 where we had three years of grinding lower. In 2002, the markets were down over 25%. So, I think it's a time to be prudent and very cautious; very careful with where you have your money.

If I look back five or ten years at your portfolio, would it be recognisable still today?

BS: Of course. A lot of the stocks that we own, we've owned for a long time. In the case of big holdings, we've owned Taiwan Semiconductor, for fifteen years, so that would have been there; Unilever Indonesia we've owned for fifteen years, that would have been there; Grupo ASUR, the Mexican airport operator, that's been there for fifteen years; CME, the Chicago Mercantile Exchange, that's a relatively new holding over the last five years or so; and Auckland Airport, in New Zealand, is also a relatively new holding.

There is more Asian growth in the portfolio than there was ten years ago. Ten years ago, there would have been a lot more consumer staples too. They got very expensive; the yields were very low. It is very difficult to grow a $200 billion company like Nestlé now. We're looking for other growth opportunities. But there's still a lot of commonality because it's a buy-and-hold strategy, and the annual turnover on our growth assets in the last five years has always been under 10%.

We haven't changed the strategy; we haven't changed the way we manage money. The US market has been flying for the last two or three years, but we don't own tech stocks; they don't pay dividends; they don't satisfy what our shareholders need, which is a rising yield and rising dividends, real income growth. The tech stocks don't really bother us, but they do drive the indices. If that's the comparison that people want to make, then that's fine. But, obviously, we have a much bigger Asian and emerging focus. We also have 18% of the portfolio in emerging market debt, which continues to look very interesting – again, because of the orthodox economics that underpins those bonds.

What sort of yields are you getting on those bonds?

BS: Around 8%. It's a mixture of sovereign debt in Brazil, Mexico, Indonesia, and corporate bonds in India, Mexico, and some Brazilian corporates as well. It's about half dollar-denominated, half in local currency. That position was built up over 2014–2015 when emerging market currencies got absolutely trashed against sterling, because of the concerns about rising interest rates.

That produced a phenomenal 2016 when our bond holdings returned over 50%, in sterling terms, over the calendar year. Then we had a good 2017. Last year, the bonds were down a couple of per cent over the year, but that was still much better than the markets, which finished down between 5–10%. They continue to perform well this year.

If you look at the bond portfolio relative to itself, it now looks quite expensive, because we always buy them below par and, today, all of them are trading above par. If you look at the bond portfolio in light of the orthodox economic policies that are unfolding in the countries issuing the bonds, it looks incredibly cheap relative to the rest of the world. The credit rating on it is arguably much higher.

What is the credit rating on HDFC Bank in India, which is a prime-quality bank, relative to say an Italian or German bank? The Italian or German bank will give you a one or one-and-a-half per cent yield and HDFC gives you six! There's just no comparison. The Indian bank is miles superior, has a better credit rating, and you have the ability to see what's on the balance sheet, which you cannot see in a German or Italian bank. It's such an interesting opportunity at this particular time.

Are you saying that they are underappreciated by the markets?

BS: Yes. I think the market is very, very quick to make the prejudiced linkages of every past period that it always makes. It was exactly the same argument that we had in 2007, when we extolled the credit-quality virtues of ICICI Bank and HDFC Bank in India, compared to the Royal Bank of Scotland and the Bank of Scotland. Our shareholders were aghast. They said, "Why would you own an Indian bank when you could own a Scottish bank that yielded 6%, and the Indian bank only yielded 3%, and it is in India for goodness sake?" Well, ten years down the line, the Indian institutions are in a lot better shape than the two Scottish institutions, I can tell you.

I'm not sure that the banking system in Europe could take another hit in terms of credit quality. It would be interesting to see how they plug their gaps this time, because I'm sure the credit quality has not improved in the last ten years.

They've just been printing money and rolling over the debt all the time. But now you get to negative yields, you don't have any choice. The bond matures; how are you going to finance it if there's no yield? I don't understand that. I wouldn't be buying a bond on minus 40 basis points. It's a difficult one to sell to your shareholders: If you give me £1,000, I'll give you £960 back in ten years' time. And no income. It is absolutely bizarre. I've never seen anything like it in my life.

So, if we could get some resolution on the trade tensions and some easing there, then I think that's the catalyst to see the rates get cut in Asia next year. Then we'll see how much operational leverage the companies have, and we'll get to see some very interesting growth dynamics in different businesses. Regardless of what happens in Europe and the UK. We might still be in the same shambles we've been in for the last three years.

Is the investment trust structure of MURRAY INTERNATIONAL *helpful or a hindrance? To what extent are your dividends having to come out of reserves?*

BS: As an income fund, it is very helpful having the trust structure. We only dip into revenue reserves (to pay the dividend) occasionally. We had to in 2012, a wee bit in 2014, and last year to the tune of about £1.6m because sterling was so strong in the first half. But every other year we've more than covered the dividend growth of 8% per annum, and the reserves have gone up from £26m to £73.5m. So, we have continued to put more in than we take out over the last 15 years, by a long way. The reserves are there for a really nasty time, but as long as we're earning the dividend over the long term, that is what is important. Earning their dividends is what we like to see from the companies we own. If you do that with an investment trust, then hopefully that will support the rating.

BRUCE STOUT *has been the portfolio manager of* MURRAY INTERNATIONAL *(MINT) since 2004, and involved in its management team since 1992. It is one of the UK's larger investment trusts, with total assets of £1.7bn, and sits in the Global Equity Income sector.*

WHAT IS THE FUTURE FOR TECH?

BEN ROGOFF, *lead manager of the* POLAR CAPITAL TECHNOLOGY TRUST, *opens up in this in-depth interview about his 25-year career as a technology investor.*

When you were a history student at Oxford did you have an idea you would end up managing a technology fund?

Ben Rogoff: No. I went to university to enjoy university and study history, which I loved, and I didn't really give very much thought to what I was going to do after that until everybody else in my final year started thinking about that. I quite liked the idea of working in the same place, but each day being different. I had a cousin who was a stockbroker at Philips and Drew and it sounded quite interesting. I ended up applying for two or three different jobs, but with no real conviction. Some of my friends were trying to be investment bankers and I'm delighted that didn't work out for me.

I applied to do a Masters degree in political science or security studies and sent out 80 letters to UK and US stockbrokers based in London, just for work experience. Two of them said I could come for an interview. About four weeks into my work experience with US stockbroker Dean Witter, two gentlemen who had heard about my plan to do a degree came to me said, "why don't you just come and work for us?" And that was that. I ended up doing two years at Dean Witter and it was a real baptism of fire. It was old-fashioned broking, effectively commission only. You are coming from this very privileged environment at Oxford, where you're one-on-one with some of the greatest minds you'll ever meet, and suddenly you're flung into, 'here's the phone book. Off you go.'

It wasn't quite as brutal as that. I was very lucky that I worked with some seriously clever people; people who have gone on to be extremely successful. Dean Witter was a forward-looking business and in the mid-1990s when I started, nobody wanted to buy US equities. Most of the asset allocators in London were ex-

Japan stars. The US had been a difficult market. My boss talked very eloquently about the great disinflationary bull market in US equities. He was an evangelist for US equities and he couldn't have been more correct.

And did you start looking into tech stocks then?

BR: Yes. I opened a few accounts – not many; about three or four, and I focused pretty much exclusively on tech stocks. I was the youngest person in the office and I have always had a natural bent towards technology. I got a Sinclair Spectrum in 1985 for my bar mitzvah; had I been a few years older it's possible that I would have missed the 8-bit computing cycle. My partner here, Nick Evans, is almost the same age as me and also got into computing at around the same time. In a very minor way, this 'luck' at having been born at the 'right time' echoes the experience of Bill Gates, Steve Ballmer and Steve Jobs who were all born within a year or two of each other, as were the great industrialists of the 19th century.

I was 13 when I got the Sinclair. Today's kids are all about smartphones and playing online, but in my youth we would go to each other's houses and play computer games. I've never got bored of it. In fact I collect old computers; I've probably got 50 1980s computers in their original boxes that I've tucked away. My late father was a huge collector of anything and everything and I've picked up some of that. I recently started putting some on the wall so I can display them.

So you had an advantage when it came to analysing tech stocks even then?

BR: Well, I arrived at Dean Witter in 1995 just in time for the Netscape IPO. I think it's fair to say that most of the people in the office didn't know what Netscape was, but I did, because we had been exposed to the internet at university. I can remember using Yahoo when its URL was a sub-directory of Stanford University. It was hugely exciting.

So I carved out a niche that ended up becoming my career. After two years Dean Witter merged with Morgan Stanley and it was a perfect moment for me to shift gears. Although I was offered a job in the combined company, I didn't want to sell things any more. What I really loved was investment, so I took a material pay cut to move to the buy side. I went to Clerical Medical for about 18 months, where I specialised as a tech analyst.

Much of what I said there fell on deaf ears. I didn't really know anything. You don't have the accumulated knowledge that you need to be able to make a genuinely informed decision, but it was a really good training ground. Some good people worked there. Then I got a job at Aberdeen Asset Management, which had a rare thing for the time, which was a tech fund. It had been launched in 1982 and so had a long track record. I joined in 1998 just before the sector exploded into life and our assets under management increased ten-fold or more.

So you lived through the whole TMT bubble experience in 1999–2000?

BR: Yes. We had some great times and some bad times. Ultimately, it all came to nought, didn't it? It is probably the most important of all observations about tech, which is that the sector overpromises and under-delivers and then when you stop looking at it, it suddenly blows you away and the whole cycle starts all over again. When you think about what this current cycle is about, it's really all about finally delivering on the promises of the late Nineties. It has just taken an extra ten or 15 years to happen.

We watched it go up, and we watched it go down. I had some formative moments going off to Asia and people signing large cheques in the back of rooms because they were so excited by tech. Unfortunately it soon transpired that much of the 'dot-com' excitement was somewhat self-fulfilling with tech companies spending disproportionately on things like servers and online advertising. Once it started to spiral downwards, those companies started spending less on advertising their products. In hindsight, the banner ad – the first wave of internet advertising – was comical. You didn't know who was clicking on them, you didn't know anything.

This confluence of positives turned into a bunch of negatives and the irrational exuberance that Alan Greenspan had talked about unwound after 2000, with pets.com and a whole bunch of specious businesses that could only have existed at that time. Looking back, what's interesting about that period was that we didn't even have smartphones. The internet was a tiny network of a few hundred million PC users compared to today with over 3.3bn smartphone users globally.

Your next move was to join this new boutique investment firm, Polar Capital.

BR: Polar Capital was formed by a team of people from Henderson's technology team: Brian Ashford Russell, Tim Woolley, and a couple of others. When the Henderson tech trust moved to Polar Capital, at the time it was the largest trust to move and follow the manager. They pretty quickly started to build up other teams because the plan was to launch a boutique investment business, not just do tech stocks. I came in to be Brian's deputy in 2003.

It was still a difficult environment. We were only halfway through the bursting of the bubble. After you've finished losing all this money for people because your sector is going down, what then happens is that the market goes up and the tech sector underperforms. It is not as painful as the initial downturn, but still very frustrating. The message when I arrived was simply 'keep your head down and focus on performance. It is not over yet'. Brian had a chart showing that the average bubble – Japanese real estate, oil, whatever it might be – takes six or seven years to unwind. Tech cycles have typically been ten years in duration. Six or seven years from the TMT bubble took us to 2007. I think the sector would have probably put in a low around when Brian had originally predicted, had the financial crisis not happened.

Brian and Tim were very alive to the need to reinvent the firm with younger blood, so with the board's approval, I took over as sole manager in 2006, just in time for the financial crisis. It was an uncomfortable beginning; we had a tricky 18 months. However, Brian and Tim understood that the universe of stocks they had been brought up on was unlikely to last, so would need to be replaced with a new pool of names, as is the norm. This dynamic – long true within tech – seems to be becoming true of other sectors today. The life expectancy of an S&P 500 company is plummeting.

Once it became slightly more obvious that we were in for a rocky ride, in early 2008 I moved the portfolio to a more defensive footing, which was a little later maybe than I would have liked, but it was still a good decision. We then had the last leg down in the cycle, where you get a complete lack of interest in tech, and the trust got out to a 28% discount, which is almost impossible to believe when you think how liquid it was even then. We bought back 2% of the company in one day, which was quite something.

But since then the performance of the trust has been very good...

BR: When we got to 2009 and the low in the market, we went all in, although we used gearing for only a handful of days. I just didn't want to lose money that wasn't ours, and there's so much natural gearing in the portfolio already. As a result, nearly all of the returns that we've generated since the crisis have come from listed companies and without using gearing.

The tech sector bottomed a few months before the S&P index, and that was the low. If you want to be very reductionist about all of this, you would say that ever since then, the tech sector has outperformed the market. We had a nice write-up recently in *The Times* that said something like, 'for the brave, this is a nice vehicle.' It was perfectly reasonable, 'brave' being I guess because it's a single sector fund and there's naturally more volatility.

But if you look at the chart that shows the performance of global equity earnings excluding the tech sector, you can see there hasn't been any growth at all since

2007. Maybe *The Times* conclusion should be flipped on its head, to say that it's pretty brave not to be a tech investor, during ten years where my sector has captured all of the growth in global equity earnings for twelve years. That's astonishing. Of course it's not just my sector. Healthcare and others have done well too, but other sectors, especially those which are cyclical, or being disrupted, or dependent on the yield curve, have found it tough going.

In 2007 we had a tough time, mostly because our Asia book performed poorly. It was exacerbated by a change in benchmark which the trust made in 2006. As sod's law would have it, 2007 was a year when three stocks in the Nasdaq 100 delivered 50% of the returns. Unfortunately we did not adjust how we built our portfolio, despite the change in benchmark. Even though I owned all three of the stocks, and outperformed the old internal benchmark, we still trailed our new benchmark that year.

From a career perspective, that experience shook me a bit. I had come in and inherited a structure and a team. It was a real learning experience for me because poor performance in Asia, which accounted for 25–30% of the portfolio, had jeopardised the whole franchise. From that point on, I decided, we were not going to have the tail wagging the dog. I told Brian, "I think we need to run the money differently."

What I ended up doing was moving the trust to become more benchmark-centric, and specifically a US-centric portfolio. I laid out an investment plan to beat the benchmark by 2–3% after fees and at least second quartile performance every year; if that could be delivered, it would likely result in top decile performance over the longer term.

This industry ultimately is like golf, isn't it? Rounds can be ruined by one or two bad holes. You see the same thing with investment. You can be the best fund one year and then very frequently the next year you are the worst fund. I never want to be the worst fund. I'm happy to be the best fund in any given year, but the chances are that I won't be.

But if you consistently deliver second-quartile performance a) people will trust you; b) they'll probably invest more with you because the value at risk is that much less; and then more importantly, as Brian explained to me years ago, the tech sector will look after itself (in terms of earnings growth) if you just steer clear of the bad stocks.

That is one of the key messages investors in tech stocks need to understand.

BR: Yes. In a sector where the underlying growth rates are materially higher than the broader market, the key is to stay away from the rubbish. The way that we think about investments is completely different to what you might think. It is not about looking for the next big thing that's going to fly out of the park. We'd love to find some of those. But most of the time you're trying to find the most important themes, trying to find sensible ways to gain exposure to them while trying to steer clear of 'jam tomorrow' companies, especially those that require capital.

Take fuel cells. When I joined Aberdeen, a Canadian fuel cell company was the biggest position in the tech fund. That company is still around; but it's 90% down from where it peaked in 2000. History is littered with companies and themes that have promised to change the world. Almost always the timeframe is wrong and the first generation of companies usually fail. Just look at all those internet search engine businesses in the Nineties! Back then we were all trying to work out which one was the winner. Was it Yahoo or Infoseek or Lycos? They all went to zero, while this company that no one had heard of back then, called Google, did not IPO until 2004.

Funnily enough, the first time I was ever quoted about the trust was at the time of the Google IPO. Brian had announced his plans to stand down and so I was asked about Google in an interview. I said it was bonkers cheap, even though it became public on a forward PE of 80 times. I think the valuation at the time was $23bn. Now the company has more than $100bn on its balance sheet in cash alone. When we bought the stock at IPO we may not have anticipated how important Google would become, but I knew even then that forward PE was a very blunt instrument when valuing a growth stock.

One problem with tech stocks is that the components of the benchmark indices keep changing, don't they?

Yes. Right now, the index we use as a benchmark, the Dow Jones world technology index, is around 70% North American. The vast majority of the rest is in Asia, and maybe 5–6% is in Europe. If you asked me the question; how confident are you that this is the right benchmark? How good a job are the benchmark people doing staying abreast of the changes that are happening in the world? I would say the answer is reasonable, but not perfect. That's because what a tech company is has become much more complicated.

If you go back to the Seventies, the Eighties, or the Sixties before it, we went from mainframes to mini computers to client-server computing. Basically technology companies sold stuff to other companies who hoped this capex would improve productivity, to sell more, whatever. That world has completely gone.

The biggest tech companies in the world now are companies that buy technology and then sell services that use it. Amazon is a retailer and a cloud computing company. It buys technology in order to be those things. Google is an advertising business. It will also move into the cloud. Google is the second biggest position in our benchmark, so credit to the index people for understanding that it's a tech company. But Amazon, which has long been our largest active investment in the portfolio, is not in the benchmark. If you ask 'why not?' the answer is 'because it's a retailer'. Which is also true.

You can only imagine the conversations that are happening at Dow Jones and MSCI, with the retail guys saying 'hands off my Amazon. It's the only stock in my sector that's working!' Joking apart, classification is not straightforward. If Revolut or any next generation fintech companies were to become public, would they be banks? Or are they tech companies? Last year there was a change in GICS classifications which saw internet stocks such as Google moved from technology into so-called 'Communication Services'. Thankfully my index hasn't adopted this change; I would be sad to see these companies reallocated away from tech.

But it's not going to stop you owning Amazon?

BR: No. But what it does do is temper the position size. Typically in my portfolios I won't be more than 3% overweight in any individual stock. The whole portfolio has about a 50% active share, but that doesn't tell you anything. Other trusts that we compete against I think are more like 70%. I've got plenty of stocks that are just ten basis points [=0.1% of the portfolio]. Amazon, which is the best example of a company that is not in the benchmark, has been limited over time to 3%, when other tech funds might have 7 or 8%.

That's the downside of constructing a portfolio around a benchmark. It's very easy to turn around and say, 'it doesn't make sense that Amazon is only 3%.' And do you know what? It doesn't. The good news is that, while avoiding the losers is crucial, the winners these days have tended to persist. When Apple was in its heyday, I was maxed out against the benchmark. I was either overweight or neutral on that stock for years. However, if it hadn't been in the benchmark, I would never have had 10 or 12% of our fund in it.

Alphabet (Google) has also become another large position in the benchmark, but Google is in the businesses of selling advertising, not in the business of selling computers. It's all about scale and the network effect. That's why the benchmark has done so well, because these large companies persist. Where is

Yahoo now? Where are the number twos? As human beings, I think everybody wants to be the guy or the girl who picks the horse that's running second in the Grand National and is going to catch the winner in the run in.

They almost never do. Most of the time the horse that's winning wins. It's particularly true today with the network effect and the value of data. There are probably six cloud computing companies left and we're only eight years into something that's probably going to persist for 30 years.

The earnings have been good, but how much of the strong tech showing in recent years is also down to a momentum effect?

BR: When you read about there being a switch from momentum to value, tech is definitely on the wrong side of that trade, but it's actually difficult to know how much of this is down to momentum. Ultimately the most important thing is the earnings growth. If you go back to the late Nineties, the last time the tech sector enjoyed this type of sustained outperformance, it wasn't about earnings at all. It was largely based on hope and the 'build it and they will come' model.

Well, they've certainly arrived; about 2.5bn people use Facebook every month. The percentage of the world population that uses Facebook each month is bigger than the British Empire at its zenith. History rhymes, it doesn't repeat. Everybody wants to be the kind of seer who says, 'this is just like the Nineties.' It isn't like the Nineties. We've got all these people on networks and there's a whole bunch of new things that Facebook might introduce to 2.5bn people that might have resonance.

When Amazon bought Whole Foods a few years back, it was a huge shot across the bow of traditional businesses. The threat is that Amazon is able to change user behaviour and expectations using payment and delivery as differentiators. Put differently, as long as price is vaguely competitive, fulfilment is becoming arguably more important than content. You're seeing that everywhere. You see it on Netflix.

Yet if you go back ten years, people were hugely excited about ITV and the value of their video assets. Content is king, they used to say. But content is not king, is it? The phrase should be, 'content is king and distribution is God.' In other words, it is about the desire people have to press a button or to click on a YouTube video. Generation Z, those who are teens to early 20s today, no longer only have an eight-second attention span. Something like 40% of them spend ten hours a day on their smartphones.

I've got some of those in the family and you probably have too.

BR: To me the backbone of everything is the internet. The disruption you're seeing is a function of this new general purpose technology around which everything is being reoriented. It was equally true for steel, electricity, automotive and containerised shipping; just as every generation thinks what's happening to it is unique, the same could be said for every industry that goes through what we're going through today.

This dynamic is not easy for smaller companies to navigate which is one reason our portfolios continue to drift away from small-caps. Only 1% of the trust is now in small-caps. Being a small-cap might have been fine when you had thousands of automakers but when you only have five automakers, or whatever the number is globally, you really need to be one of the main suppliers to those companies. The scale associated with mass production makes it so difficult for small-cap companies to break in. The internet and smartphones are all about scale. Rifle shooting in tech has always been tricky.

The big issue for tech in my mind has always been the innovator's dilemma, which I'm sure you've heard of. The idea that all technologies begin as complements and end up as substitutes. And it does that because the time to adoption is always longer than you think and because – at first – the new technology is not really fit for purpose. It's lightweight and not especially good, only cheap. The dismissive way that Larry Ellison [the founder of Oracle] was talking about the cloud in 2008 now seems comical. He was probably right at that point, because the cloud was lightweight and very feature-light. But then of course, over time, it has got better and better while remaining vastly cheaper.

What's so interesting about the cloud is that we are in a world where we're all using the same piece of software. I talked about the internet and the scale thing and everybody understands that because there are only two app stores left in the world, effectively Google and Apple. There are only two smartphone operating systems, and only two PC operating systems left which is crazy when you think about my 1980s computers on the wall when there were many more.

While everyone understands the importance of the network effect for anything related to the internet, it is less obvious as it applies to the software industry. However, the software industry is a massive beneficiary of the network effect too, because of the underlying metadata. As a business you can get to see how all of your customers are using your product. You can then iterate and make the product better all the time. What was once a productivity tool can end up becoming a critical component of the business if you're going to be able to automate processes necessary to respond to a generation of people with eight-second attention spans.

The ramifications of all this are almost endless, essentially?

BR: What you're seeing is this hackneyed phrase – 'digital transformation'. That is why software stocks have been on a tear for so long. It is partly because they don't have any China exposure, so they're not exposed to the trade war shenanigans, but more to do with the fact that in a world where you've got Amazon breathing down your neck, and you've got 300 unicorns in the States looking to try to disrupt your business, you have to reinvent yourself or risk becoming obsolete. Our best estimate is that we're probably only a third of the way through this disruptive phase.

What's so interesting about the software space is that you end up with these best-of-breed platforms that know more about your business than you do. There's a company called Fleetmatics that we didn't own. It was bought by, I think, Verizon in the end. But it used to allow you to monitor how your vans and trucks were being used. In the very basic instance, it would stop people from speeding and burning lots of fuel and having a cup of tea at the café. It gave you best practice in how to run a fleet. But if you're doing that with 500 different fleet managers around the world, you can see who the best managers are. That's profound.

That never existed before in the history of computing. Because IBM would roll out something and Oracle would roll out something, but it would be your something and it would be custom and bespoke and it might take years to roll out. But now I can sit there with cloud software and I can turn around to a client and say, 'actually, best practice looks like this. Let's build a module that will help everybody else do X, Y and Z.' And then I sell that module. Businesses that were once licence and maintenance are now producing recurring revenues, which are more valuable than one-off sales. They always were.

But in a period where the costs of capital is falling, they become particularly valuable because they look more like bond instruments. Look at Adobe. It was one of the first companies to make the transition from a licensing model to a recurring subscription business. That company is now more profitable than it was before the transition.

You said that the tech space today is different from the the TMT model, but you have also been saying that the stock market today is feeling similar to 1998 and 1999, just before the bubble inflated – how do you reconcile that?

BR: Well, there has certainly been a Nifty-Fifty feature to markets. I identified it about 20 months ago and felt that it would persist. Against the backdrop of sub-trend global growth, which is what we've had for the entirety of the post-financial crisis period, every year there's a sell side analyst writing, 'this is the year we're going to get more synchronised growth.' I almost fell for that a year ago as well.

But we haven't had it. We are still living in that post-financial crisis world. The money multiplier is not working, central bank policymakers are still more concerned about deflation than they are about inflation, and we've had a few false starts. The truth is that the global economy is operating sub whatever the old trend rate in growth was.

In the Nineties Japan experienced something like that too. They have had 30 years of stilted growth ever since. Although it might be good for tech stocks, let's hope it's not going to last that long here. When you look at what's happened in Japan after a sustained period of little or no growth, you do see genuine growth stocks elevated to very high valuations. If you're a company that can deliver 20% top line growth, you might trade at a fantastic multiple that from a distance looks insane. But if you're in Japan and there's a scarcity of growth, then a company that can deliver 20% growth is a phenomenon.

The point I'm trying to make is that people have been talking about Japanification recently. However, a backdrop where growth is underwhelming but still positive should be very good for growth stocks. That's what has played out in Japan and has certainly played out for the last ten years in the US. You haven't had the mean reversion that everybody's been looking for because we haven't had above trend growth and there has been an absence of widespread pricing power. On top of that, let's not understate how disruptive tech has been. You only have to take away 5% of footfall and you can bankrupt a retailer.

Why? Because their margins are tiny and they have enormous fixed costs. These businesses are forecast to atrophy at a modest rate but we know that technological change is not a linear thing. In practice it accelerates, a bit like armies at war. There's a point where you're trading blows on a battlefield but at some point someone suddenly wins and then you get a horrible retreat. Take the use of cash in the UK, for example. It is modelled to be falling every year in a linear fashion but in reality, it's not like that. It's now falling away at a rapid rate. You often go into shops now and they don't want the cash. Behaviour has changed. It was once fine to have cash and non-cash co-exist, but now it's not fine.

Let's go back to the question. You asked about another potential bubble. I think it's just a function of a narrowing group of companies that are able to deliver genuine growth at a time when most companies are not able to and many are struggling with disruption. Money will find its way into those assets, as the Japan experience proved, and as the earlier Nifty-Fifty period demonstrated. I wrote a paper 18 months ago to my board saying that I felt the Nifty-Fifty phenomenon was going to persist, although I admitted I wasn't sure how well we would profit from the observation, because we don't invest in companies at any price.

I'm never going to buy stocks at 30 times sales just because they have momentum. We do have the odd pricey name in our portfolio and the odd name that requires capital. But if you look at those assets in aggregate, they're a small percentage of overall assets.

There have been signs of value reasserting itself in recent weeks, have there not?

BR: Yes. That big momentum to value switch that you see in the markets has definitely put pressure on the Nifty-Fifty trade and the trust has underperformed recently. In this particular instance, it was the ten-year bond yield rallying from 1.50 to 1.80%. We took some money out of some of our higher growth names pretty quickly, because Brian taught me a long time ago, if you're going to panic, panic early. But we're not buying value stocks just because we think value is going to outperform. We're unlikely to do well in a value environment, but hopefully we can avoid enormous drawdowns because we don't have a hundred stocks that all act the same.

There are other trusts out there that are much bigger hitters, which have a handful of very big bets. If you get them all wrong, you're in real trouble. Whereas if you have a portfolio like ours where you have 110 stocks and a 50% active share, you could get them all wrong, of course you can. But we seldom have.

How does your trust compare to the other big investors in tech stocks in the investment trust universe?

BR: SCOTTISH MORTGAGE made an absolutely brilliant decision to reorient towards the tech sector and James Anderson has turned it into a pseudo tech fund. His focus is on picking the winners which means a much smaller list of holdings. The Allianz trust approach is not dissimilar to ours – they just do it in a much punchier way – much more US, more software and very growth-oriented. However, the relative drawdown that they have had in the recent momentum value switch has been at least twice ours. But Walter Price is a very good manager. If anyone's been doing this for as long as he has, or indeed how long we've done it, you're probably not too bad at what you do.

Our approach is more diversified than either SCOTTISH MORTGAGE or Allianz. My job is to identify the key technology themes and ensure they are represented within the portfolio. We try to be sensible and reallocate between them where we see value or an inflection in adoption. We also try to future-proof the trust by keeping on top of all of the emerging themes. Once the autonomous vehicle story moves from hype to reality, we will hopefully be ready to buy some stocks. Right now, we don't have any Tesla and the timeline for autonomous vehicles seems to be pushing out. There's currently a bit of exuberance in software valuations, so we've taken down our exposure in favour of semiconductor companies. But to us, that is just business as usual.

The big question for me is what can challenge technology leadership? The first thing I keep coming back to is that technology is the only sector in the US with net cash. What net cash does is it gives you flexibility. It allows you to put some cards into the deck and draw some new ones if you've got bad ones. Apple, Google particularly, Microsoft have made some really good acquisitions along the way. Microsoft is our biggest holding today. It ebbs and flows between that and Alphabet.

When you look at the other side of the coin, a lot of companies have tried to maintain a growth façade using financial engineering, particularly those on the wrong side of technology disruption. This includes buying back stock or the use of M&A which has been easy to explain to shareholders because debt has seldom been cheaper. Of course, debt has got cheaper and now you have used up all the firepower that you had just at the point where your business starts to decay at an accelerated pace.

The moment that organic growth goes negative, in my world at least, there is no way back. All you are debating is what the decay rate is likely to be. Once the British Empire peaked, it peaked. Only time will tell you what the actual decay rate was, but you reach a zenith. And that's what happens.

I think that this dynamic – long true within technology – is now happening beyond it too. Features of investment that have become second nature to us, like the lack of mean reversion, like the use of M&A to prop up and maintain appearances is spreading to other sectors.

So the question is what could change?

BR: One of the things that could change would be a very different regulatory backdrop and/or a very different backdrop for taxation. What could also change is globalisation. We could go back to a more isolationist period like the Thirties which would be bad because the tech sector has been a huge beneficiary of globalisation. It's one of the most powerful US export industries. But that is also one of the reasons why I'm relatively sanguine about regulatory risk.

If you're an American, Donald Trump or anyone, you're competing with China now for artificial intelligence (AI) which is the next big technology battlefield, isn't it? It's the next potential general purpose technology. And you are seriously thinking about breaking up the vanguard of your own forces in this area? That would be crazy at a time where the Chinese are genuinely competitive in certain areas with AI. If data is the next oil, then China might be the next Saudi Arabia.

The taxation system around the world is based on where profits are made, not where revenues are generated. If that was to change, that could have a significant impact. When we model our investments that are exposed to this risk, like Facebook and Alphabet, we conservatively model a slightly higher tax rate each year. But I think change will happen slowly. Take the digital tax that the French brought in recently. Bertelsmann came out and said, 'it's probably going to hurt us more than any of the people that you're trying to hurt', because Bertelsmann is a much lower margin business than Google.

Another change that could make a difference would be a trade deal that finally produced above-trend global growth. That could challenge the whole deflation and inflation issue, make the shape of the yield curve very different – these are the things that we watch closely. What would have us most worried? Fundamentally it's about the cost of capital. Because in a world where you can't borrow at 1 or 2%, but it's more like 4 or 5%, there won't be as many unicorns [privately owned companies with high valuations]. There won't be as much disruption. The value of these businesses would also be profoundly different when you use a discounting method with higher discount rates.

Would you agree though that at some point it's inevitable that something like that is going to happen?

BR: Well, in the long term, we're all dead, as Keynes once said. But yes, although the forces for disinflation remain very powerful: globalisation, technology disruption, the movement of labour and so on. I'm not clever enough to know when those forces will subside; what we do is find measures in the market that indicate if things are changing.

We also continue to watch the Fed closely. In January when the Fed changed course – a dramatic change of course; that doesn't happen very regularly – it felt like 1998 and you could argue it was a '98 moment, by which I mean one where you reverse course on an external factor and then ultimately wish you hadn't 18 months later! Another policy reversal seems unlikely today, but it is possible. However, when you look at the data today, more than half the world is in contraction mode, judging by PMI surveys. It looks like, on this issue at least, Donald Trump was actually right. Let's hope he concludes trade negotiations with Chinese as adroitly.

BEN ROGOFF *has been lead manager of the* POLAR CAPITAL TECHNOLOGY TRUST *since 2006.*

———————————

INVESTING IN AN AGE OF DISRUPTION

Fund manager SIMON EDELSTEN *reflects on the challenges posed by rapid technological change.*

ENGELS AND THE LUDDITES

I N 1768, THE first automated sawmill, in Limehouse, was burnt to the ground by disgruntled sawyers. The British Parliament, which was quite decisive in those days, responded by passing an act making the destruction of machines a felony punishable by death. This did not stop attacks on machines, like Cartwright's power loom or wool-combing machine, or papermaking and cotton-weaving machines.

Thought to have been named after Ned Ludd, an apprentice who allegedly destroyed two textile frames in 1779, luddite riots became common. They led Frederick Engels to argue, in his seminal book *The Condition of the Working Class in England*, that the profits from automation went to owners, and that machines impoverished workers. Writing in 1845, he had a point.

Many of the early machines undercut the costs of the home-working artisanal producers. The new factories were not only much more productive, but the equipment could be operated by young – often very young – newly-trained workers. Though some artisans did find work in the new factories, wages were often lower.

In subsequent waves of the industrial revolution, the benefits of automation were more clearly spread. But the broader benefits did not, of course, stop threatened workers from objecting – generally through strikes rather than by smashing machines. Some of the more colourful strikes included:

- **1900 – New York streetlamp lighters' strike:** policemen tried climbing up and lighting the gas lamps, but children went along behind them, turning them off again.

- **1926 – General strike in the UK:** an attempt to prevent lower pay and worsening conditions for 1.2 million locked-out coal miners.

- **1945 – New York skyscraper elevator operators' strike:** this left workers either having to climb the stairs of the Empire State Building (it has 102 floors) or go home. The owners brought forward plans to install automated lifts.

- **1958 – US longshoremen's campaign against containerisation:** a resolution was agreed with unions, but the global introduction of shipping containers could not be stalled.

- **1968 – US telephone operators' strike:** 160,000 operators refused to place calls, but automated boards were already sufficiently widespread to enable management and their allies to handle most calls.

None of these strikes could stall the adoption of new technology. Indeed, they often had the opposite effect – encouraging owners to accelerate adoption.

The sector that bore the greatest change from the introduction of machinery was agriculture. From the 1930s to the 1960s, the share of farms using tractors rose from 17% to 80%, with a parallel collapse in the use of horses. Without horses to feed and groom, farmers saw their productivity rise by 30%. Improved ploughing, sowing, and automation of the food manufacturing chain brought further leaps in productivity. Between 1870 and 2015, the percentage of the US population working in agriculture fell from 46% to 1%.

YOU'VE NEVER HAD IT SO GOOD

Periods of adjustment to new working practices certainly were distressing for those whose skills had been superseded. Many, especially the old, struggled to fit into the new economy.

Overall, however, society benefitted. Technology brought us electric light, cheaper food and goods, and the opportunities of travel. It took the drudgery out of house-cleaning and laundry. Displaced gas lamp lighters, farmhands, buggy drivers, and housemaids, generally, found new roles – often in more salubrious conditions. Many new products created their own demand and spawned new industries. Cars and aeroplanes, for example, stimulated the development of tourism and road haulage. It is startling to recognise that nearly half of current American employment is in jobs that simply did not exist in 1870.

Technology eventually improved incomes. The productivity gains from the second industrial revolution, from 1870 through to 1914, led to rapid rises in real wages across much of society. This trend continued for most of the 20th century. Strong growth in equity markets shows that capitalists continued to reap the financial benefits too.

Those who adapted better to the change tended to be the better educated and those able to learn new skills. This effect led to 'class', which used to be defined by job (manual labour, professional), now commonly being defined by educational level (degree or no degree).

Explosion of average wages, driven by industrial revolutions

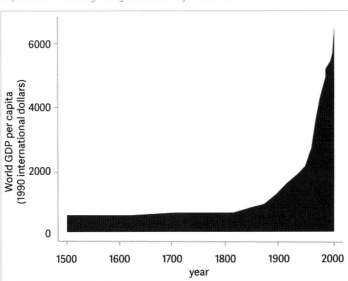

Source: Angus Maddison's World Population, GDP and Per Capita GDP, 1–2003 AD. Chart displays world average GDP per capita 1500–2003.

THE COMPUTER AGE

In my own working lifetime, technology has continued to have an impact. When I first worked in the City, I was unusual in having a pocket calculator. Most offices had slide rules and log tables. Younger generations struggle to imagine life without computers, but you do not have to have been working long to see how the rapidly-increasing power and decreasing cost of computers is threatening to put skilled jobs at risk today.

Explosion of computing power since 1980

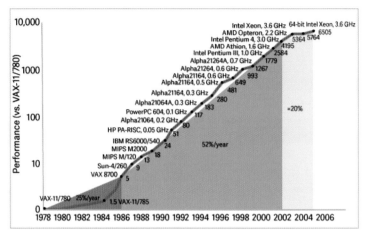

Source: cielotech.wordpress.com (05/11/2016)

Understandably, in a time of rapid change, people are nervous. Trying to assess the impact of a technology seen to replace workers is tricky, and it is easy to over-simplify – as politicians do when they instinctively decry lost jobs. Once proven, new technologies will be deployed somewhere, even if local politicians try to slow their adoption to protect jobs. So, will computers make us redundant? History suggests not. There will, however, be winners and losers.

HOW COMPUTER TECHNOLOGY IS DEVELOPING

Technological advances are taking robotics from heavy manufacturing towards a range of new sectors. Most industrial robots are currently used in automotive manufacturing, making repeat movements with heavy, metal components. Improved sensors and smaller robot arms allow automation to grow in sectors such as food handling, textiles, and even surgery, in ways previously unknown. This automation seems mainly of the productivity-enhancing type, rather than the labour-replacing type – though some low-skilled jobs, such as fruit sorting, will undoubtedly be lost.

But the new wave of automation also extends computing power into artificial intelligence. It does not mean that computers are starting to think more like people, but they are now faster at reaching the same conclusions (usually in highly-

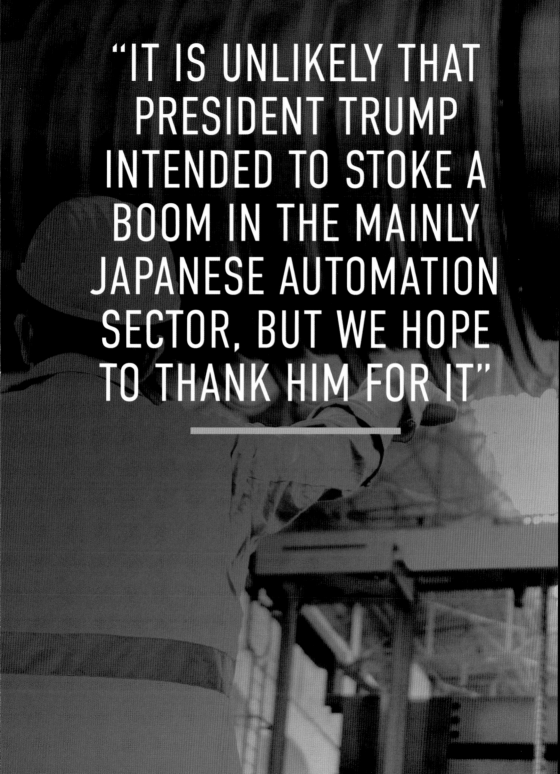

"IT IS UNLIKELY THAT PRESIDENT TRUMP INTENDED TO STOKE A BOOM IN THE MAINLY JAPANESE AUTOMATION SECTOR, BUT WE HOPE TO THANK HIM FOR IT"

specialised and technical areas). Their growing ability to learn from human-generated patterns is powering translation software, and the development of things like autonomous driving. Here, again, they are often faster than humans, but only when faced with patterns they recognise.

The Moravec paradox reflects some of these limitations. It tells us that computers are great at doing things we find difficult, yet struggle with things even a baby can do. They can win a game of chess, but cannot put the pieces back in the box. They follow rules, while we follow patterns. In Henn-na Hotel in Nagasaki, they have recently disposed of their robots; they were waking up guests who were heavy snorers and asking them to repeat their 'requests'!

Recently, computer scientists have looked at various jobs and tried to analyse how much they rely on logical processing, and how much on value judgement – the aspect that computers find hard. The idea is not so much that computers should replace humans, but supplement them.

IMPACT OF COMPUTERS ON JOBS

Since the 1980s, the growth in computerisation has driven new divisions in the labour market and the distribution of incomes. In the US, income inequality has increased – particularly over the past 20 years. Blue-collar manufacturing workers have been especially affected, and this trend will continue. The contentious list of at-risk trades for the next wave of automation includes farming, transportation, food preparation, retail, and construction.

The number of jobs that require little further education has remained the same: catering, security guards, etc. However, jobs that require value judgements – management, teachers, and other professions – have become more productive due to the support of computing. Where the value judgement is the larger part of the job, this has led to higher pay, but where the computerisation allows more candidates to qualify for the job, pay has tended not to rise. However, job numbers in these areas have all risen as the improved product attracts greater demand. Trades where automation may create more jobs than it replaces include healthcare, and financial and legal services.

POLITICAL RESPONSES

As in the past, automation is creating friction. Perhaps for political convenience, attention is being deflected towards China, with accusations of unfair trading. It is hard to separate the two issues, as offshore manufacturing savings increasingly come from automation in those locations, rather than low wages. Tariffs are unlikely to offset them. With US unemployment currently low, and wage inflation rising, we may see this issue as a more modest vote winner in the 2020 elections than it was for Trump in 2016.

In the 1920s, John Maynard Keynes predicted that productivity would rise eightfold over the next century, and that the working week would, therefore, shrink to 15 hours. In fact, productivity has risen ninefold, but the working week has not shrunk. Instead of opting for greater leisure, as incomes have risen, we have found new things to buy.

The jobs that the new wave of automation challenges may well extend further into white-collar territory than earlier waves. Politicians threatening to "tax robots" may have misunderstood the situation: computing power is hard to tax and, in manufacturing, there is little point in slowing the use of robots unless the Chinese, and others, promise to do so too.

Many jobs will be challenged and have been challenged. The working environment, today, is one that could be barely guessed at a decade, let alone two decades, ago. Many of our children and grandchildren will need to retrain mid-career and, hopefully, such opportunities will continue to expand. Some have argued that, as wealthier families invest more in their children's education, they will cope better with the changing job market than others. This seems a strong argument for the state to improve education for all, and throughout life, as social mobility may reduce as skill levels and adaptability challenges rise.

HOW WE INVEST AROUND THESE TRENDS

In our funds, one of our largest investment themes for some time has been automation. One of our larger investments, Daifuku, is a medium-sized Osaka-based business, little known amongst investors, but well known in retail and distribution as the global leader in warehouse automation.

While we remain excited about technical developments in this area, it has been a poor performer over recent years, as the US–China trade dispute has made multinational companies slow to implement their capital investment plans. This is merely delaying the inevitable. Companies with global supply chains are recognising the need to revisit, and extend, their plans for automation, to help reduce offshore manufacturing costs and accommodate recently-introduced tariffs. It is unlikely that President Trump intended to stoke a boom in the mainly Japanese automation sector, but we hope to thank him for it. It is striking how few of the world's leading automation companies are based outside Japan.

Despite sales of advanced automation being sluggish, most of our investments across the rest of the portfolio continue to benefit from technological change. Most obviously, companies in our online services theme are driven by increased computing power, especially chip design companies such as Synopsys. In our screen time theme, Vodafone and Comcast connect digital networks. From scientific equipment, makers such as Thermo Fisher to Nestlé are using big data to anticipate changing consumer trends. Most of the companies we invest in use modern technology to plan and drive their growth.

For some companies, the threats and challenges seem larger than the opportunities. We are avoiding the banking sector at present. Some banks have cleaned up their balance sheets and are finally seeing some loan growth. However, new financial operators such as PayPal, Revolut, and Square, are based on low-cost, technology-based systems that can take blocks of income from the traditional banking model. Banks are trying to keep up with modern technologies, but institutional sluggishness, and the concern of cannibalising existing profit centres, often hold them back.

CONCLUSION

We are investing during a period of very rapid technological change. Companies that make the most of the opportunities will, no doubt, thrive and provide strong investment returns for years to come. Those that lag are worth avoiding, even when they look 'cheap'. Technology does not depend on economic cycles, nor particularly on trade deals. Hopefully, our politicians will embrace the advances and will anticipate the social issues that may result. In the long run, a more productive economy can be good for us all.

SIMON EDELSTEN, *a partner at Artemis, has been the lead manager of the* MID WYND INVESTMENT TRUST *since 2014.*

THE VIEW FROM EDINBURGH

SANDY CROSS *casts an eye over the long and beneficial relationship between Scotland and the investment trust business.*

THERE WAS NO shortage of money in Scotland in the late 1800s – and no lack of evidence of it either. Huge fortunes were being made in Dundee, for example, from the super-normal profits of the jute industry – which supplied material for the sandbags used in the US Civil War, among other activities. Industrial giants were also appearing in the west in the cotton, coal, and iron industries. The money was going on elegant houses and luxury products from Princes and Bond Streets, as well as on the buying up of vast tracts of Scottish mountain and moorland, and putting up splendidly-grandiose shooting lodges all over the Highlands.

But Scotland's industrialists weren't just keen to show off their new fortunes. They wanted to find ways of both protecting and growing them – in a way that might allow them plenty of free time to spend at (and perhaps spend more money on) said lodges. They were in the right place. Scotland was jammed with legal and professional skill bases in the 1800s (we'd call it a cluster these days). It was also blessed with a couple of extraordinary innovators. Money, a professional support cluster, and a touch of genius chucked into the mix. Perfect.

And so to Robert Fleming. In 1873, the then 28-year-old Fleming persuaded a number of leading jute businessmen to invest in his new SCOTTISH AMERICAN INVESTMENT TRUST, which aimed to pool and professionally manage their wealth – initially in a (fairly) diversified portfolio of North American railroad bonds. Fleming wasn't first to the idea of pooling wealth in a corporate structure. The development of the limited liability company, and the 1862 Companies Act, had been vital precursors to ensuring the viability of the idea of an investment trust, and the FOREIGN AND COLONIAL INVESTMENT TRUST pipped him to the post with its launch, in London, in 1868.

However, he built on the idea, identified capital and investment opportunities, and laid the groundwork for the many similar entities that followed his first one. It worked: the jute barons were keen to invest in the US and elsewhere, but their attempts to do so directly had not been to their complete satisfaction, partly owing to communication difficulties, and the problems of tracking the progress of investments so geographically far away. Many of the opportunities for investing at attractive rates of return, during this era, involved exotic jurisdictions (such as Imperial Russia, Argentina, or the USA) and new industries, particularly railroads. Financial markets were also lightly regulated, with quite frequent scandals and frauds occurring. Avoiding the likes of the South Central Pacific and Mexican Railway (the fraudulent concern in Trollope's *The Way We Live Now*) was essential but not easy. So the notion that, with limited liability in the mix, they could cut their risks in a diversified vehicle, while still being in with a chance of making high returns, was very attractive.

The idea took off. Between 1909 and 1914, a particularly buoyant period, 17 new Scottish investment trusts were launched (according to John Newlands's history of investment trusts *Put Not Your Trust In Money*). Well-known Scottish investment trust managers and sponsors included William Menzies and, later, Carlyle Gifford, in Edinburgh. The latter launched THE STRAITS MORTGAGE AND TRUST CO LTD, and was the joint founder of Baillie Gifford & Co, which flourishes to this day and still manages what was the Straits and is now known as SCOTTISH MORTGAGE INVESTMENT TRUST PLC. At launch, it invested in mortgage loans to fund rubber plantations supplying the nascent auto industry. Today, it thrives in the field of long-term international growth investing, and is the largest investment trust in the UK, with a market cap of £7.7 billion.

The 20th century saw Scotland remain and grow as a centre for investment trust management, and the type of long-term investing a permanent pool of capital encourages. Firms specialising in investment trust stables grew up and were acquired. Examples include Ivory and Sime in Edinburgh, where many of Scotland's fund managers cut their teeth, and Murray Johnstone in Glasgow. As elsewhere, the industry in Scotland benefitted from the growth of financial markets, but the investment trust segment did not replicate the rate of growth of open-ended mutual funds. Some houses maintained very much of a focus on investment trusts, but most large investment management companies offered both types of fund structure.

Why? Because you could make a lot more money out of open-ended funds. It was easier to gather assets (no need to issue new shares), while the ability to create multiple trail-paying fee classes in open-ended funds made them something of a goldmine for fund management firms, in the days before the Retail Distribution Review (RDR). Investment trusts come with the problem that they are best suited as an investment for domestic investors (they are hard to market overseas), but not always easy to explain to retail investors. The inexperienced find the idea of discounts and premiums tricky, and platforms worry about how these are managed.

There have also been a few unhelpful scandals: industry problems over split caps affected Scotland's Aberdeen Asset Management, in particular, at the end of the 20th century. On the plus side, the value of the structure is still well understood in the industry. The RDR has addressed the trail commission issue, and new types of asset class, such as private equity, alternative assets, and property – with potential liquidity mismatch issues – are being bought inside trusts. With the split cap episode behind it, Aberdeen Standard Investments (Aberdeen and Standard Life merged in 2017) still has a large stable of investment trusts, and is continuing to launch new ones.

Where is Scotland today in terms of investment trusts? It is hard to give a completely comprehensive answer, given that certain trusts are domiciled in Scotland, but not managed from there (FINSBURY GROWTH AND INCOME TRUST being one example). In other cases, large companies such as Aberdeen Standard Investments are effectively to a degree UK firms, and international firms such as Templeton and Blackrock have large operations in Scotland, but do not necessarily manage trusts from here. Other large investment trusts, such as MONKS INVESTMENT TRUST, are certainly managed from Scotland but not incorporated there!

There are some 40 Scottish-incorporated investment trusts, and I calculate that investment trust assets under management of approximately £30bn are managed or controlled from Scotland. This means that Scotland remains a disproportionately large centre for investment trusts relative to its population size. The Association of Investment Trusts estimates total assets under management in investment trusts is circa £200bn, making Scotland's effective share around 15%.

For investment trusts, Scotland retains a deep resource of investment management, legal and accounting expertise, and a good pool of board talent. Broking and corporate finance expertise is perhaps more concentrated in London, in part perhaps owing to the capital requirements relating to market making. Two colossi account for the largest proportion of assets under management. The largest is nimble local behemoth Baillie Gifford, with a stable of international growth equity trusts, and a strong performance culture. Aberdeen Standard Investments is the next biggest player, with expertise in a wide range of asset classes, including alternative assets and property.

"SCOTLAND HAS AN EDGE IN THAT IT DOES NOT HAVE THE HIGH PEOPLE TURNOVER CULTURE OF THE CITY OF LONDON"

Specialist UK small-cap value manager, Aberforth, continues to plough a steady value-oriented furrow, and there continue to be thriving independent self-managed trusts, including the long-term steward of capital, the PERSONAL ASSETS TRUST. Dundee's ALLIANCE TRUST has had many column inches devoted to it over the last decade, but seems to have settled into a more stable arrangement of multi-manager investment (although not with Scottish-based managers at present, I regret to say). Notable new Scottish firm trust launches over the last couple of years include the BAILLIE GIFFORD US GROWTH TRUST and ABERDEEN STANDARD EUROPEAN LOGISTICS INCOME PLC. There are still a number of Scottish investment trusts with large family stakes, quietly held for the very long term. We should also not forget that Scotland is a centre for private client investment management, and that there is a pool of knowledgeable and supportive local investors.

Investing is about the long term and, notwithstanding the many changes I have mentioned during this piece (it does cover a century and a half!), Scotland has an edge here in that it does not have the high people turnover culture of the City of London. It offers a good lifestyle and is a pleasant place to live – ideal circumstances into which to hire good managers, and retain them throughout their careers. I don't think the investment trust structure is magic dust, but I think it has a number of distinct advantages.

I do think it can work very well because the pool of capital inside a trust is fixed, something that encourages a patient, long-term approach from those who are managing it. Talented investment managers like it as it means they can invest for the long term without the constant distraction of inflows and outflows of capital, driven by short-term market fluctuations, and advertising and marketing imperatives. They can also hold small company positions, or unusual specialist assets, which might be less liquid than large equities or bonds but offer excellent long-term opportunities. The result? You will often find that a really skilled manager will naturally gravitate towards investment trusts, hence Scotland – with established investment trust culture – has an advantage in developing, attracting and retaining good fund managers.

Despite the vicissitudes of markets and industry consolidation, investment trusts are still a Scottish strength 150 years after the first one was launched. There are strong, large industry players, and niche trusts, and a wide range of asset classes is represented – with a successful core in international equity investing which dates back to early in the 20th century. Brexit represents an existential challenge to UK financial markets, which is hard to quantify. However, the depth of skill and knowledge in the investment management industry in Scotland and the UK is likely to continue to find a market, both at home and abroad.

The ever-increasing pool of self-invested pension money in the UK matches well with investment trust managers in Scotland's long-term growth investing expertise. Scottish Independence is also a question which has returned to prominence since Brexit. As with the latter, and whatever your views on independence, political uncertainty is usually bad for business. Investment trusts have proven a pretty tough and enduring structure, and critically one which is open to evolution and innovative thinking. I feel confident investment trust directors and managers will find a way to continue to make money for their investors, as they have been doing for a century and a half – and that they will continue to do so from Scotland.

SANDY CROSS *is an investment director at Rossie House Investment Management in Edinburgh.*

THE ROLE OF THE BOARD

JONATHAN DAVIS *explains how the role of investment trust directors is changing in the face of market and regulatory challenges.*

T HE EXISTENCE OF a board of directors accountable to shareholders is widely acknowledged to be one of the great strengths that investment trusts enjoy and open-ended funds do not. To be a director of a publicly-listed company, which is what investment trusts are, is an important responsibility with obligations and duties which are laid down in law, and supplemented these days by two codes of best governance practice.

It is fair to say that corporate governance has not always been as strong and successful in protecting shareholders' interests as it should have been. Many years ago, Peter Hargreaves, the founder of the broking firm Hargreaves Lansdown, caused something of a sensation at the investment trusts' annual conference by describing trust directors as "lazy and incompetent members of a cosy gentlemen's club".

Although a deliberate intent to shock, there was more than a grain of truth in that observation, in the sense that in many cases – but by no means all – directors were chosen from a fairly small circle of City insiders and placemen whose independence was often compromised by having other commercial and business links with the trust's management company. It is difficult to believe, for example, that the split capital investment trust scandal of 20 years ago would have been allowed to develop in the way that it did, if there had been more genuinely independent directors doing their job successfully.

My observation and experience is that the days when such cavalier and cosy arrangements were the norm are rapidly receding. These days, most trusts routinely use headhunters to find new board directors, and the pool from which they are drawn is much wider and more diverse than it used to be. Although it is a slow process of change, trust boards are much less 'male, pale, and stale' (dominated by older white men) than they were. Shareholders in a trust with a well-constructed board should benefit from having a wider range of experience and expertise, in disciplines such as investment management, the law, risk management, sales and marketing, and financial reporting.

That, in itself, does not guarantee that the board will do its job of defining, overseeing, and monitoring the company's investment management arrangements successfully. To do that requires both a knowledgeable and active chairman of the board, and a group of directors who are willing to think independently but act in a collegiate manner as the occasion demands, keeping the interests of the shareholders at the forefront of their minds. According to data compiled by the broker Canaccord Genuity, the number of directors who own shares in the trusts where they are on the board is increasing, which helps to create a more direct alignment of interest with the shareholders.

Different issues arise for the small minority of trusts where the investments are managed internally but, for most trusts, the relationship with their external management company is the dominant, and most important, issue with which they are required to deal. This embraces both the vital (and somewhat tedious) business of making sure that accounting and administrative arrangements are working efficiently and cost-effectively, and the more complicated and interesting task of monitoring the performance of the investment manager or adviser.

The time taken up by the first group of responsibilities has increased, in recent years, in line with ever more intrusive financial services regulation. The board packs I see have become progressively thicker, without always adding much to the sum of human knowledge. There is a lot more box-ticking of compliance requirements to be dutifully discussed and endorsed, regardless of what practical value they may have. It is important to be cost-conscious – it is shareholders' money that is being spent after all – yet vigilant for signs of problems that can be lurking behind the blizzard of documentation.

Because the investment policy of a trust is agreed by the board, and cannot be changed without shareholder approval, the greatest risk in terms of investment performance monitoring probably lies in inertia. By common consent, it is difficult to form a judgment about an investment manager's competence and ability over periods shorter than three years. By definition, therefore, as a board it is not practical – or indeed desirable – to chop and change managers on a regular basis.

What is important is to ensure that the manager is faithfully carrying out the investment mandate he or she has been given, and is also regularly challenged about his or her decision-making. Boards also need to keep the gearing of the trust, the level of investment management fees, and the performance of the company's shares regularly under review. If and when the time does come when it is necessary to make a change, however, the directors have to bite the bullet and act decisively, regardless of their own self-interest.

Does that always happen in practice? To be honest, I suspect not, but there have been quite a few well-documented cases of boards opting to vote themselves out of existence after their trust fails to deliver what was promised, or has ceased to be relevant to investors. This can take a number of forms, including winding up the trust, agreeing to a change in management company, and/or offering a 'rollover' into another existing trust or open-ended fund (thereby avoiding the need for shareholders to realise a capital gain on transition).

One of the biggest challenges, today, concerns something that rarely concerned boards of investment trusts in days gone by, namely the management of a trust's share capital. There is little virtue in size for its own sake, save to the extent that any fixed running costs can be spread over a wider asset base, but now that boards have the power to introduce discount control mechanisms, and more flexibility in how they market themselves, there are tricky judgments to be made about whether shareholders would be best served by expanding or shrinking the issued share capital.

Investment trust share registers are increasingly dominated by two types of shareholder, discretionary wealth managers and self-directed private investors, many of whom now hold their shares on an investment platform, rather than directly or in a savings scheme offered by the trusts themselves. The liquidity of a company's shares, meaning how easily they can be bought and sold in quantity at the prices quoted by the market-makers, is an important issue for both groups.

Regulatory changes mean that wealth managers are reluctant to invest in trusts that have a market capitalisation that is under £250 million, a threshold which currently excludes more than half of the trusts in the Association of Investment Companies' (AIC) universe. Should those trusts make an effort to market themselves more widely than was either legally possible or thought cost-effective and desirable in the past? If so, how can the desire to grow the size of a trust be reconciled with the often conflicting objective of controlling the level and the volatility of the discount (or premium) at which the trust's shares are trading? Is there a risk that growing the size of a trust reaches a point where the particular investment strategy of the trust no longer works effectively, because the pool of opportunities is too small?

These are not easy questions to answer, but they are a good example of the kind of strategic issues with which investment trust boards are increasingly having to wrestle. Shrinking a trust's share capital by buying back shares is also an example of how the interests of the external management company can conflict with the board's responsibility to shareholders, since a smaller trust will generate lower management fees for the investment manager, which generally charges a fee as a percentage of assets under management. Negotiating a fair level for those fees is an important function of the board. In recent years, that has meant reducing them to stay competitive with peers and cheaper open-ended alternatives, whether or not that aligns with the manager's wishes.

My personal view is that the governance structure of investment trusts, with an accountable and independent board of directors, is one of the primary reasons that they remain the connoisseur investor's preferred investment choice. All boards, however, have to make sure that their trust remains competitive and relevant in a changing market. To do that, directors have to earn their fees and, where appropriate, take advice and utilise a broader range of specialist skills.

Retaining the loyalty of shareholders has become a much higher priority than it once was, even if it has taken some boards time to appreciate the value, and potential, of modern digital methods of marketing and communication. Ten years ago, you would have struggled to find an investment trust with a comprehensive and informative website; now they are much more common. In the not-so-good old days, underperforming trusts could stumble on for years under the less-than-watchful eye of a complacent and complicit board. Today, it is genuinely more a case of 'adapt or die'.

It is probably fair to say that most shareholders have little knowledge of what the board of a trust they own actually does, and rarely seem to make much effort to contact the chairman or directors. Attendance at AGMs is disappointingly small. If things go wrong, as a director you may come in for criticism and negative comments in the media, but that is how it should be.

Fluctuating financial markets, and changing investor preferences, make the role of the investment trust director interesting and challenging. The satisfaction that comes from being an investment trust director comes from knowing that you and your colleagues have done your honest best to advance the interests of the shareholders, of which ideally you are one yourself.

Jonathan Davis is an investment trust director, and editor of The Investment Trusts Handbook, *an annual compendium of information about the investment trust sector. A former financial journalist and columnist for* The Times, Financial Times, *and* Independent, *he is a qualified professional investor and the author of several books on investment. More information at www.investment-reader.com.*

REVOLUTION IN THE BOARDROOM?

Headhunter-turned-digital entrepreneur SUSIE CUMMINGS, *founder of fast-growing search platform Nurole, says that investment trust boards are finally becoming more diverse, but there is still further to go.*

What makes a good board director?

Susie Cummings: I've got to know hundreds of board directors over the years. The ones that really stand out for me have a natural intellectual curiosity, teamed with strong communication skills, which means they are great listeners and also great questioners. They tend to also have a good sense of humour and are articulate. There are some directors, on the other hand, who really love the sound of their own voice and talk too much. They tend to be the ones who come to a standstill at some point in their careers.

What makes a good chairman in general (do you use that term still)?

SC: I say 'chair' rather than 'chairman' but it does sound like a piece of furniture! The best chairs are great listeners. They magically create a boardroom atmosphere that gives everyone present the confidence to ask anything, even the most irrelevant-sounding questions, which are often actually the most pertinent.

Great chairs are also natural coaches, and when they hire inexperienced board members they have the patience, and put in the time, to help them get up to speed as quickly as possible. The ability to keep the conversation going in the right direction, and to bring it back on track when it's gone off-piste is also key.

Simon Fraser, who chairs MERCHANTS TRUST and F&C INVESTMENT TRUST, among other board appointments, makes the point that in the old days people used to think that the objective of a board was to come to a consensus decision. He thinks that is antiquated; the role of the board should be to arrive at the correct decision and if that means the chair listening more to those with specialist expertise, so be it.

Have you noticed anything specifically different entering the market for investment trust directors?

SC: No, not really. I think everyone should consider having an investment trust board position in their portfolio, as it's useful to understand an investor's perspective. Also, because investment trusts don't have employees, nearly all the discussion is around strategy, and there's rather less 'box-ticking' than you get on a large-cap listed board. Having said that, there is a notable trend towards recruiting new directors with specific areas of expertise, such as marketing and digital platforms.

What is the difference between Nurole and traditional headhunting firms?

SC: The key difference is that Nurole is a 'candidate-led' and totally transparent process. Traditionally, headhunters are usually very secretive about which boards they're recruiting for, and they approach a small number of candidates in their 'little black books' until they've filled their longlist of around eight to ten candidates. The client chooses a shortlist of three to five to interview. Nurole has inverted that process; we empower individuals to apply for roles and give evidence of the required competencies. Nurole then sifts all the applicants (on average, 30 per role posting) and presents a longlist of eight to 12 of the strongest fits, from which the client chooses a shortlist of three to five. Thus, the key difference is that, because we cast our net so much wider than the traditional firms, we are accessing a much broader and cognitively more diverse pool of candidates.

Can you give examples of non-executive director roles you have helped to fill in the investment trust sector?

SC: A good example would be Sarah Harvey, who joined the board of SECURITIES TRUST OF SCOTLAND last year. She is the former UK managing director of the fintech company Square (an online payment-processing business) and chief operating officer of the events business Tough Mudder. Before that, she worked in strategy roles at Diageo and Bain, and on a range of international development projects for not-for-profit organisations in Africa.

Last year, also, MERCANTILE INVESTMENT TRUST appointed Heather Hopkins to their board. She is a data and research expert who specialises in retail investment distribution, which is currently an area of great interest for investment trusts in the post-RDR world. Heather is the managing director and founder of NextWealth and, before that, the head of Platforum, a market research firm servicing the UK platform market, and the head of research for Hitwise, an internet data analytics company.

How well is the target of greater diversity being met in the investment trust sector?

SC: It depends on what you mean by diversity. If you're talking about cognitive diversity, I hope that 100% of the 100+ board members Nurole has placed on investment boards bring that. Nurole's unique algorithm enables us to cast the net much wider. Diversity is the by-product of that process.

In the last 12 months, for example, of the 30 board placements Nurole has completed in financial services, 53% have gone to women. That is more than double the 24% industry average reported in the recent Corporate Women Directors International survey, which looked at the boards of directors of the world's largest banks and financial services institutions.

While we don't have exact data, we estimate that people of colour account for about 5% of names on our platform, and a similar proportion of successful applicants. There is still much work to do as, while the Nurole data compares favourably to the 1.5% people of colour on FTSE 100 boards, we have a long way to go versus the population in the UK, which stands just shy of 20%. It's a challenge we are excited about playing a role in solving.

How do you go about justifying the benefits of having a more diverse board?

SC: We live in a global world and we aim for greater equality, and that's what a more diverse board brings. As a by-product of this, all of the research I've seen on this subject shows that greater diversity equals greater success, in whatever way you measure it. A recent survey by McKinsey found, for example, that firms which are in the top quartile for gender, or racial and ethnic, diversity are more likely to have higher financial returns than their national industry medians.

How many criteria of diversity do you think are really important?

SC: If you're hiring in a country, or for an organisation, with specific diversity quotas, then it's obviously important that you meet their different diversity criteria on a technical level. It's important that diversity does not become a tick-box exercise though. The Nurole platform is designed to find the best person for the role, and is created in such a way as to minimise box-ticking.

Whereas headhunters typically resort to a little black book of contacts, which invariably tends to be biased towards public school-educated, white males,

Nurole spreads the net far wider and so our database is, by its nature, more diverse. We have tens of thousands of cognitively diverse candidates from all walks of life, and from all over the world, for investment trust boards to draw on. We've recently launched a practice focused on impact investing, and have generated some great candidates with a background in, and passion for, the environment and sustainability.

We recently helped to appoint a 32-year-old to an investment trust board, making them probably the youngest person on a FTSE board. When you're fishing from the sea, you don't just catch the brilliant, well-connected fish, you also net some fantastic surprises, which can only add to the diversity of thinking around the board table. When we talk about diversity, however, I am referring to diversity of thought more than anything. Diversity of thought is so misunderstood. It is widely underestimated how alike people from similar backgrounds tend to think.

Yet, it has been shown that diversity of thought on boards can help identify and avoid business risk, challenge the traditional way of doing things, and encourage board members to see the business from a new and different perspective. There's a great book by Matthew Syed entitled *Rebel Ideas* that, in my view, is a must-read for any board member.

What is the optimal size of a good board?

SC: I'd say that the optimal size of an investment trust board is five, as it doesn't have any executives.

How would you like to see investment trust boards develop from here?

SC: I'd like to see investment trusts make more progress in hiring from outside the investment industry. I see a lot of benefits from taking on current-serving executives in the non-financial services sectors.

SUSIE CUMMINGS *has 30 years' experience in the headhunting business. She is the founder and managing director of Nurole, a digital platform which helps companies to recruit directors. The company has members from more than 100 countries and, this year, was listed by the* Financial Times *among Europe's fastest growing companies.*

WE ARE ALL MARKETERS NOW

Marketing expert CLARE DOBIE *explains how and why investment trusts are having to embrace a new discipline.*

INVESTMENT TRUST BOARD agendas are changing. Once focused on established staples such as performance, markets, finance and regulation, they have been joined – belatedly – by marketing.

Until recently, 'marketing' investment trusts often consisted of no more than one-to-one meetings with professional investors. While these meetings remain an essential feature of most trusts' approach to wealth managers, they are now just one tool in a much larger kitbag of communication techniques that addresses individual investors, as well as professionals.

In addition to staging annual general meetings, some trusts hold conference calls and webinars with investors. Some managers produce expensive, glossy magazines; others produce newsletters, delivered by email. Many develop content in different formats, including video, for use on platforms and elsewhere. Others advertise both in print and online. Meanwhile, trusts' websites are changing quickly, and social media is starting to figure in marketing plans.

This transformation has been brought about by an increase in the number of self-directed investors using investment platforms. Last year, Hargreaves Lansdown – the largest platform provider – reported that about 150,000 of its one million customers hold investment trusts, and Hargreaves often appears on the list of top ten shareholders in a trust. At the end of last year, its average holding was 5.7%, according to Richard Davies Investor Relations (RD:IR).

As a result of buying led by Hargreaves and other providers, including AJ Bell and Alliance Trust Savings (now part of Interactive Investor), platforms serving individuals and advisors have nearly doubled their holdings to more than 20% since 2012, while institutional and self-registered investors have fallen away (RD:IR).

Rather than a surge of new investors, drawn to the sector by its undoubted attractions, this growth in platform investing mostly reflects a switch away from traditional to DIY investing. Regulatory change, notably the Retail Distribution Review, prompted many to cease using financial advisers in favour of taking decisions into their own hands via platforms. As Jeremy Fawcett of Platforum says: "The telephone-based stockbroker has been replaced by the digital platform."

Boards have had to change their approach. Soon after I first joined an investment trust board in 2012, I was told by a non-executive director of another trust that marketing was not a proper subject for board review, and investment was the only thing that mattered. How times change! At last year's Association of Investment Companies (AIC) conference, attendees were asked which skill should have greater representation on boards. Marketing and communications gained more votes than all the other skillsets put together. Headhunters are busy trying to fill the vacancies.

What do directors with marketing backgrounds contribute? They can start by translating the marketing jargon that managers and marketing providers use all too often. Examples include CPC (cost per click), aggregators (comparison sites), and engagement (often measured in terms of website activity).

Each board needs to be clear about the appeal of their trust to each group of target investors. They need to agree with the trust's manager a handful of key messages they want to convey, that are appealing to existing and potential shareholders and differentiate the trust from its competitors. While not getting involved in implementation, directors should check that the marketing programme highlights each one, in the appropriate formats, and does so consistently. To be heard, messages must be repeated.

Where do individual investors go for information to guide their decisions? According to Research in Finance, they use third-party websites such as Morningstar and FE Trustnet most frequently, followed by research libraries on platforms, and then the national and investment press. Investment trust-specific websites are less important in this respect (but remain a vital source of consistent information carried elsewhere). Does your manager or marketing provider use all these options?

Boards are often asked to approve marketing budgets over and above the basic fee. How do directors know whether this money is well spent? For trusts with their own savings plan, the answer is simple: they can see flows into the savings scheme rise and fall, not just in the light of performance, but in response to marketing efforts. For example, campaigns on junior ISAs should result in more JISA holdings.

"WHAT DO DIRECTORS WITH MARKETING BACKGROUNDS CONTRIBUTE? THEY CAN START BY TRANSLATING THE MARKETING JARGON THAT MANAGERS AND MARKETING PROVIDERS USE ALL TOO OFTEN."

For the increasing number of trusts without their own savings scheme, the task is trickier but not impossible. Partnerships with platforms can be easily monitored, with some managers even showing an ability to learn and adapt their campaigns as they receive results. All boards should be receiving information on their website, including visits and time spent on particular pages.

With today's appetite for digital data, it is easy to overlook the older established virtues of long-term profile building, including public relations. This is still an important part of any marketing mix and, by necessity, requires patience. It is worth waiting for a great article in the *FT*. It's not easy to measure the benefit, but regular reporting and review makes the task easier.

Managers who provide marketing across a range of trusts present special challenges for directors. How to tell whether your trust is gaining its fair share of the marketing budget? Is the manager building its brand – at the trust's shareholders' expense – or is it attracting new investors to the trust cost-effectively? Might it be worth using an external provider for PR or other functions?

In my experience, many managers find it hard to report on marketing. Either they talk to directors at such a high level that they are too vague to be useful, or they send a junior to report on the detail of campaign execution. It can often be easier for a board to stipulate a reporting template.

Start with the objectives – what is your marketing trying to achieve? – and then set out measures of success. If you want more platform users on your share register then you need to get reports on progress, and measures taken to achieve the goal. What work is your manager doing with platforms to highlight your trust's advantages?

What does all this activity mean for investors? Over time, more demand should lead to lower discounts and even, in some cases, to share premiums, allowing trusts to issue shares and to reduce ongoing charges to the benefit of existing shareholders.

Investment trusts are no longer confined to the backroom; they compete with open-ended investment companies. Investors have a wider choice as a result of this marketing effort. That's a clear benefit, given the range of strategies available and performance advantages that most trusts can offer.

Clare Dobie is a non-executive director of four investment trusts: ABERDEEN NEW THAI, ALLIANCE TRUST, BMO CAPITAL AND INCOME *and* SCHRODER UK MID CAP. *She is writing in a personal capacity.*

BACK TO THE FUTURE?

Marketing expert PIERS CURRIE *explains why investment trusts are having to embrace the new digital world.*

T HE INVESTMENT MANAGEMENT industry is uncertain about how to navigate the new world of digitisation (and digitalisation). Should they prioritise their back, middle, or front office services, or apply the new methods to all of them? Administration providers are struggling to morph the systems they inherited into modern fit-for-purpose ones. New and old investment dealing systems co-exist uneasily in an effort to meet modern expectations.

Once clearly defined and delineated financial services sectors are blurring too. Savings vehicles are merging into investment products, while the lines between professional and retail communications blur in the open skies of the web. The once-clearly-prescribed segments of the industry are fragmenting and reassembling. It's become a personalised world out there, in which customers are king.

The challenges facing firms also include coping with regulatory adjustment to the new digital world, while the promotional rules from regulators are also trying to keep pace. New investment journeys for customers and investors online are increasing expectations for speed and convenience across industries. Beyond the City walls of regulated office spaces lie successful disruptors, showy, pronounced and seemingly easy winners.

Industry conferences point to case studies such as the demise of Kodak film or Blockbuster – companies which failed to recognise that Netflix was their ultimate disruptor, in the world of movies on demand. Leaders like Amazon, retail banking start-ups, Uber cabs, and Ocado groceries now offer a service whose speed and convenience was barely imaginable even five years ago. In just a couple of decades, mainstream financial services have leapt from a world of queues in banks, dusty ledgers, and cheque books, to one in which mobile payments are made on the move, and transactions at the press of a button on a phone.

Why should investment trusts be any different? They are not immune to these life-changing developments. After all, we transfer our expectations from one aspect of our lives to another, and there is no reason, as trust boards are slowly waking up to realise, why investors in closed-ended funds will not demand the same standards of speed and convenience in their dealings with those who invest their money.

GOVERNING CHANGE

Change is everywhere. The once-fixed assumptions of how asset management is meant to operate are being called into question on all sides. The decline of defined-benefit pension schemes, changing approaches to risk (as governments and companies pass the burden of retirement provision to individuals), and the fallout from the global financial crisis, create both opportunities and threats. Rational market theory has been debunked since the global financial crisis. Radically different expectations of inflation and interest rates have stymied the life industry's orthodoxies, while heightened equity volatility has confused the idea of what exactly performance returns are meant to be.

Investment trusts ownership structure has also been rapidly evolving. In what some see as a 'back to the future' moment, there has been a renaissance of the individual, self-directed investor as the most significant factor on the demand side. In an age described as 'democratisation of risk', traditional institutions, such as life companies and local authorities, have defected to other vehicles and portfolio options. For the well-to-do, increasing regulation is professionalising their wealth management advisers. The latter's compliance regimes increasingly screen out investments that are below the bar for liquidity, deemed to be too complex, or fail to pass risk screens and risk-based portfolio criteria. Competitor products such as ETFs and multi-asset funds attract capital and headlines.

The significant emergence of self-directed D2C (direct-to-consumer) platform investors, themselves not a single tribe in terms of behaviour and expectation, is a challenge to historic assumptions about investment board strategy, and long-term share register policy. It was a simpler world when 'performance' meant rating risk-adjusted returns relative to an index. Retail investor needs are often different to those of the institutional holders which dominated share registers in the past.

According to RDIR, the investment trust register analysts, self-directed private investors using consumer-friendly investment platforms (D2C) now own between a quarter and a third of investment trusts' issued share capital. More powerfully perhaps in the short term, as a group they can account for between half and three quarters of all positive annual buying liquidity.

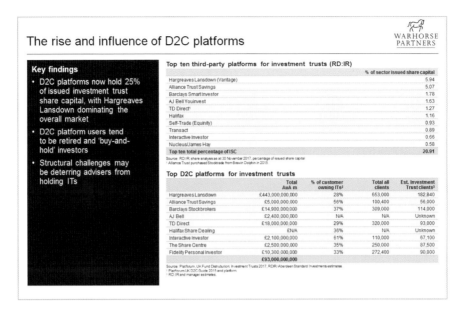

The rise and influence of D2C platforms

WARHORSE PARTNERS

Key findings

- D2C platforms now hold 25% of issued investment trust share capital, with Hargreaves Lansdown dominating the overall market

- D2C platform users tend to be retired and 'buy-and-hold' investors

- Structural challenges may be deterring advisers from holding ITs

Top ten third-party platforms for investment trusts (RD:IR)

	% of sector issued share capital
Hargreaves Lansdown (Vantage)	5.94
Alliance Trust Savings	5.07
Barclays Smart Investor	1.78
AJ Bell Youinvest	1.63
TD Direct[1]	1.27
Halifax	1.16
Self-Trade (Equiniti)	0.93
Transact	0.89
Interactive Investor	0.66
Nucleus/James Hay	0.58
Top ten total percentage of ISC	**20.91**

Source: RD:IR share analysis as at 30 November 2017, percentage of issued share capital
[1] Alliance Trust purchased Stocktrade from Brewin Dolphin in 2015

Top D2C platforms for investment trusts

	Total AuA m	% of customer owning ITs[2]	Total all clients	Est. Investment Trust clients[3]
Hargreaves Lansdown	£443,000,000,000	28%	653,000	182,840
Alliance Trust Savings	£5,000,000,000	56%	100,400	56,000
Barclays Stockbrokers	£14,900,000,000	37%	309,000	114,000
AJ Bell	£2,400,000,000	N/A	N/A	Unknown
TD Direct	£18,000,000,000	29%	320,000	93,000
Halifax Share Dealing	£N/A	36%	N/A	Unknown
Interactive Investor	£2,100,000,000	61%	110,000	67,100
The Share Centre	£2,500,000,000	35%	250,000	87,500
Fidelity Personal Investor	£10,300,000,000	33%	272,400	90,000
	£93,000,000,000			

Source: Platforum, UK Fund Distribution: Investment Trusts 2017, RD:IR/Aberdeen Standard Investments estimates
[2] Platforum UK D2C Guide 2015 and platform
[3] RD:IR and manager estimates

Source: Warhorse Partners

Understanding this important group's constituencies, and their behaviour, is more complex and behavioural than when the primary audience was small groups of professionals managing large sums by value, and judging performance on simpler, standardised metrics. In a competitive, more retail world, trusts need to be different, offer a genuine competitive advantage, and understand the shifting requirements of their more diverse clientele.

This needs grounding on strategy and shareholder targeting, managing, where possible, the tidal ebbs and flows of demand, prioritising shareholder retention and seeking to understand the risk appetite of different segments of the market. All this risks adding to price volatility and, at worst, opening weaker or inattentive trusts to demands by activist shareholders for buybacks, tenders, and shrinkage.

As well as knowing the cost of marketing to the retail world, trusts' boards understandably want numbers and key performance indicators (KPIs) in order to judge the value and effectiveness of secondary market promotion. Professional audiences, including wealth managers and financial advisers, are also increasingly impatient to manage their time, so they expect to access tailor-made intelligence online, on demand, quickly and pertinently.

CHANGING REPORTING NEEDS

The retail investor market is demanding in its own ways. Private investors do not typically use Bloomberg screens, they typically do not track regulatory news announcements, nor receive sell-side analysis and notes (which under the current regulatory regime are allowable for professional audiences only). This group therefore varies from the very engaged to the dimly aware. Surveys show that some are actively monitoring what they own daily, some weekly, some only every six months. While a few older shareholders may dive deeply into annual reports, many do not.

As the web and other channels have developed, private investors consume media and intelligence from their own sources. They also research and transact through different portals; sometimes online, sometimes by post or telephone. The driving force, in the digital age, is their convenience. They are influenced by different media too. The investment trust investor, typically retired and over 65, will read weekend newspapers, and may well subscribe to magazines they receive through their letterbox and read in depth.

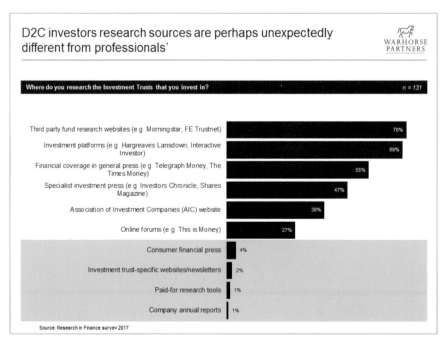

Source: Warhorse Partners

Judging the effectiveness and balance of communications and media allocation at the board level has therefore become both more pressing and more complicated. While boards are, rightly, only concerned about the direct impact of activity on their own trusts, from the investors' perspective any one trust is likely to be just a small part of their blended portfolio. For many, the convenience of tax wrappers and savings schemes are their primary reason for engagement, and the financial promotion rules available to the managers means these are seen as the mechanisms to promote.

Despite alarms raised about superstar fund managers falling to earth from time to time, the private investor seems shrewd enough to identify where responsibility for portfolio performance sits, and to expect constancy of style from their managers. Investment trusts, being classed as equities, can be low cost to acquire for self-directed investors who understand their own risk goals, and are prepared to make their own allocation decisions. This important group is helping the sector adapt to a modern age even if, at times, it feels like taking a step back to the origins of the investment trust movement, when individual investors were also the primary force on company share registers.

PIERS CURRIE *is a founding partner of Warhorse Partners Limited, and former global head of brand at Aberdeen Asset Management.*

TOP 20 INVESTMENT TRUST SECTOR BUYERS AND SELLERS (AS AT 31 DECEMBER 2018)

Buyers

BUYER	PLATFORM	% ISC
Hargreaves Lansdown, stockbrokers (EO)	Vantage	5.68
AJ Bell, stockbrokers (EO)	AJ Bell Youinvest, Sippcentre	1.84
UBS Wealth Management	N/A	0.31
Vanguard Group	N/A	0.56
Mattioli Woods	N/A	0.53
Baillie Gifford	N/A	0.45
Transact (EO)	Transact	0.83
Border to Coast Pensions Partnership*	N/A	0.10
Raymond James Investment Services	N/A	0.42
Interactive Investor (EO)	Interactive Investor	1.65
M&G Investment Management	N/A	0.82
Smith & Williamson Wealth Management	N/A	1.75
EFG Harris Allday, stockbrokers	N/A	0.86
Investec Wealth & Investment Ireland	N/A	0.31
Canaccord Genuity Wealth Management (ND)	N/A	1.22
Quilter Investors	N/A	0.81
1607 Capital Partners	N/A	0.86
Newton Investment Management	N/A	0.28
PGGM	N/A	0.05
FundsDirect, stockbrokers (EO)	Ascentric/Strawberry Invest	0.36

Sellers

SELLER	PLATFORM	% ISC
Lazard Asset Management	N/A	1.48
Investec Wealth & Investment	N/A	3.89
Barclays Smart Investor (EO)	Barclays Smart Investor	1.00
HSDL, stockbrokers (EO)	Halifax	1.54
East Riding of Yorkshire**	N/A	0.25
Cazenove Capital Management	N/A	0.93
South Yorkshire Pension Authority**	N/A	0.07
Aberdeen Standard Investments	N/A	1.85
Alliance Trust Savings	Alliance Trust / Nucleus, Stocktrade, Novia, James Hay	3.94
Speirs & Jeffrey, stockbrokers	N/A	1.95
JPMorgan Asset Management	N/A	0.54
Wells Capital Management	N/A	1.16
BMO Global Asset Management (UK)	N/A	0.45
Brewin Dolphin, stockbrokers	N/A	3.50
Architas Multi Manager	N/A	0.14
Cohen & Steers	N/A	0.01
BP Investment Management	N/A	0.02
Aberdeen Standard Capital	N/A	0.22
GLG Partners	N/A	0.00
Sarasin & Partners	N/A	0.09

*   Result of Local Government Pensions pooling
**   Local Government that has pooled into Border to Coast

Source: Richard Davies Investor Relations

"MAINSTREAM FINANCIAL SERVICES HAVE LEAPT FROM A WORLD OF QUEUES IN BANKS, DUSTY LEDGERS, AND CHEQUE BOOKS, TO MOBILE PAYMENTS ON THE MOVE AND TRANSACTIONS AT THE PRESS OF A BUTTON. WHY SHOULD INVESTMENT TRUSTS BE ANY DIFFERENT?"

HOW TRUSTS
ARE EVOLVING

ALEX DENNY, *head of investment trusts at Fidelity International, explains how the investment trust market is changing and how management groups respond when developing or expanding their range.*

Fidelity has a huge range of open-ended funds – why bother with investment trusts at all?

Alex Denny: We like to offer investors a choice. Each of the five investment trusts we have launched, over the past 30 years, has carved out its own niche. Collectively, they represent a well-diversified exposure to different regional markets – UK, Europe, Asia, Japan, and China – and they complement our open-ended fund range. We do not have a particular 'style' though. For example, FIDELITY EUROPEAN VALUES is a quality large-cap growth mandate, while FIDELITY ASIAN VALUES has a small-cap value bias.

Generally, our investment trusts seek to make use of the structural advantages of the product – through gearing, shorting, hedging, and exposure to small cap and unlisted stocks – in ways that our open-ended funds do not. The extent to which each trust does so is determined by the board, and the manager, and also reflects the results of engagement with shareholders.

We are fortunate that all our trusts have been able to sustain a clear and distinctive strategy, over the years. Assuming the strategy is sound in theory, and executed efficiently, there has been no need to change the approach. In 25 years, FIDELITY SPECIAL VALUES, for example, has had just three managers: Anthony Bolton, Sanjeev Shah, and (since 2012) Alex Wright. All three have followed the same value/contrarian investment approach, seeking to identify companies which have become undervalued by the market.

Once established, consistency in a trust's investment strategy is hugely valuable. The Special Values approach, originally pioneered by Anthony Bolton, has returned 1,809% since its launch in 1994. That is 12.6% per year over 25 years.

An equivalent investment in the FTSE All-Share index would have returned 499% (7.5% per year). If it ain't broke, don't fix it!

Do you accept that it is becoming more difficult to launch equity investment trusts?

AD: It has definitely become harder to launch a vanilla equity-focused investment trust than in the past. The cost advantage trusts once enjoyed, compared to open-ended funds, has largely been eliminated, and regulatory and structural market changes mean that you need to raise more money to make a trust viable than you did before. So, it is a more competitive and crowded space than it was when we launched our original trusts. Investors also expect a liquidity premium. They ask why they should invest in a closed-end structure, with additional broker fees, and discount volatility.

If the investment strategy is good enough to offset those factors, however, then a trust can still launch. If the new trust is just a clone of an open-ended fund, it probably won't be successful at IPO. You can see that there are successful investment trusts, which are run in an identical way to an open-ended fund, but trade at a discount. After launch, the discount may provide investors with a more attractive entry point than the open-ended fund, but it has to be launched first. There is an element of Catch 22 about this state of affairs!

In what circumstances would you consider launching a new trust?

AD: There are a number of really interesting and exciting areas that we have been exploring. I believe the correct way to approach launching a trust is the same as any other type of investment. It must be led by a client need or outcome. This will often, but not always, be coupled with evidence of client demand. If a solution is truly innovative, there may be no clients asking for a product they have not even thought of yet. (Did anyone know they wanted a car, or an iPhone, before they saw one?)

There has been a lot of talk in the last couple of years about vertical integration within financial services. What that means is that the lines between asset managers, pension providers, wealth managers, advisers, and platforms, are becoming increasingly blurred. Naturally, we think that Fidelity is well positioned to provide some of these complete investment solutions, having businesses in each of these areas already.

The investment trust industry can, and should, be adapting to this new, emerging world. There are several ways of doing so. Many investment solutions, such as targeted retirement pathways, or risk-targeted funds, need specific building blocks – meaning funds with different volatility and return profiles. There is no reason why investment trusts cannot compete in this space.

Trusts can also provide a 'pure' exposure to alternative asset classes, which cannot easily be accessed directly by many open-ended funds. Working closely with wealth managers and fund providers, investment trust managers are always on the lookout for potential demand for particular types of asset. The job, then, is to create a listed and liquid solution. Many of these products are becoming popular with individual investors looking either for income, or to diversify their portfolios.

Beyond that, I believe there are circumstances where a listed vehicle may be ideal for providing an all-in-one solution – making use of its wider investment powers, suitability for long-term or long-duration exposures, better governance, and flexibility in dividend retention/creation, to compete directly with other guided or structured products. This is an area of the market where investment trust managers have been absent, and it could be an exciting area for innovation.

When considering a new equity launch, is it more important to have a star fund manager to run it, or a new and exciting strategy idea?

AD: It is unlikely that we would launch an investment trust simply because we have a rising star manager, and want to create a clone of an existing fund. If there are specific benefits we could deliver to clients, by adapting an existing strategy, then we may do so, but only if the structure is an obvious fit. There are lessons to be learnt from the Woodford saga, both about the pitfalls of star manager culture, and the unsuitability of open-ended funds for illiquid assets.

Fidelity has a good pedigree in small and micro-cap stocks, as well as pre-IPO and early-stage venture capital investment. We also have great teams in real estate, and other specialist areas. We do not currently have investment trusts that use this expertise directly. If there is a benefit from combining these capabilities with a proven equity strategy, we would certainly consider it when developing new trust solutions.

It is worth noting, however, that the largest launch in recent years has been the SMITHSON INVESTMENT TRUST (SSON), which raised a record £822 million for what is a fairly traditional global equity investment mandate. Describing it as traditional should not be perceived as a criticism. Its success is a reminder that investors still appreciate that investment trusts are great vehicles for mainstream asset classes too.

The reason that SMITHSON was able to raise so much money from investors is, clearly, partly down to the reputation and track record of Terry Smith, the founder of Fundsmith. But there was also a perceived gap, in the global sector, for a trust with its particular style of growth investing. As long as you are offering something different and desirable, the IPO market is still open for the right product.

Would you try to launch a trust with a similar mandate to Fidelity Special Values today?

AD: No, probably not. Not because there cannot be great funds in this area, but because there are already some great ones in the space, of which FIDELITY SPECIAL VALUES is one. Launching new start-ups into a crowded, established space, where there are already good managers, is difficult for the reasons already mentioned. That is why a lot of the new launches, these days, are focused on new areas.

Many of the newcomers have been in the alternatives space. A number have obtained a high profile, and some of them are certainly interesting and different. Who could resist willing HIPGNOSIS SONGS FUND (SONG) onto success, whether an investor or not, if for no other reason than the idea of a music royalties fund being so cool? We will have to wait and see whether it works out well or not, but it is symptomatic of the innovative solutions that trusts can offer.

Fidelity Special Values uses gearing – what is the Fidelity approach to that?

AD: All of our trusts, including FIDELITY SPECIAL VALUES, have the ability to use gearing, and believe that gearing can add value over the longer term. The approaches used by the managers of each trust vary in specific detail but, generally, their exposure to the market is driven by their confidence at that time, or by the valuations of the stocks in which they invest. In practice, this means that gearing increases after market corrections, and tends to be lower when markets have sharply accelerated, or when there are specific risks.

FIDELITY SPECIAL VALUES has tended to be geared for the past few years but, at the time of writing, while UK markets have remained strong on sterling weakness, gearing has been reduced significantly in light of the continuing uncertainty over Brexit. That might change if, and when, Brexit finally happens.

This hybrid approach of strategic and tactical gearing requires a flexible approach to implementation and, for this reason, we generally use contracts for difference (CFDs) to gain additional exposure to the market – at a lower upfront cost than purchasing direct equity exposure with drawn-down debt. CFDs are a form of collateralised debt, where the credit exposure of the bank is limited to the overnight change in value of the stock.

The total cost of this kind of gearing is relatively low. In addition, it means that the trusts only pay for gearing when it is employed, as opposed to a traditional bank loan, debenture, or other long-term debt, where interest is paid on the gross sum, whether or not it is actually invested. Fidelity also has a well-established derivatives, hedging, and shorting capability, which is used to varying degrees across our trusts in line with the wishes of the boards and shareholders.

Has the make-up of your shareholder base changed over the years?

AD: Fidelity's existing investment trusts offer relatively mainstream equity market exposure, and the shareholder base reflects this. The trusts are very popular with retail investors, mainly through platforms (which now represent over one third of all share ownership), and with wealth managers investing for their clients. There is also growing interest from the financial adviser market, but this is starting from a relatively small base. Historically, defined-benefit pension assets accounted for a significant portion of the register but, unsurprisingly, these have become negligible in more recent times. Until 2011, Fidelity, in common with some other firms, ran our own 'share plans' – offering easy access to our investment trusts through a dedicated investment account. The holdings in those share plans were closed and transferred to Fidelity Personal Investing, as the online share dealing capabilities of platforms improved to such a point, that the share plan (which was paid for by all shareholders, irrespective of whether they used the service) was no longer needed.

It is a little bit different with the growing proportion of alternative asset trusts, where a greater proportion of ownership comes from fund of fund, and multi-asset, portfolio managers and institutions.

What would you most like to see happen to the investment trust market?

AD: We have been banging the drum, for some time now, about the need to widen the market for investment trusts to the pension industry. It is very rare for anyone with a defined-contribution pension to be able to invest in investment trusts, despite their long and proven track record as long-term investments. Pension trustees have had a difficult time trying to add investment trusts to the range of options open to their fund investors, often impeded by structural barriers such as inadequate platform infrastructure. Capacity constraints have also been cited as a concern in some quarters (enormous pension funds swamping relatively small investment trusts, for instance), as well as general nervousness that investors may not understand how trusts work – the discount, gearing, and so on. There is a big education job to be done, and progress is slow, but we are very much on the case. It could greatly expand the market for investment trusts, if we succeed.

Remove	Name ▲	Year to date return(%) ▼	1 year annualised(%) ▼	3 years annualised(%) ▼	5 years annualised(%) ▼	10 years annualised(%) ▼
✕	Fidelity Asian Values PLC	1.47	11.26	7.52	14.06	10.32
✕	Fidelity China Special Situations PLC	14.38	13.66	5.44	14.88	–
✕	Fidelity European Values PLC	22.55	16.90	13.09	14.32	10.14
✕	Fidelity Japan Trust PLC	22.05	3.33	15.35	18.85	11.98
✕	Fidelity Special Values PLC	18.93	7.78	12.42	13.05	11.13

Source: Association of Investment Companies (AIC), Morningstar, as at 15 October 2019.

ALEX DENNY *has been Head of Investment Trusts at Fidelity International since 2017.*

ANALYSING INVESTMENT TRUSTS

by JONATHAN DAVIS

THERE WAS A time when getting hold of good data about investment trusts was quite difficult. Brokers' research was not widely available and investment platforms did not offer much coverage of closed-ended funds. Magazines and newspapers published weekly or monthly prices and some other bits of information, but often not much more. Specialist websites such as FE Trustnet (which originated many years ago as a broking firm's investment trust research centre), Citywire and Morningstar provide lots of data, but while all of them are very useful, providing news and analysis these days as well as numbers, they have not always been the easiest sites to navigate.

The good news is that the industry's trade body, the Association of Investment Companies, has taken it upon itself to maintain an excellent and comprehensive database of investment trust information, sourced from Morningstar and Financial Express (the owner of Trustnet). The AIC website (theaic.co.uk) is updated continuously with news and performance data, as well as providing a link to the relevant website of fund management groups and (where they have their own) the trust's own sites.

All of this reflects the fact that everyone in the fund business recognises that increasing numbers of private investors are becoming interested in investment trusts as an option for their savings and investments. Research shows that investment trust shareholders tend to have larger sums to invest and are also more sophisticated than the average investor in open-ended funds.

More and more of these so-called self-directed investors use platforms such as Hargreaves Lansdown (the market leader), Interactive Investor, AJ Bell and The Share Centre, to hold their ISAs and SIPP money. The platforms in turn have responded by adding more information about investment trusts themselves, including interactive charting tools and sometimes research as well.

In this section I give some examples of the kind of information that is available on the AIC website and comment briefly on how it can be used. My advice is that any would-be investor in investment trusts should make it a first stop when embarking on research. I would also suggest registering with some of the other websites that track investment trusts in order to see what they too have to offer.

It may be, for example, that you find the charting tools on one site better or easier to use than on another, and there is no harm in using both when researching a new investment idea. You should always supplement this by reading the annual and interim reports issued by the trusts themselves. Publishing formally audited financial statements signed off by a legally accountable board of directors is one of the great safeguards that investment company shareholders enjoy.

In addition to the AIC website illustrations, this reference section of the handbook includes a number of other tables and data and finally a directory of the largest investment trusts, drawn from different sources. The aim of this is to provide you with a starting point for further research. Each entry gives the trust's stock market ticker, its name, the sector it is in and the management company or investment adviser. The directory also shows the income each trust provided (the historic dividend yield) and its approximate size, measured by its total assets (all data as at 30 September 2019). You can use Google or another search engine to track down the trusts' own websites, or use the comprehensive list of trust website addresses provided by the AIC on its website.

USING THE AIC WEBSITE

Sectors

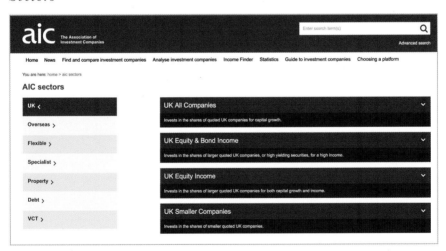

If you go to the home page and click on statistics the first item in the dropdown menu that reaches is a broad categorisation of sectors.* Each of these main sectors is broken down further into sub-sectors. The UK sector, shown here, has four sub-sectors, and there is a further dropdown menu to show the component companies in each one. Below is the list of companies in the UK All Companies sub-sector. One of the first observations you might make is that the number of

---

* The AIC tells me the layout of the home page may change slightly in 2020.

companies in each sector is quite small compared to the much larger universe of open-ended funds with a similar objective.

Individual trusts

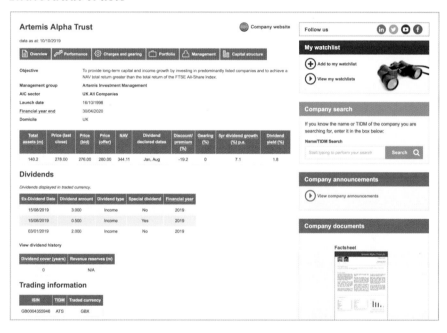

Clicking on each company name in turn will lead you to a page that provides a quick summary of what the trust does, including its dividend history, with a sidebar that has links to the trust's website, any announcements it has made recently and also the company's latest monthly factsheet and most recent annual and interim reports. The example used here is ARTEMIS ALPHA, one of the smaller trusts in the UK All Companies sector (it just happens to be the first name in the list). You can add this trust or any other trusts you are interested in to a watchlist as you go along, so that you can find your way back to the listing the next time you go to the AIC website. The tabs underneath the trust's name provide much more detail about the trust.

Performance

The first tab, 'Performance', links to a page with a chart of how the trust's share price and net asset value (NAV) have grown over the years. The difference between the two is the discount or premium at which the shares are trading. You can adjust the time period over which performance is shown – the longer the better, in general – and compare the trust's performance to its AIC sector. The share price and NAV performance figures are also shown in numerical form, as a table. The example used in this case is FIDELITY SPECIAL VALUES, one of the largest in the UK All Companies sector, with assets of just under £800 million and a track record that stretches back to 1994.

The graph shows, in this instance, how the share price and NAV of the trust have generally remained quite close together. The little graph at the bottom illustrates this in more detail. It shows that the discount (the difference between the NAV and the share price) bottomed in 2012 at around 15% when the fund manager changed and has since gradually moved back toward zero. At times the trust has traded at a premium to NAV, reflecting its generally strong performance and investor demand for more shares.

Comparing track records

Share type	Price (last close)	Price (bid)	Price (offer)	NAV	Discount/premium (%)	5yr dividend growth (%) p.a.	Dividend yield (%)
Ordinary Share	249.50	249.50	251.00	254.12	-1.8	9.4	2.1

Performance (%)

Ordinary Share	1 month	3 months	6 months	1 year	3 years	5 years	7 years	10 years
Share price total return	-2.9	-3.3	-4.7	-1.6	32.3	66.7	159.8	167.1
Share price capital return	-2.9	-3.3	-5.5	-3.7	24.6	50.6	125.2	118.3
NAV total return	-2.7	-3.0	-0.9	0.2	18.9	56.9	125.4	157.1
NAV capital return	-2.8	-3.0	-2.0	-1.9	12.3	42.5	97.8	113.7

Sector performance (%)

UK All Companies	1 month	3 months	6 months	1 year	3 years	5 years	7 years	10 years
Share price total return	-2.1	-1.0	-2.3	5.6	28.5	63.8	125.0	181.8
NAV total return	-1.9	-2.0	-0.8	5.4	22.7	57.8	110.1	170.4

Discrete annual performance (%)

Ordinary Share	10/10/14 - 15	10/10/15 - 16	10/10/16 - 17	10/10/17 - 18	10/10/18 - 19
Share price total return	25.6	0.4	25.7	6.9	-1.6
NAV total return	16.6	13.2	17.5	1.1	0.2

Volatility

Ordinary Share	3 months	6 months	1 year	3 years	5 years
Share price volatility	19.69	16.70	17.69	15.03	17.85
NAV volatility	11.81	10.33	11.92	9.82	12.20

Comparing this track record (for FIDELITY SPECIAL VALUES) to that of the average trust in the AIC's UK All Companies sector shows that its shares have outperformed this peer group over three, five and seven years, but not over one year and ten years. You would have to go to other online sources to discover whether the trust has done better than its preferred benchmark, which is the FTSE All-Share index (it has).

Charges and gearing

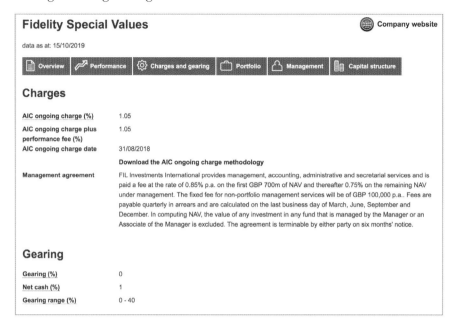

The next tab give details of the trust's charges, what the company pays for the services of the portfolio manager and some other costs, and gearing, whether it uses debt or other instruments to 'ginger up' its returns. The figure quoted here is the ongoing charge figure (or ratio), known as the OCR, which in this case is 1.05%. This means that the annual cost of running the trust's portfolio is a little over 1% of the assets of the fund.

Put another way, it means that the return the shareholder receives is around 1% per annum less than the return which the investments in the portfolio themselves have generated. That is the (approximate) cost of having your money managed for you by the trust. It is important to be aware that there is more than one way to measure cost of ownership but the OCR is now the one generally adopted by investment trusts.

The lines at the bottom show that this Fidelity trust is currently not using gearing at all, but is allowed to do so, up to a maximum of 40% of the trust's assets (which would be a very aggressive stance to take, and one the trust has never in fact employed). The manager of the trust sometimes will use gearing to improve returns if he is convinced that the market or his favoured investments have become particularly undervalued.

Geographic breakdown

data as at: 30/09/2019

Country	% of total assets
UK	76.2
Cash/Cash Equivalent	11.8
Switzerland	4.6
France	2.3
Ireland	2.3
Netherlands	1.1
Canada	0.8
USA	0.5
Australia	0.4

Top holdings

data as at: 31/07/2019

Investment	% of total assets
Royal Dutch Shell Plc	5.3
CRH PLC	4.9
Pearson Plc	4.3
Roche Holding AG	4.3
Citigroup Inc	3.9
John Laing	3.8
Meggitt PLC	3.3
Phoenix Group Holdings	3.3
BP Plc	3.0
ROYAL BK SCOTLND GRP PLC	3.0

The final tab gives a breakdown of the trust's investments on three different measures, two of which are reproduced here. The geographic and industry breakdown tables are based on the trust's most recently published monthly factsheet. There will also be a list of its top ten individual holdings, as most recently reported. Investment trusts are required to give a complete list of all their holdings at least once a year in their annual report, but vary in how frequently they publish the top ten holdings information. Don't assume therefore that they will still be the same as when you see this information published, given the time lag. It can also be useful to know how the top ten holdings compare to those of the benchmark the trust's performance is being measured against, but this information is not usually provided and cannot always be ascertained.

Data as at: 17/10/2019 | Previous working day | | PDF Archive |

Company name ⇕	Management group ⇕	AIC sector ⇕	Traded currency	Last close price	NAV
Woodford Patient Capital	Woodford Investment Management	Growth Capital	GBX	34.00	0.63
Independent Investment Trust	Independent Investment Trust	UK All Companies	GBX	538.00	5.48
Fair Oaks Income 2017	Fair Oaks Capital	Debt - Structured Finance	USD	0.76	0.78
Highbridge Tactical Credit	Highbridge Capital Management	Hedge Funds	GBX	201.00	2.17
Trian Investors 1	Trian Investors Management	Financials	GBX	101.50	1.03
Scottish Mortgage	Baillie Gifford	Global	GBX	487.40	5.08
JPMorgan American	J.P. Morgan Asset Management	North America	GBX	462.00	4.83
Invesco Perpetual Select Managed Liquidity	Invesco Asset Management	Liquidity Funds	GBX	101.50	1.05
City of London	Janus Henderson Investors	UK Equity Income	GBX	421.00	4.07
Blackstone/GSO Loan Financing	Blackstone/GSO Loan Financing	Debt - Structured Finance	EUR	0.78	0.90
Henderson Smaller Companies	Janus Henderson Investors	UK Smaller Companies	GBX	880.00	9.35
Aurora	Phoenix Asset Management	UK All Companies	GBX	208.00	2.06
Scottish Investment Trust	Scottish Investment Trust	Global	GBX	826.00	8.92

Another powerful feature of the AIC interactive statistics section is that it allows investors to filter the data to compare and contrast a range of data for any number of individual trusts or sectors. By clicking on individual columns in each table it is possible to filter and rank the data within any group of trusts you have selected.

Here is an example of one such exercise: ranking all the trusts in a selection of sectors by their ongoing charges ratio (OCR). As noted earlier, the cost of ownership is one, but only one, of a number of factors to look at when researching investment options. Note that the data is calculated on a historic, backward-looking basis, and it is important to look at the date when the information was last gathered.

Some of the other metrics which can be compared across sectors are: the discount or premium at which the shares currently trade; the level of gearing

Previous month end data will be available on the 6th working day of each month

Discount / premium (%) ⇕	SPTR 5yr (%) ⇕	NAVTR 3yr (%) ⇕	NAVTR 5yr (%) ⇕	5yr div grth (%pa) ⇕	Div yld (%) ⇕	Ongoing charge (%) ⮝	Ongoing charge inc Perf fee (%) ⇕	Ongoing charge date
-48.75	-	-32.43	-	-	0.03	0.17	0.17	31/12/2018
-3.76	116.17	47.17	108.77	6.96	1.86	0.21	0.21	30/11/2018
-3.60	34.24	22.07	42.13	-	14.72	0.25	0.25	31/12/2018
-6.77	8.71	3.84	12.07	-	-	0.28	0.28	31/12/2018
-1.35	-	-	-	-	-	0.28	0.28	31/12/2018
-3.45	131.26	57.92	147.65	1.54	0.64	0.37	0.37	31/03/2019
-4.22	99.77	38.50	111.50	19.21	1.41	0.38	0.38	31/12/2018
-2.90	0.67	2.11	1.99	-	0.79	0.39	0.39	31/05/2019
2.90	43.93	16.01	45.48	4.73	4.51	0.39	0.39	30/06/2019
-13.65	19.29	21.39	38.52	-	12.86	0.39	0.39	31/12/2018
-7.05	105.44	31.37	84.27	15.90	2.61	0.42	0.42	31/05/2019
0.18	45.76	31.99	38.30	1.30	1.92	0.44	0.44	31/12/2018
-7.78	71.25	15.43	66.55	12.82	3.05	0.45	0.45	31/10/2018

each trust employs (and the allowable range which the board has set); and the current dividend yield and the annualised rate at which dividends have grown over the previous five years.

There is also an invaluable table on the AIC website, based on research by the Lang Cat consultancy, that shows the annual cost of holding a portfolio of investment trusts on all the leading retail investor platforms. These holding costs come on top of the management fees that the funds you own in an ISA or SIPP will deduct before calculating their latest value.

GETTING HELP

Recognising that it takes some time to get the measure of the AIC's comprehensive statistics section, the AIC statistics department says it welcomes enquiries from private investors; just fill out the email enquiry form on the website.

The largest equity sectors

CONVENTIONAL SECTORS	TOTAL ASSETS (£M)	MARKET CAP (£M)	NUMBER OF COMPANIES	AVERAGE TOTAL ASSETS (£M)	AVERAGE MARKET CAP (£M)
Global	25,031	22,363	15	1,669	1,491
Private Equity	18,941	18,663	18	1,052	1,037
UK Equity Income	12,624	10,881	25	505	435
Flexible Investment	12,058	9,759	18	670	542
Hedge Funds	8,982	5,370	8	1,123	671
Global Emerging Markets	7,381	6,265	13	568	482
UK Smaller Companies	5,864	4,920	23	255	214
Asia Pacific – ex Japan	5,666	4,452	10	567	445
UK All Companies	4,676	3,887	13	360	299
Global Smaller Companies	4,548	4,132	6	758	689
Europe	3,995	3,467	7	571	495
Asia Pacific	3,527	3,120	9	392	347
Global Equity Income	3,509	3,108	5	702	622
North America	2,850	2,438	7	407	348
Japan	2,679	2,162	6	447	360
Asia Pacific Income	2,121	1,992	5	424	398
European Smaller Companies	1,860	1,540	4	465	385
Japanese Smaller Companies	1,091	890	4	273	222
Asia Pacific Smaller Companies	780	669	2	390	335
North American Smaller Companies	384	331	2	192	166
Total	**128,567**	**110,411**	**200**	**643**	**552**

There are no fixed rules for what an investment trust can invest in. The trust's strategy does, however, have to be outlined in a prospectus and approved by shareholders if, as does happen, the board wishes to change that objective at a later date. For convenience, and to help comparative analysis, trusts are grouped into a number of different sectors, based primarily on their investment focus. These are listed here and on the following two pages. It has become conventional to list very specialized investment trusts separately.

The majority of the sector categories are self-explanatory. It is worth noting, however, that individual trusts within each broad sector category will often have somewhat different investment objectives and benchmarks. The 'flexible investment' sector is a recently added one that includes a number of trusts which invest across a broad range of asset classes. Most of these were formerly included in the global sector. In 2019 the AIC reviewed its classification of sectors and introduced a number of changes to its categorisation of Asian trusts and specialist trusts in particular.

A notable feature of the table is that just under 20% of what are sometimes called conventional equity trusts have the UK as their primary investment focus. Investment trusts from the very earliest days have always had a bias towards investment outside the UK and their external focus remains one of the key attractions. ▓

Specialist sectors

SPECIALIST SECTORS	TOTAL ASSETS (£M)	MARKET CAP (£M)
Infrastructure	10,066	11,488
Renewable energy infrastructure	7,758	7,862
Leasing	4,451	1,843
Biotechnology and healthcare	4,377	4,399
Debt – direct lending	4,031	3,503
Technology and media	2,811	2,593
Debt – loans and bonds	2,698	2,562
Debt – structured finance	2,257	2,026
Commodities and natural resources	1,973	1,410
Growth capital	1,497	1,114
Financials	755	690
Environmental	723	672
Insurance & reinsurance	430	231
Royalties	373	409
Utilities	230	159
Liquidity funds	13	11
Total	**44,443**	**40,974**

The specialist sectors are also clearly identified by their name. Unlike the conventional trusts, which are mainly defined by their regional focus, the specialist sectors are grouped by industry. The specialist sector is worth looking at in more detail as it gives a flavour of the wide range of investment strategies which are available once you look beyond the conventional trusts.

It is these trusts, along with those investing in property, hedge funds and private equity, which are now commonly referred to as making up the 'alternative asset' sector. ▪

NUMBER OF COMPANIES	AVG TOTAL ASSETS (£M)	AVG MARKET CAP (£M)	% OF TOTAL ASSETS
6	1,678	1,915	22.6
12	647	655	17.5
6	742	307	10.0
6	729	733	9.8
10	403	350	9.1
4	703	648	6.3
13	208	197	6.1
8	282	253	5.1
8	247	176	4.4
4	374	279	3.4
4	189	173	1.7
3	241	224	1.6
2	215	116	1.0
1	373	409	0.8
2	115	80	0.5
1	13	11	0.0
90	**494**	**455**	**100.0%**

Source: AIC statistics as at 31 August 2019

Property sectors

PROPERTY SECTORS	TOTAL ASSETS (£M)	MARKET CAP (£M)
Property – UK commercial	10,750	7,880
Property – UK residential	2,444	2,089
Property securities	1,614	1,355
Property – Europe	1,520	1,147
Property – debt	915	902
Property – UK healthcare	776	773
Property – rest of world	412	183
Total	**18,431**	**14,328**

VCT sectors

VCT SECTORS	TOTAL ASSETS (£M)	MARKET CAP (£M)
VCT Generalist	3,547	3,315
VCT AIM Quoted	709	659
VCT Specialist: Environmental	174	166
VCT Generalist Pre Qualifying	133	133
VCT Specialist: Media, Leisure & Events	34	12
VCT Specialist: Healthcare & Biotechnology Pre Qualifying	17	17
VCT Specialist: Technology	16	10
VCT Specialist: Healthcare & Biotechnology	3	2
Total	**4,634**	**4,314**

The main distinction in the property sector table is between trusts that invest directly in property (that is, buy and sell the bricks and mortar themselves) and those that invest primarily in the shares of other listed property companies. The former by their nature are less liquid than the latter. Venture capital trusts are specialist investment companies that exist

NUMBER OF COMPANIES	AVG TOTAL ASSETS (£M)	AVG MARKET CAP (£M)	% OF TOTAL ASSETS
19	566	415	58.3%
5	489	418	13.3%
1	1,614	1,355	8.8%
6	253	191	8.2%
4	229	225	5.0%
2	388	387	4.2%
2	206	91	2.2%
39	**473**	**367**	**100.0%**

NUMBER OF COMPANIES	AVG TOTAL ASSETS (£M)	AVG MARKET CAP (£M)	% OF TOTAL ASSETS
40	89	83	76.6%
8	89	82	15.3%
5	35	33	3.8%
2	66	67	2.9%
1	34	12	0.7%
1	17	17	0.4%
4	4	2	0.4%
1	3	2	0.1%
61	**76**	**71**	**100.0%**

Source: AIC statistics as at 31 August 2019

to support companies at an early stage of their development, in return for which shareholders in the VCTs are offered some potentially attractive tax breaks. Most of these trusts will be investing in unlisted securities, although an exception are the AIM VCTs, which mostly own shares listed on the Alternative Investment Market. ■

Largest management groups

MANAGEMENT GROUP	TOTAL ASSETS (£M)	MARKET CAP (£M)
Baillie Gifford	14,580	13,381
J.P. Morgan Asset Management	11,392	9,679
BMO Global Asset Management	10,173	8,353
Aberdeen Standard Investments	9,828	8,076
3i Group	8,962	10,669
Janus Henderson Investors	6,732	5,904
Pershing Square Capital Management	6,417	3,272
InfraRed Capital Partners	4,424	4,914
FIL Investments International	4,317	3,405
Frostrow Capital	4,186	4,095
RIT Capital Partners	3,528	3,293
Invesco Asset Management	3,524	2,880
BlackRock Investment Management	3,432	2,811
Greencoat Capital	3,169	2,669
Tritax Management	3,153	2,785
Willis Towers Watson	2,995	2,633
Polar Capital Holdings	2,727	2,414
Schroder Investment Management	2,641	2,333
Witan Investment Services	2,374	2,048
Amedeo Air Four Plus	2,311	559
Total 20 largest groups	**110,865**	**96,174**
Total all management groups	**197,456**	**170,979**

The management groups with the most trust mandates are listed here. The trust sector is a competitive one, in which no management group has a dominant position. The 20 largest groups manage just over half (56%) of total industry assets, but only five firms out of more than 400 in total manage more than ten trusts. The average trust among the 20 largest management groups has £873m in assets, compared to the industry average of £495m. In 2018 Baillie Gifford, a private partnership based in Edinburgh, became the largest player in the investment trust sector for the first time, overtaking

Data sourced from AIC MIR, Morningstar and company announcements.
Data as at 31 August 2019

NUMBER OF COMPANIES	AVG TOTAL ASSETS (£M)	AVG MARKET CAP (£M)	% OF TOTAL ASSETS
10	1,458	1,338	7.4%
21	542	461	5.8%
10	1,017	835	5.2%
23	427	351	5.0%
1	8,962	10,669	4.5%
13	518	454	3.4%
1	6,417	3,272	3.2%
2	2,212	2,457	2.2%
5	863	681	2.2%
5	837	819	2.1%
1	3,528	3,293	1.8%
9	392	320	1.8%
9	381	312	1.7%
2	1,585	1,334	1.6%
2	1,576	1,393	1.6%
1	2,995	2,633	1.5%
3	909	805	1.4%
6	440	389	1.3%
2	1,187	1,024	1.2%
1	2,311	559	1.2%
127	**873**	**757**	**56.1%**
399	**495**	**429**	**100.0%**

3i and JPMorgan. Two of the larger players in the trust market, Aberdeen Asset Management and Standard Life, merged in 2018 and have the largest number of trusts between them. These range from large investment management firms to small specialist boutiques. In the case of the big firms, they will typically launch and market their own trusts to investors as well as providing portfolio management and carrying out administrative functions, often centralising them. Smaller firms, especially those managing specialist trusts, by contrast may only have one or more funds that they look after. ■

The largest trusts

		SHARE CLASS (£M)		GROSS ASS. (£M)
		MKT CAP	NET ASS.	
III	3i Group	11,351	8,171	9,046
SMT	Scottish Mortgage	7,476	7,657	8,193
PSH	Pershing Square Holdings	3,394	4,641	4,641
FCIT	F&C IT	3,838	4,044	4,327
RCP	RIT Capital Partners	3,325	3,051	3,228
HICL	HICL Infrastructure	2,977	2,809	3,009
ATST	Alliance Trust	2,636	2,790	2,930
BBOX	Tritax Big Box REIT	2,554	2,562	3,689
INPP	International Public Partnerships	2,284	2,221	2,438
BION	BB Biotech	2,773	2,200	2,200
TEM	Templeton Emerging Markets	1,935	2,160	2,182
CLDN	Caledonia	1,664	2,033	2,033
PCT	Polar Capital Technology	1,879	2,004	2,004
3IN	3i Infrastructure	2,395	1,969	2,022
WTAN	Witan	1,881	1,940	2,134
MNKS	Monks	1,975	1,909	2,005
FGT	Finsbury Growth & Income	1,892	1,879	1,897
UKW	Greencoat UK Wind	2,179	1,870	2,505
MRC	Mercantile	1,670	1,838	1,857
TFG	Tetragon Financial	1,406	1,835	1,835

While some investment trusts are managed directly by their board of directors, the great majority delegate the management of their portfolios to specialist fund managers, employed on annual or multi-year management contracts with a mandate to meet the trust's investment objectives.

Excluding the special case of 3i, which is a different kind of institution, the investment trust with the greatest net assets, SCOTTISH MORTGAGE, accounted for around 4.0% of the industry total as at 30 September 2019. The 20 largest individual trusts on this measure accounted for just under 40% of total industry assets.

In contrast, more than 100 trusts had less than £50m in assets, although this figure includes a large number of venture capital trusts, which are invariably (and by their nature) much smaller on average. The main takeaway for investors is that the investment trust sector is a genuinely diverse one, which offers a range of different kinds of opportunities.

A majority of the 50 largest trusts in the sector have been operating for many years, but that is by no means universally the case. PERSHING SQUARE, HICL INFRASTRUCTURE and TRITAX BIG BOX have all been launched or listed on the London market relatively recently.

At the same time there are regular departures from the investment trust universe, as funds either close down or return capital to shareholders, typically (though not invariably) as a result of indifferent performance or where the trust has a predetermined wind-up date. The way the universe of listed trusts looks can therefore change significantly from decade to decade. ▓

Vintage investment trusts

TICKER	COMPANY	LAUNCH DATE	SHARE CLASS £M	
			MKT CAP	NET ASS.
FCIT	F&C IT	1868	3,838	4,044
INV	Investment Company	1868	15	17
SAIN	Scottish American	1873	611	586
DIG	Dunedin Income Gwth	1873	400	436
JAM	JPMorgan American	1881	1,005	1,054
MRC	Mercantile	1884	1,670	1,838
SCIN	Scottish IT	1887	614	675
JPGI	JPMorgan Global Growth & Income	1887	456	440
ATST	Alliance Trust	1888	2,636	2,790
BNKR	Bankers	1888	1,165	1,185
AGT	AVI Global	1889	823	924
LWDB	Law Debenture	1889	698	774
BGSC	BMO Global Smaller Cos	1889	828	887
EDIN	Edinburgh IT	1889	1,092	1,228
MRCH	Merchants	1889	543	544
CTY	City of London	1891	1,606	1,581
ADIG	Aberdeen Diversified Inc & Gwth	1898	349	380
TRY	TR Property	1905	1,343	1,413
MYI	Murray International	1907	1,546	1,541
SMT	Scottish Mortgage	1909	7,476	7,657
WTAN	Witan	1909	1,881	1,940
MAJE	Majedie	1910	136	161
HAN	Hansa Trust	1912	74	111
HANA	Hansa Trust A	1912	150	223
BUT	Brunner	1927	355	393
MNKS	Monks	1929	1,975	1,909
JETG	JPMorgan European - Growth	1929	197	227
HFEL	Henderson Far East Income	1930	486	475
HEFT	Henderson European Focus	1947	268	299
CLDN	Caledonia	1905	1,664	2,033
THRG	BlackRock Throgmorton Trust	1905	417	429
MUT	Murray Income	1923	559	590
FGT	Finsbury Growth & Income	1926	1,892	1,879
TMPL	Temple Bar	1926	843	893
JFJ	JPMorgan Japanese	1927	711	803
SHRS	Shires Income	1929	80	82
III	3i Group	1945	11,351	8,171
KIT	Keystone IT	1954	208	253
RIII	Rights & Issues IT	1962	146	158
LWI	Lowland	1963	346	380
JCH	JPMorgan Claverhouse	1963	398	414
CGT	Capital Gearing	1963	445	436

Source: Numis Securities
Data as at 30 September 2019

	YIELD (%)	BID/OFFER SPREAD (%)	(DISCOUNT)/ PREMIUM 1-YEAR AVE
	1.6	0.2%	-1.6
	5.3	2.6%	-11.3
	2.8	0.8%	4.1
	4.6	1.0%	-8.2
	1.4	0.3%	-4.8
	3.1	0.3%	-10.5
	2.7	0.4%	-9.0
	4.8	0.7%	2.1
	1.7	0.2%	-5.4
	2.2	0.3%	-2.0
	1.7	0.4%	-9.4
	3.3	0.7%	-9.6
	1.2	0.3%	-3.3
	4.7	0.2%	-10.1
	5.4	0.7%	-0.4
	4.5	0.2%	1.7
	4.9	0.8%	-3.6
	3.2	0.2%	-3.2
	4.4	0.3%	0.0
	0.6	0.2%	1.9
	2.3	0.3%	-2.4
	4.5	1.7%	-15.3
	1.7	3.2%	-27.6
	1.7	3.9%	-30.1
	2.3	1.6%	-9.8
	0.2	0.2%	3.3
	3.1	1.3%	-12.0
	6.0	0.9%	2.2
	2.5	1.3%	-9.0
	2.0	0.2%	-16.9
	1.8	1.2%	-5.9
	4.0	0.6%	-6.2
	1.8	0.2%	0.5
	4.1	0.3%	-4.7
	1.1	0.3%	-8.9
	5.0	1.5%	-1.5
	3.0	0.1%	22.9
	3.1	0.7%	-12.8
	1.7	1.9%	-7.0
	4.6	0.9%	-5.6
	4.0	0.7%	-1.6
	0.5	0.4%	2.0

The first investment trust, FOREIGN & COLONIAL, was formed in 1868 and continues in existence today. It celebrated its 150th anniversary in 2018. A number of other investment companies have also been around for many years. Twelve can trace their histories back to the 19th century.

This is a list of some of the oldest vintage trusts which are still in existence. There is no obvious correlation between age and size or quality of trust, although the mere fact of having survived for so long indicates that a trust has at least successfully established a niche in the market.

A number of these trusts were started by wealthy or successful families looking to invest their fortunes in a tax-efficient manner, but have since expanded to include outside investors as well. The first Scottish investment trust, DUNEDIN INCOME GROWTH, was founded to provide a home for the savings of wealthy textile merchants in Dundee. ▨

Long-serving managers

FUND MANAGER	COMPANY	TICKER	MANAGER START DATE
Angela Lascelles	Value and Income	VIN	Jul-81
Peter Spiller	Capital Gearing	CGT	Jan-82
Simon Knott	Rights & Issues IT	RIII	Jan-84
Jacob Rothschild	RIT Capital Partners	RCP	Jun-88
James Thom	Aberdeen New Dawn	ABD	May-89
Andrew Lebus	Pantheon International	PIN	May-89
Nic Humphries	HgCapital Trust	HGT	Dec-89
Adithep Vanabriksha	Aberdeen New Thai	ANW	Dec-89
James Henderson	Lowland	LWI	Jan-90
Partners	Aberforth Smaller Companies	ASL	Dec-90
Job Curtis	City of London	CTY	Jan-91
Daniel Koller	BB Biotech	BION	Nov-93
Chris Mills	North Atlantic Smaller Companies	NAS	Jan-94
Katie Potts	Herald	HRI	Feb-94
Austin Forey	JPMorgan Emerging Markets	JMG	Jun-94
Francesco Conte	JPMorgan European Smaller Cos	JESC	Feb-95
Chris Mills	Oryx International Growth	OIG	Mar-95
Sven Borho	Worldwide Healthcare	WWH	Apr-95
Dominic Scriven	Vietnam Enterprise Investments	VEIL	Jul-95
Hugh Young	Aberdeen Standard Asia Focus	AAS	Oct-95
Matthew Dobbs	Schroder AsiaPacific	SDP	Nov-95
Jonathan Woolf	British American	BAF	Dec-95

Source: Numis Securities
Data as at 31 August 2019

Some individual trusts are also notable for having long-serving managers who have been running the trust's investments for many years. In some cases the managers also have significant personal shareholdings in the trust. This is typically regarded as a good omen for other shareholders, since it establishes a close alignment of interest between the manager and the shareholders.

Because fund management is an extremely well-paid profession, the fact that a manager continues to manage a trust after many years in harness can often be interpreted also as demonstrating exceptional commitment to the business. While some successful fund managers retire early to do other things, those who remain in post for decades are typically such enthusiasts for the challenge of investing that they cannot think of anything better to do with their time.

Against that sometimes situations arise where managers have such a large personal shareholding in a trust that they effectively control the running of the company, and may not always make the interests of other shareholders as high a priority as they should. They are effectively being paid to look after their own money.

Long-term performers

20 years

COMPANY	SECTOR
JPMorgan Russian Securities Ord	Country Specialist: Europe ex UK
Aberdeen New Thai Ord	Country Specialist: Asia Pacific ex Japan
Aberdeen Standard Asia Focus Ord	Asia Pacific Smaller Companies
Scottish Oriental Smaller Cos Ord	Asia Pacific Smaller Companies
Worldwide Healthcare Ord	Biotechnology & Healthcare
Rights & Issues Investment Trust Ord	UK Smaller Companies
TR Property Ord	Property Securities
HgCapital Trust Ord	Private Equity
JPMorgan European Smaller Comp Ord	European Smaller Companies
BlackRock Latin American Ord	Latin America

30 years

COMPANY	SECTOR
Rights & Issues Investment Trust Ord	UK Smaller Companies
ICG Enterprise Trust Ord	Private Equity
Templeton Emerging Mkts Invmt Tr TEMIT	Global Emerging Markets
Genesis Emerging Markets Fund	Global Emerging Markets
Scottish Mortgage Ord	Global
Pantheon International Ord PLC	Private Equity
North Atlantic Smaller Cos Ord	Global Smaller Companies
Canadian General Investments Unit	North America
BlackRock Smaller Companies Ord	UK Smaller Companies
AVI Global Trust Ord	Global

Longevity means that a fair number of trusts have survived long enough to post 20 and 30 year track records. These tables list the best performing trusts over those periods, measured as both the value of £100 invested and as a compound annualized rate of return, with dividends reinvested. The average annualised rate of return achieved by trusts that have survived this

Source: derived from AIC
Returns to 31 August 2019

MANAGEMENT GROUP	VALUE OF £100 INVESTED (TOTAL RETURN)	APPROX CAGR (% P.A)
JP Morgan Asset Management (UK) Ltd	£2,859	18.3%
Aberdeen Standard Investments	£1,833	15.7%
Aberdeen Standard Investments	£1,637	15.0%
First State Investments (UK) Ltd	£1,538	14.6%
Frostrow Capital LLP	£1,338	13.8%
Discretionary Unit Fund Managers	£1,282	13.6%
BMO Asset Management (Holdings) plc	£1,254	13.5%
Hg Pooled Management Limited	£1,247	13.4%
JP Morgan Asset Management (UK) Ltd	£1,107	12.8%
BlackRock	£1,050	12.5%

MANAGEMENT GROUP	VALUE OF £100 INVESTED (TOTAL RETURN)	APPROX CAGR (% P.A)
Discretionary Unit Fund Managers	£7,531	15.5%
Intermediate Capital Group PLC	£3,916	13.0%
Franklin Templeton	£3,757	12.8%
Genesis Asset Managers, LLP	£2,611	11.5%
Baillie Gifford & Co Limited.	£2,493	11.3%
Pantheon Ventures (UK) LLP	£2,493	11.3%
Harwood Capital LLP	£2,358	11.1%
MMA	£2,242	10.9%
BlackRock Investment Management (UK) Ltd.	£2,118	10.7%
Asset Value Investors	£2,112	10.7%

long is 8.2% over 20 years and 8.9% over 30 years, although this includes a wide range of outcomes and risk profiles. Because of the magical effect of compounding, any trust that can grow at 10% every year will roughly double in value every seven years. The longer the period, the harder this is to achieve. ▨

Key sector metrics

SECTOR	MARKET CAP (£M)	NAV TOTAL RETURN (10–YR) (%)
North America	2,476	265.8
Sector specialist	13,760	242.4
Japan	3,152	219.2
Global	39,510	206.6
Europe	5,016	199.2
UK	20,811	186.1
Asia Pacific	10,415	182.8
Private equity	22,062	178.7
Infrastructure	16,350	176.2
Debt	13,656	168.5
Property	29,718	107.2
Emerging markets	8,486	104.6
Hedge funds	5,283	63.9

Different sectors have very different characteristics, reflecting the different kinds of asset in which they invest. You can see this by looking at some of the key metrics for the broadest sector groupings.

So, for example, the debt and infrastructure sectors on average have the highest yields but are among the most expensive to own. UK sector trusts have the lowest management charges, and hedge funds and private equity the highest. The level of discount also varies considerably.

These metrics can be usefully compared to the performance figures for the sectors, ranked by NAV performance over the past ten years. Some of the sectors with the highest yields on average have among the the lowest returns (though this is not true of infrastructure), and those with low yields tend to have performed better in NAV terms, though again the correlation is not precise. ▪

	YIELD (%)	(DISCOUNT)/ PREMIUM (%)	OCR INC PERF FEE
	1.7	-3.3	0.76%
	2.2	0.7	1.25%
	1.0	-3.2	0.85%
	1.8	-3.2	0.82%
	2.0	-8.3	1.25%
	3.1	-6.2	0.74%
	1.8	-8.6	1.34%
	2.4	6.1	1.46%
	4.7	9.1	2.13%
	7.1	1.2	1.78%
	4.2	-0.2	1.84%
	3.0	-15.1	1.46%
	1.4	-21.8	1.86%

Returning capital

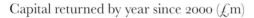

Capital returned by year since 2000 (£m)

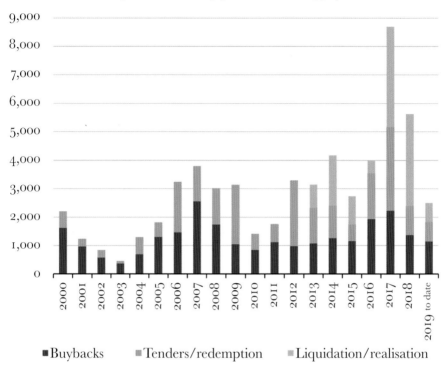

■ Buybacks ■ Tenders/redemption ■ Liquidation/realisation

Note: Excludes liquidations prior to 2013
Source: Morningstar, Numis Securities Research

There can be a number of reasons why a trust decides to return capital to its shareholders. One is to try and limit the discount at which the shares in the trust are trading. Another is because a trust has decided to liquidate itself or offer an exit to shareholders, typically because of a run of poor performance.

Many investment companies have measures in place with which they attempt to control the discount and/or reduce discount volatility. Some trusts give a specific discount target, a level at which they promise to take remedial action. Others content themselves with a more modest statement of intent to keep the discount in mind.

These measures include buying back shares in the market, making tender offers and agreeing to hold a continuation vote at some date in the future. It is fairly routine for investment companies to adopt the power to buy back their own shares. This requires shareholder approval at a general meeting and more than two-thirds of the companies in the sector have obtained this approval.

There is no doubt that many boards of investment companies are taking discount controls more seriously than in the past. As the chart shows, overall figures for the return of capital have been trending higher in recent years. One reason is the emergence of so-called professional 'activist investors' who buy a block of shares and use that as leverage in trying to force the board of poorly performing trusts to take some action. There have been some notable examples of boards giving in to this kind of pressure, including ALLIANCE TRUST and ELECTRA. ▥

New issues

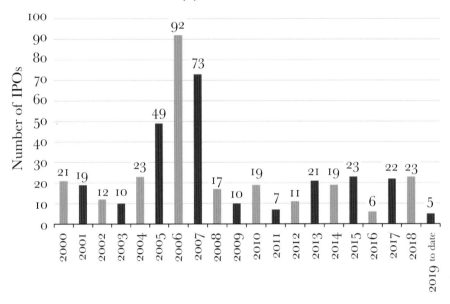

Number of investment company IPOs
by year since 2000

Note: Excludes listings where no new capital is raised.
Source: Numis Securities Research

Whereas buybacks and tender offers reduce the amount of capital invested in the trust sector, in any year they will be offset by a combination of new and secondary issues by other trusts. New trusts are launched on a regular, if cyclical, basis. Certain periods are characterised by a spurt of new issues in a particular segment of the market. Property trusts and hedge funds, for example, were popular in the run up to the financial crisis in 2008. Income-generating trusts from alternative assets, such as infrastructure, have been particularly popular since then. 2019 has been a disappointing year for new launches at the time of writing, with only five completed.

At the same time there are regular departures from the investment trust universe, as funds either close down or return capital to shareholders, typically (though not invariably) as a result of indifferent performance or where the trust has a predetermined wind-up date. The way the universe of listed trusts looks can therefore change significantly from decade to decade.

Some big-name fund managers with strong personal followings have been behind some of the largest recent new trust launches, showing the power of a star name. Examples include Anthony Bolton in 2010 (FIDELITY CHINA SPECIAL SITUATIONS), Terry Smith in 2014 (FUNDSMITH EMERGING EQUITIES) and 2018 (SMITHSON) and Neil Woodford in 2015 (WOODFORD PATIENT CAPITAL). Each one of these raised several hundred million pounds at launch.

A star name is not an automatic guarantee of success, as the Woodford example illustrates. The trust has been the worst performer of all trusts in 2019 and the investment manager Woodford Investment Management resigned as manager after being forced out of business following a series of liquidity issues in its open-ended Woodford Equity Income fund. ▦

Secondary issuance

Secondary issuance by equity mandate trusts in 2019 (Q1–Q3)

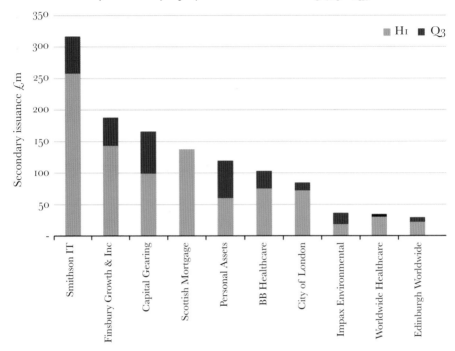

One important difference in the last two decades is that it has become easier for trusts to grow through a process known as 'secondary issuance'. Essentially trusts that are popular with investors can now, provided they have the necessary shareholder approvals, more readily issue additional shares without the need to produce an expensive legal prospectus.

It is nothing like as simple as the daily process by which open-ended funds can issue or cancel units in their funds, but it does enable trusts to tap into additional demand on a regular basis. SCOTTISH MORTGAGE is the most striking example: it has raised an additional £700m of capital in this way since January 2017. Many of the infrastructure funds have also grown rapidly through this route.

Secondary issues can take a number of different forms. The most common are placings of new shares and so-called 'C-share issues'. The first two

(Opposite page) Note: Excludes warrant exercise or ZDP issuance. Source: Numis Securities Research
(Below) Source: Winterflood Securities, Morningstar

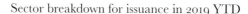

Sector breakdown for issuance in 2019 YTD

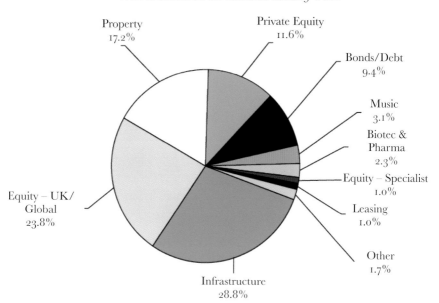

Property 17.2%

Private Equity 11.6%

Bonds/Debt 9.4%

Music 3.1%

Biotec & Pharma 2.3%

Equity – Specialist 1.0%

Leasing 1.0%

Other 1.7%

Equity – UK/ Global 23.8%

Infrastructure 28.8%

mechanisms, which are less cumbersome and time-consuming than a new issue, both have the effect of allowing an existing trust to expand its capital base by growing the number of shares in issue.

Boards that have bought back their own shares also have the option of reissuing shares that they have not yet cancelled. A number of well-known trusts whose performance or style of investing have become popular in recent years have been able to issue a steady stream of new shares at a premium to NAV.

All issues of new shares have to be approved by existing shareholders, so as to avoid dilution of their interests. Many companies seek approval at their AGMs for the flexibility to issue new shares up to certain annual limits. Property and debt funds have raised the most money with secondary issuance over the last five years, but only around a dozen equity funds have done so in 2019. ■

Closed-end fund vs open-ended funds

Performance of Closed-End Funds vs Open-Ended Funds (Equity Mandates)

	NAV total returns (annualised) Open-Ended funds			NAV total returns (annualised) Investment Cos		
	1 yr	5 yr	10 yr	1y	5y	10y
UK - Equity Income	(0.1)	5.9	8.3	2.0	7.0	10.3
UK - All Companies	0.0	6.5	8.4	(13.5)	7.0	9.8
UK - Smaller Company	(7.1)	9.2	11.9	(5.0)	9.8	14.0
UK - Equity & Bond Income	3.1	5.9	7.4	3.5	6.3	9.1
US - General	7.4	14.7	13.8	4.2	15.1	14.2
US - Smaller Company	2.2	14.6	14.5	2.1	14.6	13.6
Global - Equity	5.9	11.2	9.8	3.0	13.3	12.4
Global - Equity Income	7.4	9.8	10.2	8.1	10.1	11.1
Europe - General	2.2	9.4	8.0	4.8	12.1	11.4
Europe - Smaller Company	(5.2)	11.5	10.5	(6.3)	13.5	12.0
Asia Pacific - Ex Japan	5.8	10.0	8.4	7.2	11.4	11.2
Japan - General	(1.2)	11.8	8.8	(1.6)	15.6	11.7
Japan - Smaller Company	(4.1)	15.2	12.1	(4.1)	19.4	13.7
Emerging - Global	6.4	7.9	6.1	10.1	8.6	8.4
Technology	10.2	17.8	15.1	3.8	19.8	18.6

It is not uncommon for the investment managers of trusts to manage other funds outside the investment trust sector at the same time. In fact, a number of fund managers start their careers managing different kinds of fund (typically unit trusts and OEICs, though also hedge funds) and if successful are encouraged to take over or start an investment trust with a broadly similar investment objective.

Adding an investment trust to their responsibilities gives successful fund managers the opportunity to take advantage of the benefits of the investment trust structure, including the use of gearing and freedom from unhelpful forced selling as a result of fund flows. They can also use derivative securities such as futures and options for investment purposes.

These advantages show up regularly in comparisons between the long-term performance of investment trusts and that of open-ended funds with either the same manager or the same investment objective. Where trusts and similar funds can be directly compared in this way, trusts typically show up with superior performance records. Where a trust and an open-ended fund with

Note: Data to 30 September 2019. Blue shading indicates outperformance by ICs relative to open-ended funds.
Source: Morningstar, Numis Securities Research

| Price total returns (annualised) | | |
| Investment Cos | | |
1y	5y	10y
2.0	6.3	10.6
(17.7)	7.1	10.2
(3.8)	10.8	15.2
0.3	5.1	8.7
6.9	15.5	14.7
(1.7)	13.7	13.9
0.6	13.8	12.9
10.6	9.7	11.1
2.6	11.4	11.1
(7.2)	13.2	11.5
8.7	11.3	10.6
(2.2)	15.9	12.9
(5.7)	19.2	12.2
13.7	8.1	7.4
3.6	20.1	18.4

the same mandate are managed by the same individual, it is rare for the trust not to do better over the longer term. The degree to which comparable trusts outperform does vary markedly however from sector to sector and is not true every year (2019 being an example when the effect was less marked).

The table summarises the difference in the performance of directly comparable trust and open-ended equivalent sectors. The blue-shaded cells show the periods over which trusts in each sector have outperformed. It is fair to point out that such simple comparisons can be criticised by statisticians on the grounds that the two samples are very different in size and also may display what is called survivorship bias.

In 2018 academics at Cass Business School in London reported that a detailed analysis of investment trust returns between 2000 and 2016 appeared to support their superior performance. They found that, measured by NAV total return, directly comparable investment trusts outperformed their open-ended equivalents by an average of 1.4% per annum. However, the study has now been abandoned because of "data issues"; there is no conclusive verdict. ∎

A NOTE ABOUT INVESTMENT PERFORMANCE

Interpreting performance

There is a reason why the regulators insist that every piece of marketing literature issued by any kind of fund provider includes the phrase "past performance is no guarantee of future performance". The reason is that it is true.

While performance data gives you useful information about an investment trust's track record, and the way that it has been investing your money, that information in isolation is insufficient to tell you whether you should buy or continue to own that trust.

There are several reasons for that. They include:

• markets move in cycles and are unpredictable

• styles of investing come in and out of fashion

• superior performance in one period often does not repeat in the next

• managers of trusts can be and often are changed, making direct comparisons with earlier periods difficult

• unexpected events, such as political shocks and natural disasters, may throw a hitherto successful strategy off course.

What the regulators are keen to ensure is that less-sophisticated investors are not misled into thinking that a trust which has done particularly well in the past will continue to do so in the future. Their perspective is underpinned by many academic studies.

However, that is not the same as saying that past performance information has no value at all. Clearly it is essential for any investor to understand how a trust has performed in the past and to seek to establish why it has the track record it does.

At the very least it is important to understand the following:

• whether (and if so why) the trust's investment manager has changed over the track record period being looked at

• how far the performance of the trust has been affected by gearing

• how the trust performed during periods when markets were rising and when they were falling – it may be very different

• whether or not the trust has done better than a suitable benchmark, including the one chosen by the board

- how much risk the trust is taking relative to other comparable trusts and the markets in which it is investing.

The Financial Conduct Authority has also conducted a number of studies into the best buy lists which are produced by a number of investment platforms and broking firms. Its conclusion is that there may be some value in them, but investors would be unwise to rely solely on them when making decisions on which funds to buy. Their conclusions can be found on the FCA website.

Z scores

Z Scores

(current discount - average discount) / volatility of discount

1 year

Fund	Ticker	Discount Current	Average	Z Score
Honeycomb IT	HONY	3.4	10.7	-4.4
GRIT Real Estate Income	GR1T	-8.1	2.3	-4.1
US Solar Fund - $	USF	0.6	4.3	-3.7
Riverstone Energy	RSE	-42.2	-28.1	-3.2
Keystone IT	KIT	-17.6	-12.8	-2.7
ICG Longbow Senior Secured UK Pro|	LBOW	-0.9	1.7	-2.6
Highbridge Tactical Credit	HTCF	-7.1	-3.0	-2.5
Aberdeen Standard European Logistic	ASLI	-5.6	3.6	-2.5
CVC Credit Partners Euro Opps - £	CCPG	-5.7	-0.6	-2.5
TwentyFour Income	TFIF	-3.2	1.4	-2.5
Aberforth Split Level Income	ASIT	-13.6	-4.0	-2.4
Scottish Mortgage	SMT	-2.4	1.9	-2.4
Mobius IT	MMIT	-7.4	-0.1	-2.3
JPEL Private Equity	JPEL	-20.0	-17.9	-2.3
UK Mortgages	UKML	-16.9	-2.2	-2.3

Fund	Ticker	Discount Current	Average	Z Score
Carador Income Fund Redeemable	CIFR	35.9	0.9	4.5
Global Resources	GRIT	202.1	-22.5	3.6
Chenavari Capital Solutions	CCSL	-9.3	-15.7	3.5
Sirius Real Estate	SRE	6.8	-6.0	3.5
BB Biotech	BION	26.0	12.4	3.4
GCP Student Living	DIGS	6.9	1.7	2.7
Carador Income Fund	CIFU	0.2	-12.7	2.5
LMS Capital	LMS	-23.3	-33.0	2.3
JPMorgan Russian	JRS	-9.8	-15.1	2.3
Secure Income REIT	SIR	9.8	3.5	2.2
Greencoat UK Wind	UKW	16.5	12.0	2.2
Globalworth Real Estate	GWI	10.9	0.0	2.0
Foresight Solar	FSFL	13.1	6.0	2.0
RDL Realisation	RDL	-21.7	-55.5	2.0
Fondul Proprietatea GDR	FP/	-20.1	-31.2	1.8

Source: Numis data at 30 September 2019

Z-scores measure mathematically how far a trust's current discount or premium has diverged from its average over some previous period (days, months or even a year can be used). Brokers and other professional investors calculate the figures regularly in order to look for trading opportunities or good entry/exit points. A minus figure for a z-score suggests that a trust looks cheap relative to its past discount history; and a positive figure the reverse. There may, however, be a good reason for the change in sentiment towards a particular trust, so they are a blunt instrument without specialist knowledge and should never be used or relied on by inexperienced investors. ▪

DIRECTORY

Our directory of investment trusts includes, in alphabetical order, all trusts which had total assets of at least £50 million in the first week of October 2019. The table shows the ticker and Sedol number of the trust, its name and sector, and, where relevant, whether it constitutes a member of a market index (many do). This year we have added the date of launch, website details and the historic yield of each trust as well. Searching for the tickers on the AIC or other industry websites is the quickest way to find out more details. VCTs and other smaller trusts can also be found by searching the AIC website.

EPIC	SEDOL	NAME	AIC SECTOR
III	B1YW440	3i Group PLC	Private Equity
3IN	BF5FX16	3i Infrastructure Ltd	Infrastructure
AAIF	B0P6J83	Aberdeen Asian Income Fund Ltd	Asia Pacific Income
ADIG	129756	Aberdeen Diversified Income & Growth Trust PLC	Flexible Investment
AEMC	B45L2K9	Aberdeen Emerging Markets Investment Company Ltd	Global Emerging Markets
AFMC	B1W59J1	Aberdeen Frontier Markets Investment Company Ltd	Global Emerging Markets
AJIT	392075	Aberdeen Japan Investment Trust PLC	Japan
ALAI	B44ZTP6	Aberdeen Latin American Income Fund Ltd	Latin America
ABD	BBM56V2	Aberdeen New Dawn Investment Trust PLC	Asia Pacific
ANII	604877	Aberdeen New India Investment Trust PLC	Country Specialists: Asia Pacific ex Japan
ANW	5997	Aberdeen New Thai Investment Trust PLC	Country Specialists: Asia Pacific ex Japan
ASCI	806372	Aberdeen Smaller Companies Income Trust PLC	UK Smaller Companies
AAS	10076	Aberdeen Standard Asia Focus PLC	Asia Pacific Smaller Companies
ASEI	603959	Aberdeen Standard Equity Income Trust plc	UK Equity Income
ASLI	BD9PXH4	Aberdeen Standard European Logistics Income PLC	Property – Europe
ASL	6655	Aberforth Smaller Companies Trust PLC	UK Smaller Companies
ASIT	BYPBD39	Aberforth Split Level Income Trust PLC	UK Smaller Companies
AIF	482943	Acorn Income Fund Ltd	UK Equity and Bond Income
AEWL	BDVK708	AEW UK Long Lease REIT PLC	Property – UK Commercial
AEWU	BWD2415	AEW UK REIT PLC	Property – UK Commercial
AFRB	B3R8XC0	AFI Development PLC	Global Smaller Companies
AEFS	B6116N8	Alcentra European Floating Rate Income Fund Ltd	Debt – Loans and Bonds
ATST	B11V7W9	Alliance Trust PLC	Global
ATT	339072	Allianz Technology Trust PLC	Technology and Media

CAPITAL (£M)	INDEX	FLOAT DATE	WEBSITE	HISTORIC YIELD (%)
11,214	FTSE 100	18/07/1994	www.3i.com	3.04
2,415	FTSE Mid 250	13/03/2007	www.3i-infrastructure.com	2.90
380	FTSE Small Cap	20/12/2005	www.asian-income.co.uk	4.28
350	FTSE Small Cap	24/03/1952	www.aberdeendiversified.co.uk	4.83
265		10/11/2009	www.aberdeenemergingmarkets.co.uk	3.64
33	AIM All-Share	15/06/2007	www.aberdeenfrontiermarkets.co.uk	3.42
87	FTSE Fledgling	01/10/1998	www.aberdeenjapan.co.uk	0.89
41	FTSE Fledgling	16/08/2010	www.latamincome.co.uk	4.91
275	FTSE Small Cap	12/05/1989	www.newdawn-trust.co.uk	1.74
287	FTSE Small Cap	31/03/1994	www.aberdeen-newindia.co.uk	
102	FTSE Fledgling	22/12/1989	www.newthai-trust.co.uk	2.93
61	FTSE Fledgling	28/08/1992	www.aberdeensmallercompanies.co.uk	2.68
365	FTSE Small Cap	19/10/1995	www.asia-focus.co.uk	1.20
186	FTSE Small Cap	14/11/1991	www. aberdeenstandardequityincometrust. com	5.06
219	FTSE Small Cap	15/12/2017	www.eurologisticsincome.co.uk	3.20
1,114	FTSE Mid 250	10/12/1990	www.aberforth.co.uk	2.44
175	FTSE Small Cap	03/07/2017	www.aberforth.co.uk	5.66
55		11/02/1999	www.premierassetmanagement.co.uk	5.75
57	FTSE Fledgling	06/06/2017	www.aeweurope.com	7.77
145	FTSE Small Cap	12/05/2015	www.aeweurope.com	8.37
224		11/05/2007	www.afi-development.com	
142	FTSE Small Cap	06/03/2012	www.aefrif.com	4.56
2,627	FTSE Mid 250	17/07/1947	www.alliancetrust.co.uk	1.70
563	FTSE Small Cap	04/12/1995	www.allianztechnologytrust.com	

EPIC	SEDOL	NAME	AIC SECTOR
ARTL	B13VDP2	Alpha Real Trust Ltd	Property – Europe
AA4	BWC53H4	Amedeo Air Four Plus Ltd	Leasing
APAX	BWWYMV8	APAX Global Alpha Ltd	Private Equity
AERS	BJMXQK1	Aquila European Renewables Income Fund PLC	Renewable Energy Infrastructure
AERI	BK6RLF6	Aquila European Renewables Income Fund PLC	Renewable Energy Infrastructure
ATS	435594	Artemis Alpha Trust PLC	UK All Companies
ASPL	B1RZDJ4	Aseana Properties Ltd	Property – Rest of World
AIE	BF50VS4	Ashoka India Equity Investment Trust PLC	Country Specialists: Asia Pacific ex Japan
AJG	B61ND55	Atlantis Japan Growth Fund Ltd	Japanese Smaller Companies
AUGM	BG12XV8	Augmentum Fintech PLC	Technology and Media
ARR	63326	Aurora Investment Trust PLC	UK All Companies
AGT	133508	AVI Global Trust PLC	Global
AJOT	BD6H5D3	AVI Japan Opportunity Trust PLC	Japanese Smaller Companies
AXI	BTC2K73	Axiom European Financial Debt Ltd	Debt – Loans and Bonds
BGFD	48583	Baillie Gifford Japan Trust (The) PLC	Japan
BGS	BFXYH24	Baillie Gifford Shin Nippon PLC	Japanese Smaller Companies
BGUK	791348	Baillie Gifford UK Growth Fund PLC	UK All Companies
USA	BDFGHW4	Baillie Gifford US Growth Trust PLC	North America
BSRT	B6686L2	Baker Steel Resources Trust Ltd	Commodities and Natural Resources
BNKR	76700	Bankers Investment Trust PLC	Global
BEE	3227334	Baring Emerging Europe PLC	European Emerging Markets
BBH	BZCNLL9	BB Healthcare Trust PLC	Biotechnology and Healthcare
BHGG	B2QQPT9	BH Global Ltd	Hedge Funds
BHGU	B2QQPS8	BH Global Ltd	Hedge Funds
BHMG	B1NP514	BH Macro Ltd	Hedge Funds
BHMU	B1NPGV1	BH Macro Ltd	Hedge Funds
BBGI	B6QWXM4	Bilfinger Berger Global Infrastructure SICAV SA	Infrastructure

CAPITAL (£M)	INDEX	FLOAT DATE	WEBSITE	HISTORIC YIELD (%)
107		21/12/2006	www.alpharealtrustlimited.com	1.56
540		13/05/2015	www.aa4plus.com	9.82
764	FTSE Mid 250	15/06/2015	www.apaxglobalalpha.com	5.43
148		05/06/2019	www.aquila-european-renewables-income-fund.com	
113	FTSE Small Cap	16/10/1998	www.artemisalphatrust.co.uk	1.80
80		05/04/2007	www.aseanaproperties.com	
64	FTSE Fledgling	06/07/2018	www.ashokaindiaequity.com	
95	FTSE Fledgling	10/05/1996	www.atlantisjapangrowthfund.com	
128	FTSE Fledgling	13/03/2018	www.augmentumcapital.com	
129	FTSE Fledgling	13/03/1997	www.aurorainvestmenttrust.com	2.02
830	FTSE Mid 250	17/06/1943	www.british-empire.co.uk	1.72
99	FTSE Fledgling	23/10/2018	www.ajot.co.uk	
80	FTSE Fledgling	05/11/2015	www.axiom-ai.com	6.94
776	FTSE Mid 250	14/12/1981	www.bailliegifford.com	0.07
511	FTSE Small Cap	01/07/1985	www.bailliegifford.com	
267	FTSE Small Cap	10/03/1994	www.bailliegifford.com	2.51
309	FTSE Small Cap	23/03/2018	www.bailliegifford.com	
57	FTSE Fledgling	28/04/2010	www.bakersteelresourcestrust.com	
1,176	FTSE Mid 250	02/04/1957	www.bankersinvestmenttrust.com	2.08
104	FTSE Fledgling	18/12/2002	www.barings.com	4.05
543	FTSE Small Cap	02/12/2016	www.bbhealthcaretrust.com	3.17
345	FTSE Small Cap	29/05/2008	www.bhglobal.com	
345	FTSE Small Cap	29/05/2008	www.bhglobal.com	
439	FTSE Small Cap	14/03/2007	www.bhmacro.com	
439	FTSE Small Cap	14/03/2007	www.bhmacro.com	
998	FTSE Mid 250	21/12/2011	www.bb-gi.com	4.26

EPIC	SEDOL	NAME	AIC SECTOR
BPCR	BDGKMY2	BioPharma Credit PLC	Debt – Direct Lending
BIOG	38551	Biotech Growth Trust (The) PLC	Biotechnology and Healthcare
BERI	B0N8MF9	BlackRock Energy and Resources Income Trust PLC	Commodities and Natural Resources
BRFI	B3SXM83	BlackRock Frontiers Investment Trust PLC	Global Emerging Markets
BRGE	B01RDH7	BlackRock Greater Europe Investment Trust PLC	Europe
BRLA	505840	BlackRock Latin American Investment Trust PLC	Latin America
BRNA	B7W0XJ6	BlackRock North American Income Trust PLC	North America
BRSC	643610	BlackRock Smaller Companies Trust PLC	UK Smaller Companies
THRG	891055	BlackRock Throgmorton Trust PLC	UK Smaller Companies
BRWM	577485	BlackRock World Mining Trust PLC	Commodities and Natural Resources
BGLF	BNCB5T5	Blackstone / GSO Loan Financing Ltd	Debt – Structured Finance
BGLP	BYXL0Y1	Blackstone / GSO Loan Financing Ltd	
BGLC	BF8Q3P0	Blackstone/GSO Loan Financing Ltd	Debt – Structured Finance
BSIF	BB0RDB9	Bluefield Solar Income Fund Ltd	Renewable Energy Infrastructure
BCI	346328	BMO Capital and Income Investment Trust PLC	UK Equity Income
BCPT	B4ZPCJ0	BMO Commercial Property Trust Ltd	Property – UK Commercial
BGSC	17505	BMO Global Smaller Companies PLC	Global Smaller Companies
BMPI	B2PP3J3	BMO Managed Portfolio Trust PLC	Flexible Investment
BMPG	B2PP252	BMO Managed Portfolio Trust PLC	Flexible Investment
BPET	3073827	BMO Private Equity Trust PLC	Private Equity
BREI	B012T52	BMO Real Estate Investment Ltd	Property – UK Commercial
BHI	B1N4G29	BMO UK High Income Trust PLC	UK Equity Income
BHIB	B1N4H59	BMO UK High Income Trust PLC	UK Equity Income
BHIU	B1N4H93	BMO UK High Income Trust PLC	UK Equity Income
BGHS	B39VMM0	Boussards & Gavaudan Holdings Ltd	Hedge Funds

CAPITAL (£M)	INDEX	FLOAT DATE	WEBSITE	HISTORIC YIELD (%)
1,146		27/03/2017	www.bpcruk.com	6.43
317	FTSE Small Cap	23/06/1997	www.biotechgt.com	
82	FTSE Fledgling	13/12/2005	www.blackrock.com	5.59
318	FTSE Small Cap	17/12/2010	www.blackrock.co.uk	4.28
324	FTSE Small Cap	20/09/2004	www.blackrock.co.uk	1.50
180	FTSE Small Cap	12/07/1990	www.blackrock.com	5.42
149	FTSE Small Cap	24/10/2012	www.blackrock.co.uk	4.19
659	FTSE Mid 250	25/03/1973	www.blackrock.com	2.27
415	FTSE Small Cap	08/06/1962	www.blackrock.co.uk	1.76
626	FTSE Small Cap	15/12/1993	www.blackrock.co.uk/individual/ products/investment-trust/blackrock-world-mining-trust	5.07
286		23/07/2014	www.blackstone.com	12.53
341			www.blackstone.com	
486	FTSE Small Cap	12/07/2013	www.bluefieldsif.com	5.85
337	FTSE Small Cap	29/10/1992	www.bmocapitalandincome.com	3.34
927	FTSE Mid 250	07/07/2009	www.bmogam.com	3.88
829	FTSE Mid 250	26/06/1959	www.bmoglobalsmallers.com	1.21
133		16/04/2008	www.bmomanagedportfolio.com	
133		16/04/2008	www.bmomanagedportfolio.com	
268	FTSE Small Cap	22/03/1999	www.bmoprivateequitytrust.com	3.97
198	FTSE Small Cap	01/06/2004	www.bmogam.com	6.07
112	FTSE Fledgling	01/03/2007	www.bmogam.com	5.31
112	FTSE Fledgling	01/03/2007	www.bmogam.com	
112	FTSE Fledgling	01/03/2007	www.bmogam.com	
459		28/07/2008	www.bgholdingltd.com	

EPIC	SEDOL	NAME	AIC SECTOR
BGHL	B28ZZQ1	Boussards & Gavaudan Holdings Ltd	Hedge Funds
BPM	B0XLRJ7	BP Marsh & Partners PLC	Global Equity Income
BUT	149000	Brunner Investment Trust PLC	Global
CLDN	163992	Caledonia Investments PLC	Flexible Investment
CGT	173861	Capital Gearing Trust PLC	Flexible Investment
0P6H	B4QHGL5	Castle Alternative Invest AG	Environmental
CATC	BZ1DKY6	Catco Reinsurance Opportunities Fund Ltd	Insurance and Reinsurance Strategies
CAT	BVFCRP1	Catco Reinsurance Opportunities Fund Ltd	Insurance and Reinsurance Strategies
CCJI	BYSRMH1	CC Japan Income & Growth Trust PLC	Japan
CBA	BFMDJH1	CEIBA Investments Ltd	Property – Rest of World
TORO	BWBSDM9	Chenavari Toro Income Fund Ltd	Debt – Structured Finance
CMHY	B6RMDP6	City Merchants High Yield Trust Ltd	Debt – Loans and Bonds
CTY	199049	City of London Investment Trust (The) PLC	UK Equity Income
CTYA	199083	City of London Investment Trust (The) PLC	
CSH	BD8HBD3	Civitas Social Housing PLC	Property – UK Residential
CIC	3369872	Conygar Investment Company (The) PLC	Hedge Funds
CYN	35392	CQS Natural Resources Growth & Income PLC	Commodities and Natural Resources
NCYF	B1LZS51	CQS New City High Yield Fund Ltd	Debt – Loans and Bonds
CRS	B1Z2SL4	Crystal Amber Fund Ltd	UK Smaller Companies
CREI	BJFLFT4	Custodian Reit PLC	Property – UK Commercial
CCPE	B9G79F5	CVC Credit Partners European Opportunities Ltd	Debt – Loans and Bonds
CCPG	B9MRHZ5	CVC Credit Partners European Opportunities Ltd	Debt – Loans and Bonds
NBDD	BDFZ6F7	Distressed Debt Investment Fund Ltd	Debt – Loans and Bonds
DIVI	B65TLW2	Diverse Income Trust (The) PLC	UK Equity Income
DNA3	B92LHN5	Doric Nimrod Air Three Ltd	Leasing
DNA2	B3Z6252	Doric Nimrod Air Two Ltd	Leasing
DPA	BBP6HP3	DP Aircraft Ltd	Leasing

CAPITAL (£M)	INDEX	FLOAT DATE	WEBSITE	HISTORIC YIELD (%)
459		28/07/2008	www.bgholdingltd.com	
97	AIM All-Share	02/02/2006	www.bpmarsh.co.uk	1.83
358	FTSE Small Cap	03/04/1950	www.brunner.co.uk	2.16
1,664	FTSE Mid 250	18/07/1960	www.caledonia.com	1.97
445	FTSE Small Cap	13/02/1973	www.capitalgearingtrust.com	0.53
77		17/06/2005	www.castleai.com	
179		20/12/2010	www.catcoreoppsfund.com	
179		20/12/2010	www.catcoreoppsfund.com	14.72
206	FTSE Small Cap	15/12/2015	www.ccjapanincomeandgrowthtrust.com	2.45
112		22/10/2018	www.ceibalimited.co.uk	6.05
226		08/05/2015	www.chenavaritoroincomefund.com	9.82
191	FTSE Small Cap	02/04/2012	www.invescoperpetual.co.uk	5.15
1,604	FTSE Mid 250	04/05/1955	www.cityinvestmenttrust.com	4.43
1,604	FTSE Mid 250	04/05/1955	www.cityinvestmenttrust.com	
536	FTSE Small Cap	18/11/2016	www.civitassocialhousing.com	4.36
74	AIM All-Share	23/10/2003	www.conygar.com	
60	FTSE Fledgling	04/11/1994	www.ncim.co.uk	5.81
254	FTSE Small Cap	07/03/2007	www.ncim.co.uk	7.42
184	AIM 100, AIM All-Share	17/06/2008	www.crystalamber.com	2.58
482	FTSE Small Cap	26/03/2014	www.custodianreit.com	5.58
465		25/06/2013	www.ccpeol.com	
463	FTSE Small Cap	25/06/2013	www.ccpeol.com	5.56
146		04/03/2014	www.nbddif.com	
346	FTSE Small Cap	28/04/2011	www.mitongroup.com	3.99
191		02/07/2013	www.dnairthree.com	9.51
314		14/07/2011	www.dnairtwo.com	9.92
138		04/10/2013	www.dpaircraft.com	11.08

EPIC	SEDOL	NAME	AIC SECTOR
DUKE	BYZSSY6	Duke Royalty Ltd	Leasing
DNE	577656	Dunedin Enterprise Investment Trust PLC	Private Equity
DIG	340609	Dunedin Income Growth Investment Trust PLC	UK Equity Income
EGL	BD3V464	Ecofin Global Utilities And Infrastructure Trust PLC	Utilities
EFM	294502	Edinburgh Dragon Trust plc	Asia Pacific
EDIN	305233	Edinburgh Investment Trust (The) PLC	UK Equity Income
EWI	BHSRZC8	Edinburgh Worldwide Investment Trust PLC	Global Smaller Companies
EPIC	BNGMZB6	Ediston Property Investment Co PLC	Property – UK Commercial
EJFI	BF0D1M2	EJF Investments Ltd	Financials
EJFZ	BDG12N4	EJF Investments Ltd 2022 ZDP NPV	Financials
ELTA	308544	Electra Private Equity PLC	Private Equity
ESP	BLWDVR7	Empiric Student Property PLC	
EPG	3386257	EP Global Opportunities Trust PLC	Global
ESO	BYW49X3	EPE Special Opportunities PLC	Private Equity
EAT	BHJVQ59	European Assets Trust NV	European Smaller Companies
EUT	329501	European Investment Trust PLC	Europe
FCIT	346607	F&C Investment Trust PLC	Global
FAIR	BF00L34	Fair Oaks Income Ltd	Debt – Structured Finance
FAS	332231	Fidelity Asian Values PLC	Asia Pacific
FCSS	B62Z3C7	Fidelity China Special Situation PLC	Country Specialists: Asia Pacific ex Japan
FEV	BK1PKQ9	Fidelity European Values PLC	Europe
FJV	332855	Fidelity Japanese Values PLC	Japan
FSV	BWXC7Y9	Fidelity Special Values PLC	UK All Companies
FGT	781606	Finsbury Growth & Income Trust PLC	UK Equity Income
FSFL	BD3QJR5	Foresight Solar Fund Ltd	Renewable Energy Infrastructure
FEET	BLSNND1	Fundsmith Emerging Equities Trust	Global Emerging Markets
GMP	BD8P074	Gabelli Merger Plus+ Trust PLC	Hedge Funds
GVP	BTLJYS4	Gabelli Value Plus+ Trust PLC	North America

CAPITAL (£M)	INDEX	FLOAT DATE	WEBSITE	HISTORIC YIELD (%)
97	AIM All-Share	09/07/2012	www.dukeroyalty.com	5.77
70	FTSE Fledgling	01/04/1987	www.dunedinenterprise.com	0.59
397	FTSE Small Cap	21/11/1949	www.dunedinincomegrowth.co.uk	4.65
148	FTSE Small Cap	26/09/2016	www.ecofin.co.uk	3.99
520	FTSE Small Cap	07/09/1987	www.edinburghdragon.co.uk	0.99
1,094	FTSE Mid 250	08/02/1952	www.invescoperpetual.co.uk	4.73
552	FTSE Small Cap	10/07/1998	www.edinburghworldwide.co.uk	
181	FTSE Small Cap	28/10/2014	www.epic-reit.com	6.73
109			www.ejfi.com	5.99
			www.ejfi.com	
127	FTSE Small Cap	18/02/1976	www.electraequity.com	
566	FTSE Small Cap	30/06/2014	www.empiric.co.uk	5.32
128	FTSE Small Cap	15/12/2003	www.epgot.com	1.79
59	AIM All-Share	16/09/2003	www.epespecialopportunities.com	
370	FTSE Small Cap	12/10/1983	www.europeanassets.co.uk	
327	FTSE Small Cap	28/06/1972	www.eitplc.com	3.32
3,838	FTSE Mid 250	21/03/1952	www.fandcit.com	1.56
277		12/06/2014	www.fairoaksincomefund.com	14.07
311	FTSE Small Cap	13/06/1996	www.fidelity.co.uk	1.30
1,175	FTSE Mid 250	19/04/2010	www.fidelity.co.uk	1.80
1,014	FTSE Mid 250	06/11/1991	www.fidelity.co.uk	2.55
214	FTSE Small Cap	15/03/1994	www.fidelity.co.uk	
718	FTSE Mid 250	17/11/1994	www.fidelity.co.uk	1.92
1,870	FTSE Mid 250	24/12/1953	www.finsburygt.com	1.64
665	FTSE Mid 250	29/10/2013	www.foresightgroup.eu	5.44
308	FTSE Small Cap	25/06/2014	www.feetplc.co.uk	0.17
74		19/07/2017	www.gabelli.co.uk	5.31
131	FTSE Fledgling	19/02/2015	www.gabelli.co.uk	0.56

EPIC	SEDOL	NAME	AIC SECTOR
GABI	BYXX8B0	GCP Asset Backed Income Fund Ltd	Debt – Direct Lending
GCP	B6173J1	GCP Infrastructure Investments Ltd	Infrastructure
DIGS	B8460Z4	GCP Student Living PLC	Property – UK Residential
GSS	B4L0PD4	Genesis Emerging Markets Fund Ltd	Global Emerging Markets
GWI	B979FD0	Globalworth Real Estate Investments Ltd	Property – Europe
GRN	BC9LJD3	Green REIT PLC	Property – UK Residential
GRP	BF4TVJ3	Greencoat Renewables PLC	Renewable Energy Infrastructure
UKW	B8SC6K5	Greencoat UK Wind PLC	Renewable Energy Infrastructure
GRID	BFX3K77	Gresham House Energy Storage Fund PLC	Renewable Energy Infrastructure
GRIO	B8K0LM4	Ground Rents Income Fund PLC	Property – UK Commercial
GIF	B1Z4070	Gulf Investment Fund PLC	Global Emerging Markets
HWSL	BYMYC34	Hadrian's Wall Secured Investments Ltd	Debt – Direct Lending
HAN	BKLFC18	Hansa Investment Company Ltd	Flexible Investment
HANA	BKLFC07	Hansa Investment Company Ltd	Flexible Investment
HVPE	BR30MJ8	Harbourvest Global Private Equity Ltd	Private Equity
HAST	121600	Henderson Alternative Strategies Trust PLC	Flexible Investment
HDIV	BF03YC3	Henderson Diversified Income Trust PLC	Debt – Loans and Bonds
HEFT	526885	Henderson European Focus Trust PLC	Europe
HNE	419929	Henderson EuroTrust PLC	Europe
HFEL	B1GXH75	Henderson Far East Income Ltd	Asia Pacific Income
HHI	958057	Henderson High Income Trust PLC	UK Equity and Bond Income
HINT	B3PHCS8	Henderson International Income Trust PLC	Global Equity Income
HOT	853657	Henderson Opportunities Trust PLC	UK All Companies
HSL	906506	Henderson Smaller Companies Investment Trust PLC	UK Smaller Companies
HRI	422864	Herald Investment Trust PLC	Global Smaller Companies
HGT	BJ0LT19	HgCapital Trust PLC	Private Equity

CAPITAL (£M)	INDEX	FLOAT DATE	WEBSITE	HISTORIC YIELD (%)
479	FTSE Small Cap	23/10/2015	www.graviscapital.com	5.62
1,106	FTSE Mid 250	22/07/2010	www.graviscapital.com	6.03
710	FTSE Mid 250	20/05/2013	www.gcpstudent.com	3.58
927	FTSE Mid 250	06/07/1989	www.genesisemf.com	1.93
1,647		25/07/2013	www.globalworth.com	5.65
1,187		18/07/2013	www.greenreitplc.com	1.47
529	AIM 100, AIM All-Share		www.greencoat-renewables.com	5.25
2,170	FTSE Mid 250	27/03/2013	www.greencoat-ukwind.com	4.73
172		13/11/2018	www.newenergy.greshamhouse.com	
			www.groundrentsincomefund.com	
93		31/07/2007	www.gulfinvestmentfundplc.com	
106		20/06/2016	www.hadrianswallcapital.com	8.11
224		25/03/1951	www.hansaicl.com	8.43
224		25/03/1951	www.hansaicl.com	
1,426	FTSE Mid 250	09/10/2013	www.hvgpe.com	
104	FTSE Small Cap	01/01/1930	www.janushenderson.com	1.86
173	FTSE Small Cap	18/07/2007	www.hendersondiversifiedincome.com	4.82
268	FTSE Small Cap	08/12/1971	www.hendersoneuropeanfocus.com	2.49
249	FTSE Small Cap	06/07/1992	www.janushenderson.com	2.60
484	FTSE Small Cap	18/12/2006	www.janushenderson.com	5.89
221	FTSE Small Cap	01/12/1989	www.hendersonhighincome.com	5.59
311	FTSE Small Cap	21/04/2011	www.henderson.com	3.20
72	FTSE Fledgling	16/10/1985	www.hendersonopportunities.com	2.30
644	FTSE Small Cap	29/03/1955	www.janushenderson.com	2.67
880	FTSE Mid 250	21/02/1994	www.heralduk.com	
928	FTSE Mid 250	13/12/1989	www.hgcapitaltrust.com	2.00

EPIC	SEDOL	NAME	AIC SECTOR
HICL	BJLP1Y7	HICL Infrastructure PLC	Infrastructure
SONG	BFYT9H7	Hipgnosis Songs Fund Ltd	Royalties
HONY	BYZV3G2	Honeycomb Investment Trust PLC	Debt – Direct Lending
ICGT	329200	ICG Enterprise Trust PLC	Private Equity
LBOW	B8C23S8	ICG-Longbow Senior Secured UK Property Debt Investments Ltd	Property – Debt
IHR	BYXVMJ0	Impact Healthcare REIT PLC	Property – UK Healthcare
IEM	3123249	Impax Environmental Markets PLC	Environmental
IIT	81168	Independent Investment Trust (The) PLC	UK All Companies
IGC	B0P8RJ6	India Capital Growth Fund Ltd	Country Specialists: Asia Pacific ex Japan
INL	B1TR031	Inland Homes PLC	Technology and Media
IBT	455934	International Biotechnology Trust PLC	Biotechnology and Healthcare
INPP	B188SR5	International Public Partnership Ltd	Infrastructure
IAT	453530	Invesco Asia Trust PLC	Asia Pacific
IPE	B05NYM3	Invesco Enhanced Income Ltd	Debt – Loans and Bonds
IVI	358572	Invesco Income Growth Trust PLC	UK Equity Income
IVPB	B1DQ669	Invesco Perpetual Select Trust PLC	Flexible Investment
IVPG	B1DQ647	Invesco Perpetual Select Trust PLC	Global Equity Income
IVPM	B1DQ670	Invesco Perpetual Select Trust PLC	Liquidity Funds
IVPU	B1DPVL6	Invesco Perpetual Select Trust PLC	UK All Companies
IPU	B1FL3C7	Invesco Perpetual UK Smaller Companies Investment Trust PLC	UK Smaller Companies
JLEN	BJL5FH8	JLEN Environmental Assets Group Ltd	Renewable Energy Infrastructure
JAM	BKZGVH6	JPMorgan American Investment Trust PLC	North America
JAI	132077	JPMorgan Asian Investment Trust PLC	Asia Pacific Income
JMC	343501	JPMorgan Chinese Investment Trust PLC	Country Specialists: Asia Pacific ex Japan
JCH	342218	JPMorgan Claverhouse Investment Trust PLC	UK Equity Income
JPE	852814	JPMorgan Elect PLC	Global

CAPITAL (£M)	INDEX	FLOAT DATE	WEBSITE	HISTORIC YIELD (%)
2,973	FTSE Mid 250	29/03/2006	www.hicl.com	4.85
419			www.hipgnosissongs.com	2.09
406		23/12/2015	www.honeycombplc.com	7.77
599	FTSE Small Cap	23/07/1981	www.icg-enterprise.co.uk	2.53
119	FTSE Small Cap	05/02/2013	www.lbow.co.uk	6.14
318	FTSE Small Cap		www.impactreit.uk	5.41
607	FTSE Small Cap	22/02/2002	www.impaxenvironmentalmarkets.co.uk	0.95
278	FTSE Small Cap	18/10/2000	www.independentinvestmenttrust.co.uk	1.38
83	FTSE Fledgling	22/12/2005	www.indiacapitalgrowth.com	
164	AIM All-Share	03/04/2007	www.inlandhomes.co.uk	2.78
231	FTSE Small Cap	06/05/1994	www.ibtplc.com	4.60
2,410	FTSE Mid 250	09/11/2006	www.internationalpublicpartnerships.com	4.53
192	FTSE Small Cap	11/07/1995	www.invesco.co.uk	2.07
129		15/10/1999	www.invesco.co.uk	6.58
159	FTSE Small Cap	28/03/1996	www.invescoperpetual.co.uk	4.21
133		23/11/2006	www.invesco.co.uk	
133		23/11/2006	www.invesco.co.uk	
133		23/11/2006	www.invesco.co.uk	
133		23/11/2006	www.invesco.co.uk	
174	FTSE Small Cap	08/03/1988	www.invescoperpetual.co.uk	3.52
589	FTSE Small Cap	31/03/2014	www.jlen.com	5.49
1,005	FTSE Mid 250	09/03/1955	www.jpmamerican.co.uk	1.36
337	FTSE Small Cap	12/09/1997	www.jpmasian.co.uk	4.38
224	FTSE Small Cap	19/10/1993	www.jpmchinese.co.uk	1.14
391	FTSE Small Cap	24/04/1963	www.jpmclaverhouse.co.uk	3.96
354		24/11/1999	www.jpmelect.co.uk	1.55

EPIC	SEDOL	NAME	AIC SECTOR
JPEC	3408009	JPMorgan Elect PLC	Liquidity Funds
JPEI	3408021	JPMorgan Elect PLC	UK Equity Income
JMG	341895	JPMorgan Emerging Markets Inv Trust PLC	Global Emerging Markets
JETI	B17XWW4	JPMorgan European Investment Trust PLC	Europe
JETG	B18JK16	JPMorgan European Investment Trust PLC	Europe
JESC	BMTS0Z3	JPMorgan European Smaller Companies Trust PLC	European Smaller Companies
JPS	316581	JPMorgan Fleming Japanese Smaller Cos Inv Tr PLC	Japanese Smaller Companies
JPSS	BSFWJ54	JPMorgan Fleming Japanese Smaller Cos Inv Tr PLC	
JGCI	B96SW59	JPMorgan Global Convertibles Income Fund Ltd	Debt – Loans and Bonds
JARA	BJVKW83	JPMorgan Global Core Real Assets Ltd	Flexible Investment
JEMI	B5ZZY91	JPMorgan Global Emerging Markets Income Trust PLC	Global Emerging Markets
JPGI	BYMKY69	JPMorgan Global Growth & Income PLC	Global Equity Income
JII	345035	JPMorgan Indian Investment Trust PLC	Country Specialists: Asia Pacific ex Japan
JFJ	174002	JPMorgan Japanese Investment Trust PLC	Japan
JMF	235761	JPMorgan Mid Cap Investment Trust PLC	UK All Companies
MATE	BFWJJT1	JPMorgan Multi-Asset Trust PLC	Flexible Investment
JPEL	BFMX1M0	JPMorgan Private Equity Ltd	Private Equity
JRS	3216473	JPMorgan Russian Securities PLC	Country Specialists: Europe ex UK
JMI	BF7L8P1	JPMorgan Smaller Companies Investment Trust PLC	UK Smaller Companies
JUSC	BJL5F34	JPMorgan US Smaller Companies IT PLC	North American Smaller Companies
JEFI	BDR0575	Jupiter Emerging & Frontier Income Trust PLC	Global Emerging Markets
JEO	19772	Jupiter European Opportunities Trust PLC	Europe

CAPITAL (£M)	INDEX	FLOAT DATE	WEBSITE	HISTORIC YIELD (%)
354		24/11/1999	www.jpmelect.co.uk	
354		24/11/1999	www.jpmelect.co.uk	
1,196	FTSE Mid 250	15/07/1991	www.jpmemergingmarkets.co.uk	1.27
346	FTSE Small Cap	23/06/1955	www.jpmeuropean.co.uk	5.98
346	FTSE Small Cap	23/06/1955	www.jpmeuropean.co.uk	
573	FTSE Small Cap	24/04/1990	www.jpmeuropeansmallercompanies.co.uk	1.87
224	FTSE Small Cap	12/04/2000	www.jpmjapansmallercompanies.co.uk	4.39
	FTSE Small Cap	12/04/2000	www.jpmjapansmallercompanies.co.uk	
104	FTSE Small Cap	11/06/2013	am.jpmorgan.com	4.99
154		24/09/2019	am.jpmorgan.com	
391	FTSE Small Cap	29/07/2010	www.jpmglobalemergingmarketsincome.co.uk	3.80
458	FTSE Small Cap	23/10/1968	www.jpmoverseas.co.uk	3.68
777	FTSE Mid 250	26/05/1994	www.jpmindian.co.uk	
718	FTSE Mid 250	20/10/1955	www.jpmjapanese.co.uk	1.12
266	FTSE Small Cap	30/06/1972	www.jpmmidcap.co.uk	2.63
84	FTSE Fledgling	02/03/2018	www.jpmmultiassettrust.co.uk	4.09
210		30/06/2005	www.jpelonline.com	
322	FTSE Small Cap	20/12/2002	am.jpmorgan.com	3.77
174	FTSE Small Cap	06/08/1990	www.jpmsmallercompanies.co.uk	2.43
186	FTSE Small Cap	12/01/1982	www.jpmussmallercompanies.co.uk	0.77
89	FTSE Fledgling	15/05/2017	www.jupiteram.com	6.30
941	FTSE Mid 250	20/11/2000	www.jupiteram.com	0.66

EPIC	SEDOL	NAME	AIC SECTOR
JGC	B120GL7	Jupiter Green Investment Trust PLC	Environmental
JUKG	BFD3V96	Jupiter UK Growth Investment Trust PLC	UK All Companies
JUS	346340	Jupiter US Smaller Companies PLC	North American Smaller Companies
JZCP	B403HK5	JZ Capital Partners Ltd	Flexible Investment
KIT	491206	Keystone Investment Trust PLC	UK All Companies
LWDB	3142921	Law Debenture Corp (The) PLC	UK Equity Income
LSAA	BF1Q4B0	Life Settlement Assets PLC	Insurance and Reinsurance Strategies
LTI	3197794	Lindsell Train Investment Trust (The) PLC	Global
LIV	B08N4M0	Livermore Investments Group Ltd	Flexible Investment
LWI	536806	Lowland Investment Co PLC	UK Equity Income
LXI	BYQ46T4	LXI REIT PLC	Property – UK Commercial
MGCI	BFYYL32	M&G Credit Income Investment Trust PLC	Debt – Loans and Bonds
MPO	BGDYFV6	Macau Property Opportunities Fund Ltd	Property – Rest of World
MAJE	555522	Majedie Investments PLC	Global
MNL	225847	Manchester & London Investment Trust PLC	Global
MPLF	BF1Q4G5	Marble Point Loan Finance Ltd	Debt – Structured Finance
MCP	569512	Martin Currie Asia Unconstrained Trust PLC	Asia Pacific Income
MNP	537241	Martin Currie Global Portfolio Trust PLC	Global
MVI	BYTRG23	Marwyn Value Investors Ltd	UK Smaller Companies
MVIR	BF39V83	Marwyn Value Investors Ltd Realisation	UK Smaller Companies
MHN	BZ0XWD0	Menhaden PLC	Environmental
MRC	BF4JDH5	Mercantile Investment Trust (The) PLC	UK All Companies
MRCH	580007	Merchants Trust (The) PLC	UK Equity Income
MERI	BGJYPP4	Merian Chrysalis Investment Co Ltd	Growth Capital
MWY	B6VTTK0	Mid Wynd International Inv Trust PLC	Global

CAPITAL (£M)	INDEX	FLOAT DATE	WEBSITE	HISTORIC YIELD (%)
36	FTSE Fledgling	08/06/2006	www.jupiteram.com	1.14
44	FTSE Fledgling	02/07/1987	www.jupiteram.com	2.55
149	FTSE Small Cap	11/03/1993	www.jupiteram.com	
417		26/06/1998	www.jzcp.com	
209	FTSE Small Cap	19/11/1954	www.invesco.co.uk	3.62
690	FTSE Mid 250	10/07/1946	www.lawdebenture.com	3.24
78			www.lsaplc.com	
275	FTSE Small Cap	22/01/2001	www.lindselltrain.com	2.03
82		15/06/2005	www.livermore-inv.com	
343	FTSE Small Cap	05/04/1966	www.lowlandinvestment.com	4.25
678	FTSE Small Cap	27/02/2017	www.lxireit.com	4.16
140	FTSE Fledgling	14/11/2018	www.mandg.co.uk	
80	FTSE Small Cap	05/06/2006	www.mpofund.com	
135	FTSE Small Cap	05/03/1941	www.majedieinvestments.com	2.75
160	FTSE Small Cap	08/12/1997	www.mlcapman.com	2.64
132		13/02/2018	www.mplflimited.com	8.91
			www.martincurrie.com/uk/asia-unconstrained-trust	
242	FTSE Small Cap	22/03/1999	www.martincurrieglobal.com	1.45
215		22/02/2006	www.marwynvalue.com	1.63
215			www.marwynvalue.com	
65	FTSE Fledgling	31/07/2015	www.menhaden.com	0.86
1,674	FTSE Mid 250	21/07/1952	am.jpmorgan.com	2.98
545	FTSE Small Cap	09/03/1954	www.merchantstrust.co.uk	5.27
408	FTSE Small Cap		www.merian.com/Chrysalis	
247	FTSE Small Cap	21/10/1981	www.midwynd.com	1.00

EPIC	SEDOL	NAME	AIC SECTOR
MCT	B15PV03	Middlefield Canadian Income Trusts Investment Company PCC	North America
MIGO	3436594	Miton Global Opportunities PLC	Flexible Investment
MINI	BWFGQ08	Miton UK Microcap Trust PLC	UK Smaller Companies
MMIT	BFZ7R98	Mobius Investment Trust PLC	Global Emerging Markets
MNKS	3051726	Monks Investment Trust (The) PLC	Global
MTE	454351	Montanaro European Smaller Companies Trust PLC	European Smaller Companies
MTU	BZ1H9L8	Montanaro UK Smaller Companies Inv Tr PLC	UK Smaller Companies
MUT	611112	Murray Income Trust PLC	UK Equity Income
MYI	611190	Murray International Trust PLC	Global Equity Income
NBDG	BFZ5JM9	NB Distressed Debt Investment Fund Ltd	Debt – Loans and Bonds
NBDX	BFZ5JL8	NB Distressed Debt Investment Fund Ltd	Debt – Loans and Bonds
NBLS	B3KX4Q3	NB Global Floating Rate Income Fund Ltd	Debt – Loans and Bonds
NBLU	B3P7S35	NB Global Floating Rate Income Fund Ltd	Debt – Loans and Bonds
NBPE	B28ZZX8	NB Private Equity Partners Ltd	Private Equity
NBPS	BD96PR1	NB Private Equity Partners Ltd 2024 Zero Div Pref Shares NPV	Private Equity
NBPP	BD0FRW6	NB Private Equity Partners Ltd/Fund ZDP	Private Equity
NSI	263104	New Star Investment Trust PLC	Flexible Investment
NESF	BJ0JVY0	NextEnergy Solar Fund Ltd	Renewable Energy Infrastructure
NAIT	BJ00Z30	The North American Income Trust plc	North America
NAS	643900	North Atlantic Smaller Companies Inv Trust PLC	Global Smaller Companies
OCI	B23DL39	Oakley Capital Investments Ltd	Private Equity
OIT	BFFK7H5	Odyssean Investment Trust PLC	UK Smaller Companies
OIG	B3BTVQ9	Oryx International Growth Fund Ltd	UK Smaller Companies
PAC	667438	Pacific Assets Trust PLC	Asia Pacific
PHI	666747	Pacific Horizon Investment Trust PLC	Asia Pacific
PIN	414850	Pantheon International PLC	Private Equity

CAPITAL (£M)	INDEX	FLOAT DATE	WEBSITE	HISTORIC YIELD (%)
108	FTSE Small Cap		www.middlefield.co.uk	5.05
74	FTSE Fledgling	06/04/2004	www.mitongroup.com	
65	FTSE Fledgling	30/04/2015	www.mitongroup.com	0.43
90	FTSE Fledgling		www.mobiusinvestmenttrust.com	
1,975	FTSE Mid 250	29/01/1952	www.monksinvestmenttrust.co.uk	0.21
173	FTSE Small Cap	13/05/1981	www.montanaro.co.uk	0.87
185	FTSE Small Cap	16/03/1995	www.montanaro.co.uk	3.52
561	FTSE Small Cap	17/09/1953	www.murray-income.co.uk	4.01
1,538	FTSE Mid 250	21/06/1945	www.murray-intl.co.uk	4.31
146		10/06/2010	www.nbddif.com	0.95
146			www.nbddif.com	
484	FTSE Mid 250	20/04/2011	www.nbgfrif.com	4.47
394		20/04/2011	www.nbgfrif.com	
497	FTSE Small Cap	30/06/2009	www.nbprivateequitypartners.com	3.50
81	FTSE Fledgling	02/05/2000	www.nsitplc.com	1.23
706	FTSE Mid 250	25/04/2014	www.nextenergysolarfund.com	5.50
440	FTSE Small Cap	21/10/1952	www.northamericanincome.co.uk	2.76
431	FTSE Small Cap	31/01/1973	www.harwoodcapital.co.uk	0.99
461		03/08/2007	www.oakleycapitalinvestments.com	2.00
90	FTSE Fledgling	01/05/2018	www.oitplc.com	
107		02/03/1995	www.oryxinternationalgrowthfund.co.uk	
357	FTSE Small Cap	29/01/1985	www.pacific-assets.co.uk	1.02
183	FTSE Small Cap	22/09/1989	www.pacifichorizon.co.uk	
1,260	FTSE Mid 250	21/09/1987	www.piplc.com	

EPIC	SEDOL	NAME	AIC SECTOR
PGHZ	BDHXP96	PCGH ZDP PLC	Biotechnology and Healthcare
PLI	679842	Perpetual Income & Growth Investment Trust PLC	UK Equity Income
PNL	682754	Personal Assets Trust PLC	Flexible Investment
PSDL	BVG2VP8	Phoenix Spree Deutschland Ltd	Property – Europe
PCTN	B0LCW20	Picton Property Income Ltd	Hedge Funds
PCFT	B9XQT11	Polar Capital Global Financials Trust PLC	Financials
PCGH	B6832P1	Polar Capital Global Healthcare Growth & Income PLC	Biotechnology and Healthcare
PCT	422002	Polar Capital Technology Trust PLC	Technology and Media
PSSL	BLP57Y9	Pollen Street Secured Lending PLC	Debt – Direct Lending
PGIZ	BYP98L6	Premier Global Infrastructure Trust PLC	Utilities
PHP	BYRJ5J1	Primary Health Properties PLC	
PEY	B28C2R2	Princess Private Equity Holding Ltd	Private Equity
PEYS	BF012D4	Princess Private Equity Holding Ltd	Global Equity Income
PRSR	BF01NH5	PRS REIT (The) PLC	Property – UK Residential
RAV	B0D5V53	Raven Property Group Ltd	Insurance and Reinsurance Strategies
RAVP	B55K7B9	Raven Property Group Ltd	
RECI	B0HW536	Real Estate Credit Investment PCC Ltd	Property – Debt
RLE	B45XLP3	Real Estate Investors PLC	
RGL	BYV2ZQ3	Regional REIT Ltd	Property – UK Commercial
RESI	BYSX150	Residential Secure Income PLC	Property – UK Residential
RIII	739207	Rights and Issues Inv Trust PLC	UK Smaller Companies
RCP	736639	RIT Capital Partners PLC	Flexible Investment
RMMC	BZ8VFG0	River & Mercantile UK Micro Cap Investment Co Ltd	UK Smaller Companies
RCOI	BJHPS39	Riverstone Credit Opportunities Income PLC	Debt – Loans and Bonds
RSE	BBHXCL3	Riverstone Energy Ltd	Commodities and Natural Resources
RMDL	BYMTBG5	RM Secured Direct Lending PLC	Debt – Direct Lending
RICA	B018CS4	Ruffer Investment Company Ltd	Flexible Investment

CAPITAL (£M)	INDEX	FLOAT DATE	WEBSITE	HISTORIC YIELD (%)
132			www.polarcapitalhealthcaretrust.com	
699	FTSE Mid 250	21/03/1996	www.invesco.co.uk	4.65
1,115	FTSE Mid 250	02/09/1983	www.patplc.co.uk	1.32
310	FTSE Small Cap	15/06/2015	www.phoenixspree.com	2.19
480	FTSE Small Cap	25/10/2005	www.picton.co.uk	4.00
282	FTSE Small Cap	01/07/2013	www.polarcapitalglobalfinancialstrust.com	2.99
264	FTSE Small Cap	15/06/2010	www.polarcapitalhealthcaretrust.com	1.39
1,874	FTSE Mid 250	16/12/1996	www.polarcapitaltechnologytrust.co.uk	
606		30/05/2014	pollenstreetsecuredlending.com/	5.91
		04/11/2003	www.premierfunds.co.uk	
1,610	FTSE Mid 250	05/11/1998	www.phpgroup.co.uk	4.07
600		01/11/2007	www.princess-privateequity.net	5.74
438			www.theprsreit.com	5.65
225	FTSE Small Cap	25/03/2009	www.theravenpropertygroup.com	
225	FTSE Small Cap	25/03/2009	www.theravenpropertygroup.com	
334	FTSE Small Cap	13/12/2005	www.recreditinvest.com	7.16
99	AIM All-Share	10/06/2004	www.reiplc.com	6.72
439	FTSE Small Cap	06/11/2015	www.regionalreit.com	7.89
156	FTSE Small Cap		www.resi-reit.com	3.29
144		28/07/1966	www.maitlandgroup.com	1.67
3,349	FTSE Mid 250	01/08/1988	www.ritcap.com	1.53
74	FTSE Fledgling	02/12/2014	microcap.riverandmercantile.com	
79		28/05/2019	www.riverstonecoi.com	
463	FTSE Mid 250	24/10/2013	www.riverstonerel.com	
114	FTSE Fledgling	15/12/2016	www.rm-funds.co.uk	6.40
400	FTSE Small Cap	08/07/2004	www.ruffer.co.uk	0.81

EPIC	SEDOL	NAME	AIC SECTOR
SAFE	B1N7Z09	Safestore Holdings PLC	
SIT	BMPHJ80	Sanditon Investment Trust PLC	UK All Companies
MNTN	BJ0CDD2	Schiehallion Fund Ltd (The)	Growth Capital
ATR	871079	Schroder Asian Total Return Investment Company PLC	Asia Pacific
SDP	791887	Schroder AsiaPacific Fund PLC	Asia Pacific
SERE	BY7R8K7	Schroder European Real Estate Investment Trust Ltd	Property – Europe
SCF	791586	Schroder Income Growth Fund PLC	UK Equity Income
SJG	802284	Schroder Japan Growth Fund PLC	Japan
SOI	B0CRWN5	Schroder Oriental Income Fund Ltd	Asia Pacific Income
SREI	B01HM14	Schroder Real Estate Investment Trust Ltd	Property – UK Commercial
SCP	610841	Schroder UK Mid & Small Cap Fund PLC	UK All Companies
SAIN	787369	Scottish American Investment Co (The) PLC	Global Equity Income
SCIN	782609	Scottish Investment Trust PLC	Global
SMT	BLDYK61	Scottish Mortgage Investment Trust PLC	Global
SST	783613	Scottish Oriental Smaller Companies Trust PLC	Asia Pacific Smaller Companies
SEIT	BGHVZM4	SDCL Energy Efficiency Income Trust PLC	Renewable Energy Infrastructure
SIR	BLMQ9L6	Secure Income REIT PLC	Property – UK Commercial
STS	B09G3N2	Securities Trust of Scotland PLC	Global Equity Income
SIGT	876999	Seneca Global Income & Growth Trust PLC	Flexible Investment
SEQI	BV54HY6	Sequoia Economic Infrastructure Income Fund Ltd	Infrastructure
SHRS	805250	Shires Income PLC	UK Equity Income
SRE	B1W3VF5	Sirius Real Estate Ltd	Global Smaller Companies
SCRF	BYYJCZ9	SME Credit Realisation Fund Ltd	Debt – Direct Lending
SSON	BGJWTR8	Smithson Investment Trust PLC	Global Smaller Companies
SQN	BN56JF1	SQN Asset Finance Income Fund Ltd	Leasing
SQNX	BFXYHJ1	SQN Asset Finance Income Fund Ltd C Shares NPV	Leasing

CAPITAL (£M)	INDEX	FLOAT DATE	WEBSITE	HISTORIC YIELD (%)
1,415	FTSE Mid 250		www.safestore.co.uk	2.42
59	FTSE Fledgling	27/06/2014	www.sanditonam.com	0.62
456		27/03/2019	www.schiehallionfund.com	
345	FTSE Small Cap	26/11/1987	www.schroders.com	1.72
732	FTSE Mid 250	20/11/1995	www.schroderasiapacificfund.com	2.17
150	FTSE Small Cap	09/12/2015	www.schroders.com	5.86
196	FTSE Small Cap	09/03/1995	www.schroderincomegrowthfund.com	4.14
243	FTSE Small Cap	11/07/1994	www.schroders.com	2.06
676	FTSE Mid 250	28/07/2005	www.schroders.co.uk	3.82
285	FTSE Small Cap	16/07/2004	www.schroders.com	4.65
192	FTSE Small Cap	18/05/1983	www.schroders.com	2.97
610	FTSE Small Cap	26/02/1953	www.bailliegifford.com	2.76
617	FTSE Mid 250	20/08/1952	www.thescottish.co.uk	2.54
7,483	FTSE 100	12/01/1953	www.bailliegifford.com	0.62
306	FTSE Small Cap	29/03/1995	www.scottishoriental.co.uk	1.12
188	FTSE Small Cap	11/12/2018	www.sdcleeit.com	0.91
1,466	AIM UK 50, AIM 100, AIM All-Share	05/06/2014	www.SecureIncomeREIT.co.uk	3.46
207	FTSE Small Cap	28/06/2005	www.securitiestrust.com	3.15
88	FTSE Fledgling	04/04/1996	www.senecaim.com	3.73
1,605	FTSE Mid 250	03/03/2015	www.seqifund.com	5.15
80	FTSE Fledgling	26/01/1972	www.shiresincome.co.uk	5.05
745	FTSE Mid 250	04/05/2007	www.sirius-real-estate.com	4.12
246	FTSE Small Cap	30/11/2015	www.smecreditrealisation.com	6.73
1,362	FTSE Mid 250	19/10/2018	www.smithson.co.uk	
406	FTSE Small Cap	14/07/2014	www.sqnassetfinance.com	9.06
121	FTSE Small Cap	12/12/2016	www.sqnassetfinance.com	

EPIC	SEDOL	NAME	AIC SECTOR
SLI	3387528	Standard Life Investments Property Income Trust Ltd	Property – UK Commercial
SLPE	3047468	Standard Life Private Equity Trust plc	Private Equity
SLS	295958	Standard Life UK Smaller Companies Trust plc	UK Smaller Companies
SWEF	B79WC10	Starwood European Real Estate Finance Ltd	Property – Debt
STP	BDR8FC4	Stenprop Ltd	
SEC	B0BDCB2	Strategic Equity Capital PLC	UK Smaller Companies
SUPR	BF345X1	Supermarket Income Reit PLC	Property – UK Commercial
SIHL	B231M63	Symphony International Holdings Ltd	Private Equity
SYNC	B8P59C0	Syncona Ltd	Biotechnology and Healthcare
THRL	BJGTLF5	Target Healthcare REIT Ltd	Property – UK Healthcare
TMPL	882532	Temple Bar Investment Trust PLC	UK Equity Income
TEM	882929	Templeton Emerging Markets Investment Trust PLC	Global Emerging Markets
TFG	B28ZZS3	Tetragon Financial Group Ltd	Flexible Investment
TFGS	BFNSMW1	Tetragon Financial Group Ltd	Flexible Investment
TRIG	BBHX2H9	The Renewables Infrastructure Group Ltd	Renewable Energy Infrastructure
TPOU	B1YQ721	Third Point Offshore Investors Ltd	Hedge Funds
TRG	906692	TR European Growth Trust PLC	European Smaller Companies
TRY	906409	TR Property Investment Trust PLC	Property Securities
TI1	BF52MW1	Trian Investors 1 Ltd	Financials
SOHO	BF0P7H5	Triple Point Social Housing REIT PLC	Property – UK Residential
BBOX	BG49KP9	Tritax Big Box REIT PLC	Property – UK Commercial
BOXE	BG43LH0	Tritax Eurobox PLC	Property – Europe
TIGT	370866	Troy Income & Growth Trust PLC	UK Equity Income
SHIP	BDFC164	Tufton Oceanic Assets Ltd	Leasing
TFIF	B90J5Z9	TwentyFour Income Fund Ltd	Debt – Structured Finance
SMIF	BJVDZ94	TwentyFour Select Monthly Income Fund Ltd	Debt – Loans and Bonds
UTL	BZ4BVN3	UIL Ltd	Flexible Investment

CAPITAL (£M)	INDEX	FLOAT DATE	WEBSITE	HISTORIC YIELD (%)
358	FTSE Small Cap	19/12/2003	www.slipit.co.uk	5.40
540	FTSE Small Cap	29/05/2001	www.slpet.co.uk	3.53
486	FTSE Small Cap	19/08/1993	www.standardlifeuksmallercompaniestrust.co.uk	1.59
417	FTSE Small Cap	17/12/2012	www.starwoodeuropeanfinance.com	6.44
301		15/06/2018	www.stenprop.com	6.34
140	FTSE Small Cap	19/07/2005	www.strategicequitycapital.com	0.45
251			www.supermarketincomereit.com	5.39
252		03/08/2007	www.symphonyasia.com	4.15
1,460	FTSE Mid 250	26/10/2012	www.synconaltd.com	1.05
515	FTSE Small Cap	07/03/2013	www.targethealthcarereit.co.uk	5.84
843	FTSE Mid 250	15/04/1952	www.templebarinvestments.co.uk	3.71
1,937	FTSE Mid 250	19/06/1989	www.temit.co.uk	2.03
899		01/10/2009	www.tetragoninv.com	5.78
1,831	FTSE Mid 250	29/07/2013	www.trig-ltd.com	5.13
537		25/07/2007	www.thirdpointpublic.com	
432	FTSE Small Cap	29/08/1990	www.treuropeangrowthtrust.com	2.20
1,341	FTSE Mid 250	11/03/1953	www.trproperty.com	3.20
273		27/09/2018	www.trianinvestors1.com	
333	FTSE Small Cap	08/08/2017	www.triplepointreit.com	5.24
2,526	FTSE Mid 250	09/12/2013	www.tritaxbigboxreitplc.co.uk	4.50
406		09/07/2018	www.tritaxeurobox.co.uk	
246	FTSE Small Cap	18/07/1988	www.tigt.co.uk	3.18
211		20/12/2017	www.tuftonoceanicassets.com	6.90
570	FTSE Small Cap	06/03/2013	www.twentyfourincomefund.com	5.92
172	FTSE Small Cap	10/03/2014	www.twentyfouram.com	7.06
227		20/06/2007	www.uil.limited	2.90

EPIC	SEDOL	NAME	AIC SECTOR
UKCM	B19Z2J5	UK Commercial Property REIT	Property – UK Commercial
UKML	BXDZMK6	UK Mortgages Ltd	Debt – Structured Finance
SHED	BYV8MN7	Urban Logistics REIT PLC	Property – UK Commercial
USF	BJCWFX4	US Solar Fund PLC	Renewable Energy Infrastructure
UEM	BD45S96	Utilico Emerging Markets Ltd	Global Emerging Markets
VIN	848471	Value & Income Trust PLC	UK Equity Income
VEIL	BD9X204	Vietnam Enterprise Investments Ltd	Country Specialists: Asia Pacific ex Japan
VNH	BJQZ9H1	Vietnam Holding Ltd	Country Specialists: Asia Pacific ex Japan
VOF	BYXVT88	VinaCapital Vietnam Opportunity Fund Ltd	Country Specialists: Asia Pacific ex Japan
VTA	B28Y104	Volta Finance Ltd	Debt – CLOs
VSL	BVG6X43	VPC Specialty Lending Investments PLC	Debt – Direct Lending
WHR	BD2NCM3	Warehouse REIT PLC	Property – UK Commercial
WKOF	B933LL6	Weiss Korea Opportunity Fund Ltd	Country Specialists: Asia Pacific ex Japan
WTAN	BJTRSD3	Witan Investment Trust PLC	Global
WPC	365602	Witan Pacific Investment Trust PLC	Asia Pacific
WPCT	BVG1CF2	Woodford Patient Capital Trust PLC	Growth Capital
WWH	338530	Worldwide Healthcare Trust PLC	Biotechnology and Healthcare

CAPITAL (£M)	INDEX	FLOAT DATE	WEBSITE	HISTORIC YIELD (%)
1,092	FTSE Mid 250	21/09/2006	www.ukcpreit.com	4.38
184		07/07/2015	www.ukmortgagesltd.com	8.89
111	AIM All-Share	13/04/2016	www.urbanlogisticsreit.com	5.57
160		16/04/2019	www.ussolarfund.co.uk	
546	FTSE Small Cap	20/07/2005	www.uemtrust.co.uk	3.01
114	FTSE Small Cap	14/07/1981	www.olim.co.uk	4.70
1,090	FTSE Mid 250	05/07/2016	www.veil-dragoncapital.com	
97	FTSE Fledgling	15/06/2006	www.vietnamholding.com	
632	FTSE Mid 250	30/09/2003	www.vinacapital.com	3.44
219		29/05/2015	www.voltafinance.com	6.97
255	FTSE Small Cap	17/03/2015	www.vpcspecialtylending.com	10.09
250	AIM 100, AIM All-Share	20/09/2017	www.warehousereit.co.uk	5.77
120	AIM All-Share	14/05/2013	www.weisskoreaopportunityfund.com	2.80
1,876	FTSE Mid 250	27/10/1950	www.witan.com	2.18
208	FTSE Small Cap	11/02/1952	www.witanpacific.com	2.07
408	FTSE Small Cap	21/04/2015	www.woodfordfunds.com	
1,404	FTSE Mid 250	28/04/1995	www.worldwidewh.com	1.00

PARTNERS

AberdeenStandard
Investments

ABERDEEN STANDARD INVESTMENT TRUSTS

Searching widely to discover more investment opportunities

Aberdeen Standard Investments is a leading global asset manager dedicated to creating long-term value for our clients.

We manage assets worth £525.7bn on behalf of clients in 80 countries (as at 30 June 2019). In managing these assets, we employ over 1,000 investment professionals and provide client support from 48 client relationship offices globally. This ensures we are close to our clients and the markets in which they invest.

We are high-conviction, long-term investors who seek to realise the value of our investments over time. In our view, teamwork and collaboration between investment managers and across asset classes is key to delivering repeatable, robust investment performance. We are also resolute in our commitment to active asset management.

If you're keen to capture the potential offered by global investment markets, turn to Aberdeen Standard investment trusts. Managed by teams of experts, each trust is designed to bring together the most compelling opportunities we can find to generate the investment growth or income you're looking for.

You can choose from trusts investing in the UK, in specific overseas regions such as Asia or the Americas, or that give you a global spread of investments. With a flexible multi-asset fund, a diversified private equity trust, three property funds and two UK smaller companies funds to choose from too, there's plenty of choice to target your specific investment goals.

Important information:

- The value of investments and income from them can go down as well as up and you may get back less than the amount invested.
- Past performance is not a guide to future results.

- Investment trusts are specialised investments and may not be appropriate for all investors. We recommend you seek financial advice prior to making an investment decision.

- There is no guarantee that the market price of a Trust's shares will fully reflect its underlying Net Asset Value.

- As with all stock exchange investments the value of the Trust shares purchased will immediately fall by the difference between the buying and selling prices, the bid-offer spread. If trading volumes fall, the bid-offer spread can widen.

- Investment trusts can borrow money in order to enhance investment returns. This is known as 'gearing' or 'leverage'. However, the use of gearing can result in share prices being more volatile and subject to sudden or large falls in value. Where permitted an investment trust may invest in other investment trusts that utilise gearing which will exaggerate market movements, both up and down.

- The value of tax benefits depends on individual circumstances and the favourable tax treatment for ISAs may not be maintained. If you are a basic rate tax payer and you do not anticipate any liability to Capital Gains Tax, you should consider if the advantages of an ISA investment justify the additional management cost/charges incurred.

Issued by Aberdeen Asset Managers Limited which is authorised and regulated by the Financial Conduct Authority in the UK. Registered Office: 10 Queen's Terrace, Aberdeen AB10 1XL. Registered in Scotland No. 108419.

Find out more at www.invtrusts.co.uk

ABOUT FIDELITY INTERNATIONAL

Fidelity International provides world class investment solutions and retirement expertise to institutions, individuals and their advisers – to help our clients build better futures for themselves and generations to come. As a private company, we think generationally and invest for the long term. Helping clients to save for retirement and other long-term investing objectives has been at the core of our business for 50 years.

We offer our own investment solutions and access to those of others, and deliver services relating to investing: For individual investors and their advisers we provide guidance to help them invest in a simple and cost-effective way. For institutions, including pension funds, banks and insurance companies, we offer tailored investment solutions, consultancy, and full-service outsourcing of asset management to us. For employers, we provide workplace pension administration services on top of, or independently from, investment management. We are responsible for total client assets of £329.7bn from 2.4m clients across Asia Pacific, Europe, the Middle East and South America.

OUR INVESTMENT APPROACH

Investing requires a continuous research commitment to build a deep understanding of what is driving industries and individual businesses. This is where our global research capabilities with 410 investment professionals and research support staff around the world come in: Fidelity International is committed to generating proprietary insights and our analysts work together across asset classes, e.g. combining insights from equity, credit, macro and quantitative research, to form a 360° view on the health and prospects of companies.

- Our analysts carry out their research on the ground – visiting the shop floor, speaking to customers, competitors, suppliers, and independent experts to form conviction.

- Over the course of a year, we estimate across the entire Fidelity research group, covering fixed income and equities, that we conduct in excess of 15,000 company meetings each year – or one every 8 minutes on average between them.

- We commission a number of bespoke projects and surveys to understand the market potential of companies' product and service innovations. As part of our fixed income research, we run 15 top-down systematic overlay models as well as generating a wide range of quantitative tools and nudges to complement our fundamental credit analyst output.

OUR UK INVESTMENT TRUST BUSINESS

Fidelity has over 25 years' experience managing investment companies and manages around £3.3bn in assets across five investment trusts. These are all focused on equity growth strategies.

As a major platform distributor, Fidelity is able to offer its own investment trusts and those managed by third parties to professional investors and retail investors alike through a range of different product wrappers. Fidelity also promotes its range of trusts directly to institutions and wealth managers through its highly experienced in-house sales teams.

JUPITER
Asset Management

ABOUT JUPITER

Jupiter was founded in 1985 and has since become one of the UK's most respected and successful fund management groups. From our origins as a manager primarily of investment trust and private client portfolios, we expanded into institutional fund management before mutual funds became the key engine of growth.

In 2007, Jupiter's employees bought the Jupiter Group from its parent company Commerzbank through a management buyout supported by private equity firm TA Associates, and other minority investors. In June 2010 Jupiter listed on the London Stock Exchange. Many of our fund managers and other employees continue to hold shares in the Company and in addition, we encourage our fund managers to invest their own money into Jupiter funds, helping to create what we believe to be a stable environment in which the interests of our fund managers and other employees are aligned with those of our customers.

ABOUT POLAR CAPITAL

Polar Capital Holdings plc is a specialist, investment-led, active fund management company offering investors a range of predominantly long-only and long/short equity funds.

The company's investment strategies are based on long-term investment themes, specialist sectors and global, regional or single country geographies. The majority of these assets including the three investment trusts are in long only equity strategies. There are also long/short and convertible bond strategies. They all have a fundamental, research-driven approach, where capacity is rigorously managed to enhance and protect performance.

The three investment trusts are in the specialist sectors of technology, healthcare and financials. In fact, Polar Capital was founded in February 2001 by fund managers Brian Ashford-Russell and Tim Woolley, together with corporate partner Caledonia Investments, with the Polar Capital Technology Trust (PCT) as the first portfolio it managed.

PCT has access to the growth potential of companies in the global technology sector and is managed by one of the largest technology investment teams in Europe. The Trust's longevity has seen it enjoy a multi-cycle/multi-year track record.

Polar Capital Global Healthcare Trust (PCGH) is run by an investment team of five senior fund managers looking at healthcare's long-term, secular growth sector as ageing populations drive the demand and the need for increased healthcare provision. Something for us all to consider as we all live longer.

The largest investable equity sector globally is the financial sector which is where the Polar Capital Global Financials Trust (PCFT) invests. Their universe includes banks, life and non-life insurance companies, asset managers, stock exchanges, specialty lenders and fintech companies.

The company's investment teams are all based in Polar Capital's principal location in London, with investment staff in offices in Connecticut, Edinburgh, Jersey, Paris and Shanghai.